THE LAST
JEFFERSONIAN

Grover Cleveland and the Path
to Restoring the Republic

Ryan S. Walters

WestBow
PRESS
A DIVISION OF THOMAS NELSON

WestBow Press books may be ordered through booksellers or by contacting:

WestBow Press
A Division of Thomas Nelson
1663 Liberty Drive
Bloomington, IN 47403
www.westbowpress.com
1-(866) 928-1240

Because of the dynamic nature of the Internet, any web addresses or links contained in this book may have changed since publication and may no longer be valid. The views expressed in this work are solely those of the author and do not necessarily reflect the views of the publisher, and the publisher hereby disclaims any responsibility for them.

Any people depicted in stock imagery provided by Thinkstock are models, and such images are being used for illustrative purposes only.

Certain stock imagery © Thinkstock.

ISBN: 978-1-4497-4049-8 (sc)
ISBN: 978-1-4497-4050-4 (hc)
ISBN: 978-1-4497-4048-1 (e)

Library of Congress Control Number: 2012902819

Printed in the United States of America

WestBow Press rev. date: 2/28/2012

To all the Tea Party Patriots who strive each and every
day to restore our constitutional republic.

CONTENTS

ACKNOWLEDGMENTS

As any author will tell you, a literary work can only be successful with some outside assistance and my book is no exception. Each and every day, young and unproven writers struggle to find publishers for their manuscripts. I encountered similar obstacles as I embarked on the same lonely trail. After several rejections, I discovered Westbow Press, a division of Thomas Nelson Publishers. Staff members at Westbow were extraordinarily helpful and optimistic about the potential success of my book from the very beginning, while the superb editorial team helped me iron out the rough spots in the manuscript. I can't praise the professionals at Westbow Press enough.

Though I am a historian of American political history, that does not mean I know everything. Far from it. Those areas with which I felt inadequate to the task, I sought the aid of experts within a more narrowed field and within disciplines of which I am untrained. Dr. Joseph Salerno, an economist at Pace University in St. Louis, very kindly examined parts of the manuscript on the cumbersome monetary issues regarding the Panic of 1893. He had good things to say about my work and his advice kept me from making a few minor mistakes.

Lawrence W. Reed, the president of the Foundation for Economic Education, and a fellow fan of Grover Cleveland, generously took his time to read the manuscript in its entirety. His advice on numerous areas made the manuscript much better and kept me from making a few more errors.

Mississippi Senator Chris McDaniel, my good friend and a rising star in the Republican Party, also read the complete manuscript, though his legislative and legal workload was enormous. His aid and encouragement helped me through the process, while giving me a much-needed boost of confidence as the book went to press.

Although I have acknowledged those who assisted me in making this book the best that it can be, any mistakes within its pages I take full responsibility for. They are mine and mine alone.

"The historian is a prophet looking backward."

Friedrich Schlegel

INTRODUCTION:
WHY GROVER CLEVELAND IS IMPORTANT

At first glance, it might seem odd that a nineteenth-century president could have any bearing on the modern world. How could the record of a president who served more than a century ago have any influence on contemporary politics or impact a political movement like conservatism? Should we even care about what happened in bygone eras? Many economists, politicians, and pundits believe there's nothing to gain from studying the past. We live in a new world, they often say, and should look to the future and to new ideas. But that is where we make a great mistake. There are lessons we as a society can learn by viewing modern times through the prism of history, and conservatives can gain much by examining the historic presidential administration of Jeffersonian Democrat Grover Cleveland.

The conservative movement, once the dominant political force in America, found itself, after the electoral debacles in 2006 and 2008, in a state of disarray. Conservatives struggled to find a solid leader or a unified agenda and seemed to have no solid prospects for the immediate future. In the days after Barack Obama's historic victory, the right appeared to be a ship adrift at sea without a rudder, as many politicians and the media capitulated to "Obama-mania." Even Christopher Buckley, son of the late conservative icon William F. Buckley, shocked the Republican world in the fall of 2008 by announcing his support for Obama, while others in the GOP flirted with the possibility of getting behind the smooth-talking candidate, disgusted as they were with their party and nominee.

The recent Tea Parties, though, have started a pushback with a groundswell of resistance to Obama's encroaching government, a movement instrumental in the 2010 midterm election landslide. Yet even since the advent of the Tea Party, many rank-and-file members, the heart and soul of the conservative movement, have been disillusioned, depressed, and in search of a champion. There are numerous reasons for the state of perplexity and lack of direction, the absence of an inspirational, unifying leader among them. This is especially true when Republican presidential candidates tout Lincoln or Teddy and Franklin Roosevelt as heroes, while major conservative publications endorse moderates as preferred nominees.

Along with leadership, the lack of a coherent, consistent message is another major problem. Conservative leaders themselves often question and disagree on what conservatism actually is. Many have succumbed to the never-ending leftwing assault that conservatism is extreme and mean-spirited. To counter that attack, a multitude of new books, theories, and catchy slogans, such as "compassionate conservatism," have emerged in the last several years attempting to redefine the movement for the purpose of bringing in new supporters, seemingly by lessening conservatism's supposed harshness.

But conservatives need not fear the assaults of liberals, nor should conservatism be retooled or redefined. It should be advocated in its original Jeffersonian purity. The Jeffersonians believed in all the major tenets of what modern conservatism actually is, known at the time as classical liberalism: limited government; respect for the states; economy and accountability; strict construction of the Constitution; sound money; low taxes and tariffs; no national debt; and a noninterventionist foreign policy.

When these ideals of pure Jeffersonian conservatism are expressed, as they were so eloquently by Ronald Reagan, the right wins and wins big; when they are not, as in the recent case of John McCain, Republicans are beaten and, generally, beaten badly. We often hear from many thinkers and commentators on the right that conservatives must look to the future for new ideas about governing, for the present is much too complex to rely on a distant, simplistic past. Many of these new theories put trust in a governmental structure to fix problems. But it was not government that made America great; it was the people, who possess individual liberty, a capitalistic economic system, and a government that remained on the sidelines and out of their back pockets. We need only to look to the past to what worked and to those principles that made the United States the greatest nation on Earth.

"For conservatism is grounded in the past," writes Pat Buchanan. "Its principles are derived from the Constitution, experience, history, tradition, custom, and the wisdom of those who have gone before us—'The best that has been thought and said.' It does not purport to know the future. It is about preserving the true, the good, the beautiful."[1]

Or as Chuck Norris wrote in *Black Belt Patriotism*, "Go back to go forward."[2]

But perhaps our Lord said it best in Jeremiah 6:16: "Stand at the crossroads and look; ask for the ancient paths, ask where the good way is, and walk in it, and you will find rest for your souls."

But rarely do we hear candidates discuss our glorious past. Today's conservative leaders express new ideas, new solutions, and new ways of doing things, trying to impress voters with how innovative they are when we should be looking for our answers in the past, at the old ways of doing things. For this reason we study history. To students, both past and present, as well as those in the future, history should not be seen as simply a bunch of facts, names, and dates; nor is it, as one critic suggested, "Just one damn thing after another."[3] The study of history has a purpose. We must learn from it because if we don't, we become irrelevant as a people and as a great civilization.

As Ronald Reagan reminded the American people in his 1989 Farewell Address, "If we forget what we did, we won't know who we are."[4] How right he was. Consider for a moment an absence of history. What if we had no knowledge of the past, no stories, no facts, no records, nothing but ignorance? What if we knew nothing that had happened before our lifetimes and beyond the grasp of our memories or that of our elders? A scary thought indeed.

History can intellectually enrich one's life and can be an excellent guide to understanding present events and to correct existing problems. "What … is the solution to our current woes?" asks Professor Larry Schweikart in his recent book *What Would the Founders Say? A Patriot's Answers to America's Most Pressing Problems*. "It helps, when you are lost, to find out where you made the wrong turn. But if you don't know where you started, how can you discover where you went off course?"[5] The study of our history will show us the answers, allowing us to understand where we have come from as a society so we will know where we are going as a society. So it is important that the study of history, as well as the writing of it, reflects modern times.

A thorough understanding of American history can also make one a better citizen and a more enlightened voter. Discussing posterity, Thomas Jefferson wrote in 1784 that the people would derive tremendous benefits from studying the past. "History, by apprising them of the past, will enable them to judge … the future; it will avail them of the experience of other times and other nations; it will qualify them as judges of the actions and designs of men; it will enable them to know ambition under every disguise it may assume; and knowing it, to defeat its views."[6]

Grover Cleveland would have agreed. He held strongly to what he believed, passionately advocating the principles of Jeffersonian conservatism, ideals that resided in the Democratic Party in his day. He held that those standards should be freely championed, not concealed or watered down, while the history of those beliefs could be an excellent judge for the present and future. "The Democratic cause need have no fear of the most complete discussion of its principles, and the history of its great leaders and their achievements cannot fail to inspire the members of the party with pride and veneration," he wrote a friend during his first year as president. "It is well in these latter days to often turn back and read of the faith which the founders of our party had in the people—how exactly they approached their needs and with what lofty aims and purposes they sought the public good."[7]

We have definitely lost sight of the history of our political fathers and must look to them for our future path. Grover Cleveland was one of those patriarchs, a Jeffersonian Democrat who served as mayor of Buffalo, New York, governor of the Empire State, and two nonconsecutive terms as the twenty-second and twenty-fourth president of the United States, holding the White House from 1885 to 1889 and again from 1893 to 1897. The American public and the conservative movement have largely forgotten Cleveland, mainly because he has received scant attention by academic historians and political writers. Only a handful of biographies have been authored, and few academic journals and magazines contain articles with Cleveland as the principle subject.

But with such a lack of scholarship, why should we even bother studying Cleveland? Would Jefferson not be a better subject? For one, Cleveland is much closer to modern times and as a result faced many of the same domestic challenges we do today, including one of the worst economic calamities in our history, a depression similar to our own. As the nation edged closer to the modern world, he also faced new problems in foreign policy, issues that earlier presidents scarcely had to contend with but which every contemporary president certainly does. But in facing his challenges, he continued to embody Jeffersonian values more fully than anyone, every bit as strong as Jefferson himself, making him one of the most conservative of presidents and, perhaps, as I hope to demonstrate, the greatest conservative statesman in American history.

As the title of this book proclaims, Cleveland should rightly be regarded as the last Jeffersonian, the last president to espouse the purity of those ideals. Though many may argue the point, what cannot be argued is that he was certainly the last Democrat to serve as president in the Jeffersonian mold and perhaps one of the last national figures in his party advocating the classical liberal persuasion, now a relic of a forgotten past. In fact, David N. Mayer, a scholar of Thomas Jefferson, also regards Cleveland as the "last Jeffersonian." Economics Professor Thomas J. DiLorenzo labeled him "the last good Democrat," while Paul Whitefield, in *Investor's Business Daily*, recently dubbed him "the last libertarian president." Conservative historians Larry Schweikart and Michael Allen point out in *A Patriot's History of the United States* that he was "the last small-government candidate the Democrats would ever run" for the presidency. And though Calvin Coolidge and Ronald Reagan had many Jeffersonian qualities, Cleveland should be considered, in the opinion of this historian, without question, the last authentic Jeffersonian president. He is deserving of serious study by conservative scholars, as well as the general public.[8]

I became seriously interested in Grover Cleveland in my first semester of graduate school at the University of Southern Mississippi in the fall of 2001. Being assigned the task of finding a suitable topic for my MA thesis, I initially chose Cleveland and drew up a research prospectus that focused on his trade policy. However, I eventually settled on a theme more in line with my field of study at the time, the politics of the Antebellum Period, due in no small measure to the prodding of my major professor. But Cleveland never strayed far from my mind, and I decided to write my doctoral dissertation on his political life as I broadened my scope to include the political history of all of nineteenth-century America when I entered the PhD program. I purchased biographies and collections of Cleveland's speeches, writings, and letters for study in my very limited free time.

With the recent disorder on the political right, I decided to write this book, culled from my dissertation research, to reexamine a truly great president and to point out what we in the conservative movement, as well as the nation as a whole, can learn from him today. Recent years have seen the publication of various books by conservative and libertarian scholars that criticize many of our former statesmen and presidents, as well as the policies they advocated, namely Alexander Hamilton's betrayal of the ideals of the American Revolution, Abraham Lincoln and his war policy toward the South, Teddy Roosevelt's progressivism, Woodrow Wilson's foreign and economic policies, and FDR's New Deal. Such critiques are extremely important to our understanding of history, to warn us what paths we should not take, but I chose a different method. While it's essential to point out flawed leaders and disastrous policies, it's also equally important to examine exemplary statesmen and demonstrate why they are worthy of consideration, admiration, and emulation. This book attempts to do just that.[9]

In the course of my research, I have been captivated by Cleveland's political courage, character, honesty, and strict adherence to political principles, all extreme rarities in this day and age. These characteristics are particularly admirable when you consider that the post–Civil War era was one of widespread dishonesty and selfishness. And yet there was absolutely no hint of corruption in Grover Cleveland. As mayor of Buffalo, he fought and defeated the corrupt ring that controlled the city. As governor, he stared down Tammany Hall, the great New York Democratic political machine and a major engine of corruption. During his first run for the presidency in 1884, his political opponents, unable to tag him as corrupt in an age of unbridled deceitfulness, instead questioned his morality. But in so doing, Republicans succeeded only in demonstrating that he was a man of great morals, integrity, and goodness. Some in the press even labeled him "Grover the Good."

Cleveland was perhaps the most honest man ever to occupy the White House and certainly the most straightforward in the century since he left office in 1897. Even his political enemies conceded this fact. This was a major reason Democrats turned to him in 1884. Yet he was not a man of extraordinary talent or ability. Biographer Allan Nevins stated it best, writing that "in Grover Cleveland, the greatness lies in typical rather than unusual qualities. He had no endowments that thousands of men do not have. He possessed honesty, courage, firmness, independence, and common sense. But he possessed them to a degree other men do not."[10]

And because he possessed moral character to such a degree, he would never involve himself, or his campaigns, in the "politics of personal destruction" that is so prevalent today. In fact, he would not tolerate his campaign managers engaging in such practices during his 1884 presidential race with the inherently corrupt James G. Blaine. When a scandal broke that might embarrass and humiliate Blaine's wife, Cleveland ordered his managers to accept Blaine's side of the story and drop the matter, an unthinkable act in the history of American political campaigning.

Cleveland was also one of the most philosophically consistent statesmen in American history. He remained the same, no matter what office he held or sought. Unlike today's politicians, whose morals and platforms change with the wind, Cleveland stuck to his principles. He held so fast to his Jeffersonian principles that he often likened it to religion, referring to it as "my Democratic faith."

And he kept his campaign promises to reform government. Cleveland was a man and statesman who said what he meant and meant what he said, willing to lose an election rather than betray his cherished ideals. Such traits make him, perhaps, the greatest statesman in American history.

Like Jefferson, he was a fierce advocate of economy and accountability in government. In Buffalo, he was known as the "Veto Mayor"; in Albany, the "Veto Governor"; and in Washington the trend continued as the "Veto President." In the previous 100 years of presidential history, from George Washington to Chester A. Arthur, Cleveland's immediate predecessor, the twenty-one prior chief executives cast a total of 204 vetoes.

But in his first term alone Cleveland vetoed 414 bills, mainly extravagant spending measures. His second term saw the rejection of another 170 bills, including 49 on his last day in office, giving him a total of 584 in eight years, the most by far of any president until FDR, who eclipsed him by bypassing Washington's unofficial two-term tradition. And of Cleveland's many vetoes, Congress overrode only seven. Unlike our more recent presidents, President Cleveland aggressively used the veto pen to keep the federal government within its constitutional and fiscal bounds.

As for the Constitution and its interpretation, Cleveland strongly advocated strict construction, following the original meaning of the Founders, not the progressive "living document" theory that was becoming more prevalent in his day, as well as our own. In his many veto messages to Congress, Cleveland echoed a consistent theme: "I can find no warrant for such an appropriation in the Constitution."[11] To him, like Jefferson, the president had just as much right and authority to interpret the Constitution as did the Supreme Court, and he exercised that power rigorously.

At the start of his second term, Cleveland faced a severe economic depression, known as the Panic of 1893. Though economic statistics of that time were not as plentiful as they are today, the limited data suggests, and many economists and historians agree, that the downturn was one of the worst of the nineteenth century and even rivaled the Great Depression in its severity, especially in the area of unemployment. President Cleveland responded to the emergency in an entirely different manner than one would expect from modern presidents. Unlike Herbert Hoover, FDR, George W. Bush, Barack Obama, or a majority of his presidential successors who did everything they could when economic problems arose, Cleveland did not mobilize the full powers of the federal government to fight the depression. There was no talk of bailouts for any of the 16,000 businesses that went bankrupt during the Depression's first year, the 500 banks that closed, or the 70 railroads that went into receivership.

Nor were there any programs or "stimulus" to relieve the unemployment rate, which has been estimated as high as 25 percent among industrial workers and more than 18 percent nationwide. The government under Cleveland stopped the inflation that caused the downturn, cut taxes and spending, and allowed the free market to correct itself. As a result, the crisis was short-lived and did not devolve into a Great Depression. However, this has not stopped many historians from raking him over the coals for his seemingly uncaring attitude toward those hit hardest by the panic, yet his actions were honorable, just, and in perfect keeping with Jeffersonian ideals.

Cleveland was born in 1837, the year of the worst financial panic and depression to strike the young nation, presided over by President Martin Van Buren, a former New York governor. Cleveland, also hailing from New York and serving as the state's governor, would preside over the Panic of 1893, which rivaled 1837's in its severity and could easily have eclipsed it.

While president, Cleveland met the young son of one of his New York supporters, a five-year-old lad named Franklin Delano Roosevelt, who came to the White House with his father, James, a strong Cleveland man the president wanted to appoint as minister to Holland, a position the elder Roosevelt respectfully declined. The president, exacerbated by all the work he faced and the constant throng of office-seekers, placed his hand on the small boy's head and said, "My little man, I am making a strange wish for you. It is that you may never be president of the United States."[12] But the young man would indeed become president nearly fifty years later, after two terms as the governor of New York, and preside over the nation's worst economic depression, a panic that surpassed both 1837 and 1893 in its harshness. Yet Van Buren and Cleveland treated their respective calamities much differently than FDR had and had much better results.

Because of his excellent statesmanship, Cleveland should be of particular importance for conservatives and an icon for the political right. He provides us with an outstanding example not only for our presidents but for our state and local officials as well. He was a superb officeholder and managed the affairs of his local and state offices, that of sheriff of Erie County, mayor of Buffalo, and governor of New York, with as much careful attention as he gave his White House duties. He was also well-liked by the public, winning record-breaking majorities in his victories as mayor and governor as well as a plurality of the popular vote in three successive presidential elections, the first president to do so, and the only other besides Andrew Jackson and Franklin D. Roosevelt, all because he stuck to his principles.

But why have modern political leaders, particularly in the conservative movement, shunned Cleveland? Or if not shunned, outright forgotten. It didn't help that he served in an era academic historians have characterized as one of weak and mediocre presidents, those chiefly falling between Abraham Lincoln and Theodore Roosevelt, a time when Congress held most of the influence, though Cleveland was far from a weak or mediocre president. Richard Hofstadter has written that Cleveland "stood out, if only for honesty and independence, as the sole reasonable facsimile of a major president between Lincoln and Theodore Roosevelt."[13] Most of the chief executives during this period can be regarded, in the words of an old political science professor of mine, "postage-stamp presidents," for if they had not appeared on postage stamps, no one would know who they were. Rutherford B. Hayes, James A. Garfield, Chester A. Arthur, and Benjamin Harrison are generally not on the lips of most Americans when thinking of their presidential favorites but were, by no means, horrible executives, just not outstanding ones. But Cleveland far outclassed all presidents in the late nineteenth century and should, by any reasonable account, fall in the top five of any presidential poll. He was determined to keep the country on a proper heading, the course set forth by the Founders, no matter what direction Congress or the courts sought to steer it.

Professional historians, however, most often place President Cleveland in the realm of mediocrity. In articles discussing presidential greatness, he is usually never mentioned. In many presidential polls, he generally ranks in the top twenty but typically never in the top ten, the threshold for greatness and near-greatness. Of all the major historical surveys, he ranked in the top ten just once, coming in at number eight (the "near-great" category) in Arthur M. Schlesinger Sr.'s 1948 poll in *Life* magazine, the first such study ever undertaken. Schlesinger repeated his poll in 1962, this time in the *New York Times*, but Cleveland had slipped to eleventh place, generally an "above average" rating.[14]

In a 1981 poll conducted by historian David L. Porter, Cleveland finished fifteenth, an "average" ranking. In 1982, a poll came out in the *Chicago Tribune Magazine* in which Cleveland finished thirteenth. Scholars

Robert K. Murray and Tim H. Blessing conducted their own presidential performance study, published in 1982 in the *Journal of American History*. Cleveland came in at number seventeen, again in the "above average" category. Murray and Blessing make note of the fact that Cleveland has fallen consistently in polls from 1948, where he stood at number eight, to their poll, which listed him in seventeenth place. "Cleveland is rated more harshly by the younger historians than by the older historians," they write, and "will probably not rise above his current ranking as older historians die off." This is particularly true since the older generation of historians were more conservative than their younger counterparts. A more recent survey conducted in 2005 by the more conservative *Wall Street Journal* in conjunction with the Federalist Society pegged Cleveland at number twelve, his latest listing in the "above average" category.[15]

But in the end, Murray and Blessing's analysis has been proven correct, as more recent polls have not been sympathetic. A 2002 Siena College Research Institute survey ranked him number twenty, a frequent spot and almost exactly in the middle. On President's Day in 2009, C-SPAN released a new presidential survey, its first since 2000. In overall ranking, Cleveland also came in twentieth. The poll of sixty-two historians also ranked each president in ten separate categories, where Cleveland also remained largely in the middle. He ranked highest in "Public Persuasion," coming in at number seventeen, and lowest in "Relations with Congress," at twenty-seventh. In the important categories of "Crisis Leadership" and "Economic Management," he ranked twentieth and twenty-first respectively.[16]

On July 1, 2010, Siena College Research Institute released its latest presidential survey. Cleveland again, as he did in 2002, ranked at number twenty, five spots *behind* Barack Obama, who had served just eighteen months in office when the poll was taken. This review by 238 scholars also ranked each president in twenty separate categories, everything from background and experience to communications and handling the economy. Cleveland ranked nineteenth in overall leadership and highest in the categories "Avoid Crucial Mistakes," placing at number fourteen, in "Relations with Congress" at number fifteen, and "Party Leadership" at sixteen. In his handling of the economy he ranked twenty-second, close to the twenty-first spot he polled in the C-SPAN survey. But even though many historians praise him for his legendary honesty, strangely he placed nineteenth in "Integrity," meaning there were eighteen presidents that scholars believe were more sincere than Grover Cleveland.[17]

Although these findings are perplexing, two of the most puzzling categories in both the C-SPAN poll and the recent Siena College survey were those dealing with leadership and economic management. Cleveland's lower rankings are most peculiar since he managed the Panic of 1893 with considerable skill and under intense pressure while maintaining law and order, which had begun to break down, and placing the nation on the road to economic recovery far better than did FDR, who ranked second and fifth in those respective categories in the C-SPAN poll, and first and third in the 2010 Siena College survey. It is quite mystifying that a president who managed to keep the United States mired in a severe Depression for more than a decade as much of the world was coming out of it, while using the opportunity to transform a capitalistic nation into a social welfare state, received such high rankings. Perhaps this says more about the scholars being polled than it does about their rankings.

Alvin Stephen Felzenberg, who holds a PhD in politics from Princeton and is a fellow with the Kennedy School of Government at Harvard, recently conducted his own study and gave Cleveland mediocre marks. Using a five-point scale to determine presidential success, with five representing the highest grade and one the lowest, Felzenberg, in his book, *The Leaders We Deserved (And A Few We Didn't)*, rates Cleveland at 2.83, roughly in the middle, in six separate categories. Cleveland ranked a five, the highest grade possible, for character, along with the likes of George Washington, Abraham Lincoln, James Madison, and John and John Quincy Adams, to name a few.[18]

In other categories, Cleveland did not fare nearly as well. For vision, Felzenberg rated Cleveland a two, along with such presidents as Martin Van Buren, William Howard Taft, and George H. W. Bush because they were primarily "managers" and "responded to events as they unfolded," rather than taking control of events and inspiring the nation with a far-reaching vision. In the category for competence, Cleveland also rated a two, placing him in the same company with Ulysses S. Grant, Taft, Van Buren, Chester A. Arthur, and John and John Quincy Adams, an insulting and degrading score. In economic policy he again rated a two, pairing him with Andrew Johnson, Lyndon Baines Johnson, James Buchanan, and John Tyler, none of whom ever faced the level of economic turmoil that Cleveland did. For preserving and extending liberty, he also rated a two, ranking him with the likes of Woodrow Wilson and Richard M. Nixon, two presidents who did not hold liberty in the highest regard. And finally, for defense, national security, and foreign policy, he received a grade of three, along with such chiefs as Thomas Jefferson, Andrew Jackson, and Van Buren. Though his high-ranking grade in character is beyond argument, the other positions are inaccurate and unfair.[19]

Other, more recent scholarly examinations by intellectuals in non-historical fields have generally provided a more favorable ranking. Ivan Eland, the director of the Center for Peace & Liberty at the Independent Institute, published in 2009 *Re-carving Rushmore: Ranking the Presidents on Peace, Prosperity, and Liberty*, in which he graded each president according to how their policies promoted peace, ensured prosperity, and safeguarded liberty. Eland ranked Cleveland at number two, Cleveland's highest placement ever.[20] But such praise is limited in academic circles.

So for a myriad of reasons, Cleveland ranks low in presidential greatness, at least in the eyes of most academic historians and political scholars. Perhaps there is a simple reason for this disrespect, aside from purely ideological ones. Historians Schweikart and Allen, who hold a more favorable opinion of Cleveland, referring to him as a "presidential giant," write that "Republicans have ignored him because he was a Democrat; Democrats downplayed his administration because he governed like a modern Republican."[21] Or, as I would add, as a modern Republican *should* govern. But the Republican Party, we should keep in mind, is not the conservative movement, nor is the conservative movement the Republican Party. The GOP has only served as a recent vehicle, crashed on the side of the road most of the time, it would seem. Though Cleveland was a Democrat, I am not advocating a return of conservatives to their original home in the Democratic Party. That ship has sailed, and good riddance. This book is about the purity of a historical conservatism, not about party politics.

But to put the movement back on solid footing, it is less important where conservatism resides and more imperative to find the right leader and the right principles. If conservatism should remain with the Republican Party, then we must select, for all future presidential nominees, a strong, proven, unflinching conservative in the mold of Cleveland—steadfastly principled, fiscally rock-solid, and ethically pure, a leader who will not sacrifice his principles for any political gain whatsoever. We cannot abide any more Bob Doles, John McCains, or even George Bushs for that matter. Compromising principles will no longer suffice. Those days must end and end forever. Conservatives must prevail in the choice for president in all future elections, or we might all go down with the ship.

"The problem for conservatives with the arrival of our 'hour' is leadership," R. Emmett Tyrrell, Jr. has written. "It appears that we are not flush with the kind of leadership that we had in the Reagan years or even in the 1990s."[22] But we must not lose heart. A great leader will emerge, perhaps one we know or someone not yet in the national spotlight. Cleveland was not a solid candidate for the presidency in 1884. He was fairly strong in New York but relatively unknown around the country. In most lists of potential presidential nominees, he was placed no higher than third. Yet when finally discovered, the people rallied around him because he was a true, honest reformer.

This book is not a full biography of Grover Cleveland. It does not look at the man's life in detail but instead how he, as a public official, dealt with the major issues of his day during his capacity as mayor of Buffalo, governor of New York, and president of the United States. The issues tackled within these pages are as relevant today as they were in his time—public character and behavior of our candidates; the role of government in the everyday lives of the people; the burden of taxation; the distribution of wealth; government involvement in an economic Depression; monetary policy; and complex foreign affairs. It is hoped that this book can awaken the American people to the realization of exactly how far off the cliff we have driven. We should not continue to ignore our political forebears, great statesmen such as Grover Cleveland; we should embrace him. A reexamination of his career can help blow a fresh wind into the conservative movement, re-strengthen the party, and hopefully get us back on track toward righting our ship of state.

Preface:
Parallels of History:
"The Billion-Dollar Congress"

In 1884, after twenty-four years of Republican White House rule, Grover Cleveland became the first Democrat elected to the presidency since before the Civil War. A quarter century of corruption, profligate spending, high taxes, and ever-expanding government had become the norm. When Cleveland entered office, he instituted honest government; ended presidential luxury; slashed the bureaucracy; halted out-of-control spending by vetoing a record 414 bills; protected the massive budget surplus that Republicans were all too eager to spend; attempted to cut taxes by a significant margin only to come up short in the US Senate; and reduced the national debt by 20 percent. After four years of Cleveland Conservatism, voters gave him a plurality of popular votes in his 1888 reelection bid, but he lost the presidency in the Electoral College to Benjamin Harrison. Big Government Republicans were back in charge.

The Republican Party, where liberalism resided in those days, believed it had the support of the majority of the country, and party leaders had every reason to think just that. During the previous quarter century, as the Civil War nearly destroyed the Democratic Party, the GOP held the White House for twenty-four of twenty-eight years. The makeup of Congress was nearly as one-sided. From the midterm elections in 1858, until 1888, Democrats, with a strengthening Northern wing, coupled with its steadfast Southern stronghold, managed to control the House for only twelve years; the Senate just four. It seemed as if the "Grand Ole Party" had been and would be in power forever.

When Harrison entered office in 1889, with a Congress controlled by the GOP, liberals wasted little time in getting its Big Government agenda back on track. The Jeffersonian interlude of Grover Cleveland only made liberal Republicans more eager, and with full control of the federal government once again, they embarked on an ambitious, far-reaching agenda, seemingly to make up for lost time. The new House Speaker, Thomas "Czar" Reed of Maine, summed up the Republican attitude about governance. "The danger in a free country is not that power will be exercised too freely," he said, "but that it will be exercised too sparingly."[23] Such a statement could have been the official slogan for the Obama-Pelosi-Reid Administration from 2009-2011.

During the first session of the Fifty-First Congress from 1889–90, Republicans enacted several major pieces of legislation, which have an eerie similarity with government actions under Obama. Liberals went after corporations, inflated the currency, raised taxes, massively increased spending, squandered the surplus, and tried to assert federal control over the electoral process. They even played "sectional warfare" by passing laws to increase the premiums paid to bondholders and to return federal tax money paid by the Northern states during the Civil War.[24] It would be a classic case of political overreach.

First, succumbing to pressure from its Western base, Republicans authorized the Sherman Antitrust Act, a strong measure that gave the federal government more control over big business. Authored by Senator John Sherman of Ohio, brother of the famous Civil War general, the bill stated in its very first sentence: "Every contract, combination in the form of trust or otherwise, or conspiracy, in restraint of trade or commerce among the several States, or with foreign nations, is hereby declared to be illegal." Such vague language in the new law allowed future administrations, namely that of Theodore Roosevelt, to expand it and use it in wide-ranging ways. With this bill, the federal government could essentially seize and break up any company it deemed a monopoly. It "was one of the most important enactments ever passed by Congress," wrote Republican Senator Shelby Cullom of Illinois, but "if it were strictly and literally enforced, the business of the country would come to a standstill."[25] The federal power grab was enormous.

Second, to provide more inflation in the currency, pressure that also came from the West, Congress passed the Sherman Silver Purchase Act, which required the government to buy 4.5 million ounces of silver per month, the total amount produced by the nation's silver mines in the western states. Under the previous silver law, the Bland-Allison Act of 1878, the government purchased just 2 million ounces per month. Though not all of the silver was coined and put into circulation, the Sherman Act authorized new treasury notes to purchase the bullion, greenbacks that could be redeemed for gold. The infusion of new money produced a boom period, but it also caused a slow drain on the nation's gold reserve, which, along with too much cheap money in the economy and increased spending, led to a severe depression in 1893.

Third, protectionist Republicans wanted higher tariffs, even though rates were already at all-time highs. Ohio Congressman William McKinley, chairman of the House Ways and Means Committee, authored a new tariff law that raised duties to their highest level in history. By doing so, it was hoped the McKinley Act would keep out most foreign imports, which would take away all competition for American businesses and also help alleviate the growing federal budget surplus, ongoing since 1866. With such high rates, imports would fall, thereby diminishing revenue. Western Republicans, not necessarily in favor of higher tariffs, supported the measure in exchange for eastern support for the antitrust and silver acts. But despite its intentions, the bill's high duties effectively raised taxes on everyone by making products more expensive for consumers.

Fourth, in another effort to get rid of the pesky surplus, Congress passed an extravagant pension bill, the Dependent Pension Act, to provide help to Union army veterans and their dependents. Older, more stringent requirements were loosened tremendously so that anyone who had served at least ninety days in the Union army during the Civil War and had a disability, regardless of how the handicap occurred, could receive a pension. During his first term in 1887, President Cleveland had vetoed a similar measure, calling it a raid on the treasury, but the new Republican Congress, now in conjunction with a Republican president, was determined to place it on the law books and reward one of its favored constituent groups with funds from the public trough.

Under Harrison and the Republican Congress, spending on pensions rose from $80 million in 1888, Cleveland's last full year of his first term, to $160 million by 1893, when Cleveland resumed the presidency. The pension list also swelled from 489,725 recipients in 1889 to 966,012 in 1893 as the Pension Bureau added 19,000 new pensioners per month, whereas before just 19,000 per year were placed to the rolls, as everyone with army experience rushed to get on the dole.[26]

In addition to the increased spending on pensions, Congress appropriated a wealth of money for other schemes, earmarking funds for additional naval vessels and various internal improvements projects, such as river and harbor development, the main pork barrel project of the day. With all the spending, Democrats quickly dubbed it the "Billion-Dollar Congress," the first Congress in American history to spend a billion dollars. Czar Reed, in his smug, arrogant manner, responded to Democratic criticism of the splurge by noting, "It's a billion-dollar country!"[27] But ordinary Americans weren't buying it.

Under liberal governance, the nation saw its hard-earned surplus, accumulating in the treasury at a rate of $100 million per year, vanish with scarcely a return. While in office, President Cleveland watched over it like a protective mother and tried on many occasions to return it to the people, but Republicans squandered it with little regard for its rightful owners. In 1888, Cleveland's final year in office, the surplus amounted to $111 million; after Harrison's administration it had dwindled to just $2 million.[28] Political cartoons depicted President Harrison pouring Cleveland's surplus into a large hole in the ground.

Congress also attempted to assert federal control over traditionally local areas. One bill, authored by Republican Senator Henry W. Blair of New Hampshire, provided $15 million in federal aid to education, a proposal he had submitted in every Congress since 1881. President Harrison supported the measure, but it was defeated in the Senate by a narrow vote of 42 to 36. Today, in contrast, the government spends roughly $70 billion a year on public education, a budget that has continued to grow by leaps and bounds with no effort to stop it.[29]

Like support for public schools, voting has always been a state and local matter, but liberals in Washington always seek means to control it, as Democrats have in recent years with the group ACORN, an Obama administration-supported community organization that sought to control voter registration. The 1890s were no different. A bill authored by Congressman Henry Cabot Lodge of Massachusetts would have given the federal courts jurisdiction over state and local elections as well as registration efforts, presumably to aid disenfranchised blacks in the South. But Democrats feared the measure would enhance the GOP's hold on power through fraud. Southerners, reminded of the hated days of Reconstruction, were outraged, calling the act the "Force Bill." It passed the House by a close party-line vote but later died in the Senate. Cleveland himself called the effort to control elections "a dark blow at the freedom of the ballot."[30]

Democrats across the country were perplexed at Republican efforts to gain more power in Washington, and Cleveland, as the only living ex-president from that party, was much sought after for advice and support on how to stop it. Hesitant to actively campaign for candidates, the former chief executive counseled his party to remain on the sidelines. There was no need to offer Democratic alternatives, he told them. Republicans had sought control of the government, and now they had it. It wouldn't be long, Cleveland believed, before the people were alerted to GOP shenanigans.

Though he counseled restraint, the Republican legislative program, particularly the spending, greatly concerned Cleveland, who saw his four years of hard work going down the drain. But in the end he thought it might work out for the best. "You and others used to say that our administration of affairs would be remembered long by the American people," he wrote to William Vilas, one of his former cabinet secretaries, who became a close friend and pen pal during these intervening years. "I could not see why this should necessarily be so; but our successors have made it so, I am sure. I feel badly and sad to see the result of so much hard labor undone. And yet I sometimes think that God has ordered it all for the enlightenment and awakening of our people."[31]

On another occasion he wrote to Vilas, "In these days, the people who occupy in Washington are so fast running off the rope, which I believe is bound to get about their necks." So why interfere with a party that was in the process of committing suicide? "I have thought as I have seen the Republicans getting deeper and deeper into the mire that our policy should be to let them flounder," he wrote Congressman John Carlisle. For Cleveland, it was okay to be a "Party of No."[32]

No one really wanted to be a party of do-nothingism, but Cleveland's political instincts proved to be right, as the massive GOP program proved too much for the American people. In the midterm elections in 1890, Republicans were trounced in one of the greatest midterm landslides, losing more than 90 seats in the House. Conservative Democrats won an astonishing 238 of 332 congressional races. When the Fifty-Second Congress opened in 1891, only 86 Republicans remained in the US House of Representatives. Among the vanquished: staunch progressive and future presidential candidate Robert M. LaFollette of Wisconsin; future House Speaker Joseph Gurney "Uncle Joe" Cannon of Illinois; and William McKinley himself, who was punished for his massive tax hike. One of the new Democratic arrivals was a young, thirty-six-year-old populist from Lincoln, Nebraska, named William Jennings Bryan. And though they did not reclaim the Senate, Democrats gained four seats there as well. Happily relaxing in retirement, Cleveland was overjoyed with the electoral success and wrote a close friend, "Election news and fishing rods make me quite happy in these days. Did you ever see such a landslide?"[33] This set the pace for the presidential election of 1892.

As the leading Democrat in the country, Cleveland was asked to again be a candidate for the White House, but he had no desire to return to what he often referred to as a "killing office." But two things changed his mind. He did not like what the Republicans were doing to the country, and he was greatly disturbed by the movement within the Democratic Party to emulate GOP policies, a nineteenth-century version of modern-day "me too" Republicanism. Leading Democratic presidential candidates in 1892 were moving toward the GOP on the issues of protectionism and currency inflation with an advocacy of free coinage of silver. These policies, Cleveland believed, would hurt the nation and destroy his party. That he could not and would not allow.

Soon he began giving public speeches articulating the philosophy that set Democrats apart from Republicans and made it the party that should be in power in Washington. On January 8, 1891, he gave a Jackson Day public address in Philadelphia at the Young Men's Democratic Association, a speech titled "The Principles of True Democracy," a clear enunciation of Jeffersonianism. The true principles of the Democratic Party were a creed, he told his assembled audience, a creed that had the significance of religious dogma, not to be violated. The Democratic Creed was not "uncertain or doubtful" but came straight from the "illustrious founder of our party," Mr. Jefferson:

> Equal and exact justice to all men; peace, commerce, and honest friendship with all nations—entangling alliance with none; the support of the State governments in all their rights; the preservation of the general government in its whole constitutional vigor; a jealous care of the right of election by the people; absolute acquiescence in the decisions of the majority; the supremacy of the civil over the military authority; economy in the public expenses; the honest payment of our debts and sacred preservation of the public faith; the encouragement of agriculture,

and commerce as its handmaid, and freedom of religion, freedom of the press, and freedom of the person.[34]

But the party had begun moving away from these timeless principles, he believed, and Washington now seemed to be engaged in government paternalism, siding with one class of Americans over another, in exorbitant spending, and in crushing the rights of the states and the people. When "we see the functions of government used to enrich a favored few at the expense of many," he continued, "and see also its inevitable result in the pinching privation of the poor and the profuse extravagance of the rich; and when we see in operation an unjust tariff which banishes from many humble homes the comforts of life, in order that, in the palaces of wealth, luxury may more abound, we turn to our creed and find that it enjoins "equal and exact justice to all men." He continued:

> When we see our farmers in distress, and know that they are not paying the penalty of slothfulness and mismanagement, when we see their long hours of toil so poorly requited that the money lender eats out their substance, while for everything they need to pay a tribute to the favorites of governmental care, we know that all this is far removed from the "encouragement of agriculture," which our creed commands.

> When we see the extravagance of public expenditure fast reaching the point of reckless waste, and the undeserved distribution of public money debauching its recipients, and by pernicious example threatening the destruction of the love of frugality among our people, we will remember that "economy in the public expense" is an important article in the true Democratic faith.

> When we see our political adversaries bent upon the passage of a Federal law, with the scarcely denied purpose of perpetuating partisan supremacy, which invades the States with election machinery designed to promote Federal interference with the rights of the people in the localities concerned, discrediting their honesty and fairness, and justly arousing their jealousy of centralized

power, we will stubbornly resist such a dangerous and revolutionary scheme, in obedience to our pledge for "the support of the State governments in all their rights."

With strict adherence to such principles, the party, once back in power, and "by an intelligent study of existing conditions, should be prepared to meet all the wants of the people as they arise, and to furnish a remedy for every threatening evil." The government existed, he believed, and the people supported it "for the sake of the benefits of all," not to the chosen few, whomever they may be. The protection of the people's rights and the promotion of their welfare and happiness was the object of good government, and, he believed, only the Democratic Party, with its adherence to "time-honored principles," could obtain it.

The American people, who always stood with him, agreed. Two years after the Republicans and their Billion-Dollar Congress came to an end in November 1890, the Harrison Administration met a similar fate and felt the wrath of the American people. Cleveland would occupy the White House for a second time and was once again determined to keep the ideals of the American Revolution, embodied in the Party of Jefferson, alive and well in the United States.

I

Grover Cleveland: The Man and His Age

Your patriotic virtues have won for you the homage of half the nation and the enmity of the other half. This places your character upon a summit as high as Washington's. ... When the votes are all in a public man's favor the verdict is against him. It is sand, and history will wash it away. But the verdict for you is rock, and will stand.
—Mark Twain to Grover Cleveland[35]

THE MAN

Grover Cleveland's story is a purely American tale, where a man of less than modest means, with no political connections, rose to the highest office in the land. He was born Stephen Grover Cleveland on March 18, 1837, in Caldwell, New Jersey, named for a former family pastor, Stephen Grover, who had died the year before. The fifth child of the Reverend Richard Falley Cleveland and Anne Neal, the Cleveland family had a long and illustrious line of success and distinction. The first Cleveland to arrive on American shores was Moses Cleveland, a Puritan from Ipswich, England, who sailed to Massachusetts in 1635 at the age of eleven to serve as an indentured servant. Many in the Cleveland family believed that the present-day city of Cleveland, Ohio, was named after a descendent of Moses.[36]

Once his term of indentured service ended, Moses Cleveland settled in the town of Woburn, Massachusetts working as a carpenter. In 1648, at the age of twenty-five, he married Ann Winn and gained enough prominence to reach the status of "Freeman" in Puritan society, which brought with it all the rights of citizenship. He also belonged to the local militia unit. Moses and Ann had eleven children, and the third son, Aaron, began a sting of four consecutive Aaron Clevelands, most of them members of the clergy.[37]

Grover Cleveland descended from a line of ministers and clergymen, with the most famous among them being his great-great-grandfather, Aaron Cleveland, who died in Philadelphia in 1757 at the home of his good friend Benjamin Franklin. Franklin eulogized the late Cleveland in his newspaper, the *Pennsylvania Gazette*, writing that his death "is greatly lamented by all who knew him, as a loss to the public, a loss to the Church of Christ, and in particular to that congregation who had proposed to themselves so much satisfaction from his late appointment among them." Dr. Franklin went on to call Aaron Cleveland "a gentleman of humane and pious disposition, indefatigable in his ministry, easy and affable in his conversation, open and sincere in his friendship, and above every species of meanness and dissimulation." His great-great-grandson would exhibit many of the same qualities.[38]

The familial line continued from the next Aaron Cleveland, who was a member of the Connecticut legislature and introduced a bill to abolish slavery, to William Cleveland, Grover's paternal grandfather, who worked as a watchmaker in Westfield, Massachusetts. William married Margaret Falley of Norwich, Connecticut, in 1793. Their son, Richard, Grover's father, was born in 1804. Richard attended school first in Norwich and then went on to Yale College, graduating with high honors in 1824, and later enrolled at the Princeton Theological Seminary, completing his studies in 1829. He served briefly as a tutor in Baltimore, where he met and married Ann Neal and then accepted the call to preach. In keeping with the family tradition, Richard served as a Presbyterian minister, settling first in Windham, Connecticut, then in Caldwell, New Jersey in 1835.[39]

Grover Cleveland's oldest brother, William, the firstborn child, would pursue his father into the ministry, continuing the Cleveland family legacy. Although he did not follow in the footsteps of his forebears, being the son of a preacher meant that Grover was raised on the same Puritan values, consisting of firm discipline, obedience, reverence, a strenuous work ethic, and a strict observance of the Sabbath. In 1841, when Grover was four, the family moved to Fayetteville, New York, near Syracuse, where Richard took a job as pastor of the local Presbyterian church. There Grover lived for the next ten years of his life.[40]

As a pastor, Richard Cleveland's salary usually never rose above $600 a year, making it difficult to provide for a family with nine children. Grover, along with his other siblings, attended a local academy in Fayetteville but also relied heavily on his well-educated father, who excelled in Latin and mathematics, as well as other important subjects, for their education. This vast home-schooling curriculum was necessary, for in the family's state of near-poverty, a college education would be almost impossible for Grover to obtain. But like many of America's early presidents, Grover Cleveland received most, if not all, of his education at home, a fact he delighted in telling his friends and companions.[41]

By 1851 prospects looked brighter, as Richard moved the family to Clinton, New York, where he would head the American Home Missionary Society, a job that would pay $1,000 a year, quite a tidy sum in those days. This would be more than enough to provide for the growing family and send the boys to college. In Clinton, Grover attended a better school than he had in Fayetteville, thereby allowing him to begin a preparatory course for nearby Hamilton College. He had dreams of attending with his brother William, who had already enrolled.[42]

But his father's perpetually declining health forced Grover to return to Fayetteville to work in a country store for two years, where he would earn $150 as well as his room and board, which would help pay his college expenses. He returned to Clinton in 1853, after a two-year hitch, only to find that his still-ailing father had quit his more lucrative and increasingly stressful job to accept a position as a pastor in nearby Utica for much less money. His father had an extremely strong work ethic, typical of a Puritan, often working himself ill on many occasions. Such a trait would be carried on by his son Grover. But soon after the move to Utica, Richard Cleveland finally succumbed to his sickness and died. Grover was just sixteen years old and, with his mother and sisters to care for, all hope for college evaporated.[43]

The young Grover, now fatherless, never possessed a burning desire or ambition to accomplish great things, only a driving sense of duty, ingrained in him by his Presbyterian father. As Richard Hofstadter has written, "The son took on his father's moral imperatives and accepted his lack of ambition as normal. In him the balance between the call of duty, as he saw it, and the call of ambition was heavily weighted in favor of duty." In fact, the "hardship of being thrown on his own resources at an early age made Cleveland neither bitter nor rebellious."[44] He wanted to succeed in any field of endeavor, for that was what duty required of him. If his road was blocked in one area, he looked for another. His sense of duty led him to look for new opportunities. "He did not differ from other boys of his town save one thing," wrote journalist and friend William Allen White. "He always had a job."[45]

After the death of his father, Grover spent a year in New York City, working as a bookkeeper and assistant to the superintendent at the Institution for the Blind, where brother William had taken a job as head teacher. But the position paid very little and offered no hope of advancement. Miss Fanny Crosby was a very well-known pupil and a teacher at the institute, and a remarkable woman in her own right. Blind from birth, she was the first woman to address the US Congress, personally met every president from John Quincy Adams to Woodrow Wilson, and wrote the lyrics to more than 8,000 songs and hymns. She remembered the young Grover. "His mind was unusually well developed for his years," she recalled to George F. Parker in 1892. "Every moment of his spare time was given to the hardest kind of study. He was a persistent reader, devoting most of his attention to history and … the law." She also noted his outstanding character, that no one had "a kinder heart" than he, particularly remarkable at that young age, she recalled.[46]

After his unhappy year in the city concluded, Grover, as so many Americans had done before him, decided to head west, perhaps to Cleveland, Ohio, to seek better opportunities and, hopefully, great success. But before he could begin his journey, he needed money. So he arranged to borrow $25 from an old friend of his father's, Ingham Townsend, who readily made the loan on the condition that the young Grover pay it back by lending a helping hand to someone in need when he became a success. But the steadfastly honest young man, even at age eighteen, would not accept the money or depart on his trip without first getting a promissory note from Townsend.[47]

He set out for the West in the spring of 1855 and decided first to visit an uncle, Lewis P. Allen, in Buffalo before continuing his journey. Allen, a prosperous landholder, farmer, and cattle breeder, persuaded Grover to stay in Buffalo by offering him a job in the revising and editing of a book, the *American Shorthorn Herd Book,* which Allen published every few years. In the 1861 edition, after Grover entered his legal practice, Allen credited his nephew's assistance. "I take great pleasure in expressing my acknowledgment of the kindness, industry, and ability of my young friend

4

and kinsman, Grover Cleveland, Esq., of Buffalo, a gentleman of the legal profession who has kindly assisted my labors...." It was Allen who arranged an opportunity for his nephew to study law in the excellent Buffalo firm of Rogers, Bowen & Rogers, a career Grover had already considered pursuing. Allen, founder of the Erie County Agricultural Society, was well respected throughout Buffalo and the surrounding county. Henry Rogers accepted the young man into his firm, though reluctantly so.[48]

His law studies began near the end of 1855, while earning four dollars a week working at the firm. On his first day, December 3, after arriving early for work, he was given a copy of *Blackstone's Commentaries on the Laws of England.* "That's where they all begin," Rogers told him as he handed the young man the dusty book. He sat down at his desk and began to read. At noon, as the rest of the firm departed for lunch, they locked the doors, imprisoning their new, and forgotten, employee. *Some day I will be better remembered,* he thought.[49]

Cleveland studied law for four years at Rogers, Bowen & Rogers, which, incidentally, was located next to the firm of former President Millard Fillmore, to whom the young Grover had developed a casual acquaintance. He worked long and hard preparing to take the bar exam. One evening, while at his studies, he was again locked in the office, as one of the clerks mistakenly believed everyone was out of the building. Having no key of his own, Cleveland simply worked all night and was still at it when everyone returned the next morning. He had an "inordinate capacity for work," wrote biographer Denis Tilden Lynch. "Hours meant nothing to him." He even moved from his uncle's farm outside the city to the Southern Hotel to be closer to his office. The hard work paid off, as he gained admittance to the New York Bar during the May term of the New York Supreme Court in 1859. But rather than leave the firm to begin a private practice, he remained for four additional years, eventually rising to the position of chief clerk.[50]

It was during these early years, the tumultuous 1850s, that he attached himself to the Democratic Party, even though Uncle Lewis, a former Whig, belonged to the newly formed Republicans. The partners at Rogers, Bowen & Rogers, who were in a position to exert much influence on the young man, all belonged to the Whig Party as well. However, when the Whigs collapsed, Henry W. Rogers and nephew Sherman S. Rogers both supported former president and fellow Buffalonian, Millard Fillmore, as the Know Nothing Party candidate, while Denis Bowen joined the Democrats.[51]

With a divided firm, it would have been wise for a young up-and-coming law student to remain neutral, particularly when he could not yet vote. But that was never Grover Cleveland's way. Not as a law student and not as president of the United States. He openly declared himself a Democrat. In 1856, at the age of nineteen, he worked on the presidential election campaign of Democrat James Buchanan, despite the fact that Cleveland was still too young to vote. He marched in torchlight parades and stood outside polling places to hand out ballots. Later in life, he told his close friend Richard Watson Gilder that he chose the Democrats because it seemed to him "to represent greater solidity and conservatism." The Republican candidate in 1856, John C. Fremont, "repelled" him, while the GOP campaign struck him "as having a good deal of fuss and feathers about it."[52]

Cleveland's early years working on behalf of the party provided much training and experience that he would utilize later in his public life. "I had no aspiration to be a boss," he told his presidential secretary George F. Parker, "but I only followed the custom of my time in taking my place at the polls and distributing ballots to all those who asked for them, using my influence to convince the wavering, or to confirm those who belonged to my household of faith." And because he spent so much time working for the party on the grassroots level, Cleveland came to understand the great game of politics—the politicians and how they operated. Later, when he held public office, seekers of patronage jobs would request an audience with him, believing him naïve with little understanding of the sport of politics, thereby making it easier to persuade him to dole out favors. But "these men little knew how thoroughly I had been trained, and how I often laughed in my sleeve at their antics."[53]

It is interesting to note that Grover Cleveland's first foray into presidential politics was on behalf of James Buchanan, who won his 1856 White House race over Fremont by a close vote. No Democrat would be elected to the office of president of the United States until Grover Cleveland himself some twenty-eight years later. In 1858, after reaching the voting age of twenty-one, he cast his first ballot for the Democratic slate in the midterm elections that fall. His hard work on behalf of the party and its candidates over the next five years earned him a position as assistant district attorney, an office he held for three years. On January 1, 1863, he left Rogers, Bowen & Rogers to accept the position with an annual salary of $600. And because of the advanced age of his boss, District Attorney

C. C. Torrance, Cleveland did the majority of the work and argued most of the cases.[54]

His excellent work in the district attorney's office won him praise, but new worries emerged during that crucial time period. A horrendous war with the South broke out in 1861, and Cleveland, though of military age, did not volunteer to fight for the Union cause as so many Northern men had done. He was quite content to continue his life in Buffalo, far removed from the fighting. As biographer Horace Samuel Merrill has noted, Cleveland's behavior during the war "was not conducive to political advancement. While others were profoundly moved by the crisis, he remained almost coldly calm."[55]

The situation changed in 1863, as President Abraham Lincoln signed a conscription law instituting a military draft, making the twenty-six-year-old Grover eligible for the army. And sure enough, on the first day, he was chosen. But he elected not to fight and followed the example of many professionals, including John D. Rockefeller and future political nemesis James G. Blaine by hiring a substitute to take his place, which the law allowed. There are a couple of possible reasons for his decision. Perhaps, according to Merrill, "his innate conservatism and inherent independence caused him to resist a popular crusade," which was how the war seemed for many Northerners, especially since Lincoln changed the war's aim that year from one of preserving the Union to liberating slaves. Or, perhaps, he had a much more practical reason. With older brother William now a minister living in New York City caring for a family of his own and trying to make a living on a meager pastor's salary, someone had to stay home and care for his mother and sisters. Since Grover had a good job and no obligations of his own, the family decided that he should occupy that role while two other Cleveland brothers joined the fight.[56]

Scholars Larry Schweikart and Michael Allen, though praiseworthy of Cleveland, heavily criticize him for this act, calling him "the first draft-dodger president, no matter the legality of the purchase [of the substitute]."[57] This is an obvious comparison to Bill Clinton and a false one at that. The differences could not be clearer. Clinton's actions may very well have violated US law during the Vietnam era, but Cleveland's was perfectly legal and in accordance with the conscription statute as written and passed by Congress, which was then signed by President Lincoln. It may have been politically unpopular, but it was well within the law.

To fulfill his part of the conscription requirements, Cleveland, like so many of his peers, hired a newly arrived Polish immigrant, a seaman named George Benninsky. The conscription act allowed the hiring of substitutes for $300, but Cleveland did not have the money, so he borrowed it from his boss, District Attorney Torrance. It took him some time to repay the loan, and he was able to do so only after he left his job for private practice. He chose this path even though he had the right, as an assistant district attorney, to procure the services of a convict, who would have readily agreed to fight rather than face the full jail sentence or execution. The real tragedy of the draft exception was that most substitutes were poor, ignorant immigrants who had little choice. Arriving in America with no friends, no money, and no job or living arrangements, the army offered "three hots and a cot." Many took the chance, only to end up mangled or dead in a war they had no stake in. But Cleveland's substitute survived the war unharmed, and the two remained acquaintances afterward.[58]

As for the war's most contentious issue, as a young man Cleveland had a very indifferent attitude toward slavery, precisely because the Southern institution did not directly affect him. He had never been around slavery, never came into contact with it, and never joined an abolitionist organization. In fact, his family practiced the same indifference. Neither his father nor his mother held abolitionists in high regard, so it's no surprise that Cleveland did not seem interested in the issue. However, he considered himself a War Democrat and did not side with the Copperheads, those Democrats who advocated peace with the Confederacy. Furthermore, it is believed by members of his family that he crossed party lines and voted for Lincoln in 1864, though there is no direct evidence of a claim that seems dubious for such a rock-solid Democrat.[59]

Because of his impressive work as an assistant district attorney during the war years, Democrats selected him as their candidate for the office of district attorney in 1865, even though the elderly Torrance wanted another term. Cleveland faced off against a close friend, Lyman K. Bass, the Republican candidate. When leaders of the GOP approached Bass about running for the office, he talked it over with Cleveland first. "Well, Cleve," he said, "I have been offered the nomination for district attorney against you." Cleveland replied without hesitation, "Well, why don't you take it?" Bass did and would enjoy huge advantages—a heavy Republican county, and, with the end of the war, the projection of an extraordinarily successful year for the GOP. But despite the disadvantages, Cleveland lost by just 600 votes. Soon after the failed bid, he went into private practice, joining a law firm as a partner with Albert P. Lanning and Oscar Folsom.[60]

It would not be long, however, before his name was put forward for another political office. For the local elections in 1870, Democrats needed a sound candidate for the important post of sheriff of Erie County. Though it had been five years since he lost his bid for district attorney, the fact that he made a strong showing in a county with a large Republican majority was not lost on his supporters. William Williams, manager of the Lake Shore Railroad and a client of Rogers, Bowen & Rogers when Cleveland clerked there, sought a congressional seat but wanted a strong Democratic ticket to help carry him to victory. He chose Cleveland for the sheriff slot.[61]

When asked by fellow Democrats to accept the nomination, Cleveland hesitated for some time, mainly because such an office was generally never given to lawyers. He eventually relented because he realized that should he win, he would have more free time for personal study, and the office of sheriff paid, in salary and fees, much more than he made in his private law practice, money he needed for the continued care of his mother and sisters. On Election Day he won the race against Colonel John B. Weber, a Union army veteran, by the slim majority of just 303 votes, a remarkable feat in such a Republican-dominated county.[62]

Once settled into the sheriff's office, on January 1, 1871, Cleveland had to contend with a multitude of difficulties. Buffalo, the third largest city in New York, as well as the whole of Erie County, had a crime problem. This was due to a variety of reasons but mainly because the area was constantly inundated with strangers, as it sat on Lake Erie and attracted everyone involved in the shipping industry, from out-of-town sailors to local dockworkers. Buffalo, at that time, had, according to Alyn Brodsky, "the highest concentration of lowlifes east of the Ohio River." Of course, the "lowlifes" probably couldn't help but be enticed by the 673 bars, a multitude of gambling halls, and scores of brothels and independent "women of the night" who propagated the city. The jail held more prisoners than any in the entire state of New York, housing every kind of criminal from petty thieves to violent felons. And those who weren't caught or convicted had most likely paid off one of the many corrupt local officials, or so it was believed.[63]

In addition to problems on the streets, Sheriff Cleveland also had headaches with the management of the office he now held. His predecessors ran the department like it was a joke. It was grossly inefficient and abhorrently corrupt. But he dived right in and began the cleanup of large-scale mismanagement and corruption. He personally oversaw how expenses were appropriated and put an end to much of the dishonesty, even from contractors who happened to be Democrats. He stopped suppliers of food who "short-weighted" the products and even used a tape measure to determine if the county received the right amount of wood it had paid for. No one got a free ride with this new sheriff in town.[64]

As unpleasant as wading through endless corruption seemed, perhaps Cleveland's most distasteful task as sheriff was the personal supervision of the execution of two prisoners. The local court had scheduled the hanging of two convicted murderers during Cleveland's tenure. He thought the task disagreeable, for in those days the sheriff pulled the lever himself. Yet he took on his responsibility rather than hiring someone to carry it out, which he had the authority to do. This is not to say that he opposed capital punishment, for he did not, but he felt it was his solemn duty to conduct the affairs of his office, not pass the buck to someone who had not been elected by the people. Judge Albert Haight of Buffalo recalled that to dodge duty "wasn't Grover Cleveland's way. He recognized his duty and was not disposed to shirk it or transfer his own responsibility to the shoulders of a subordinate." It also saved the county money by not having to pay an executioner. He also decided to carry out the sentences in a more private setting, ending what had become, in his mind, a public spectacle.[65]

Despite the objectionable executions, Cleveland's term as sheriff was successful. The people of Erie County loved the reformer in the sheriff's office and were quite pleased with the results of his tenure. According to Samuel Horace Merrill, he "conducted the office efficiently and honestly and found the role rather pleasant." Even his former opponent, Weber, who succeeded him, noted that Cleveland had administered the office "with marked efficiency." But as pleasant as it was, at least a majority of the time, once his service was over he declined a second term in 1873, though he more than likely would have easily gained reelection. He had served honorably, had done a fine job for the people, and made $40,000 on top of it all. It was time to get back to the practice of law.[66]

In 1873, Cleveland returned to his profession full time in a new firm of Bass, Cleveland & Bissell, the same Lyman K. Bass who had defeated him for district attorney eight years before. He continued to lead the life of a bachelor, living alone in a small apartment above his law office, relishing in the comforts of his station. During this period, he was, according to William Allen White, "[a] tall, burly, hard-faced, soft-voiced, but quick-spoken fellow; hard-headed, hard-living, hard-working, close-fisted, honest, sturdy, manly." Among his closest friends during these years were Folsom, Bass, and Powers Fillmore, son of the former president Millard Fillmore.[67]

Though a bachelor, he did not mix with the younger crowd or attend any of the lavish social functions held in Buffalo. He had, according to fellow Buffalonian Charles H. Armitage, "few of the truly social instincts and fewer of the social graces." Instead, during after-hours with no legal work pending, he could be found in a local saloon enjoying the company of his close friends, eating, and drinking. He delighted in large plates of sausage and sauerkraut, washing it down with numerous steins of beer, and afterward a good cigar. Years later, political enemies would tar him as the "town drunk," but alcoholic beverages were consumed in moderation. He also enjoyed a good game of cards or fishing and hunting on his off days, which were few and far between.[68]

He was also an exceptional attorney. According to his law partner and close friend, Wilson S. Bissell, himself a Yale graduate and later postmaster general, Cleveland had the best qualities a partner could ask for. "He was in the best sense a successful lawyer. He never belonged to the class of 'money-making' lawyers.... He always met his personal obligations promptly, and he abhorred debt; but he never had any desire to accumulate a fortune, and he was generous to a degree." He also had a strict policy against defending murderers and known crooks. According to an early biography written in 1889, Cleveland, as an attorney, "was fluent, terse, and forcible. His clear apprehension of legal principles, and his logical statement of them, rendered him successful." And "he was never so industrious as when working for the rights of some poor man."[69]

Showing traits from his father, Cleveland was a workaholic despite enjoying the fun of bachelorhood. As Samuel Horace Merrill has noted, he "could more than hold his own as a hard worker. He possessed phenomenal physical energy and power of concentration, at times working continuously for twenty-four hours without feeling tired." William Allen White described him as possessing a "great, hulking body [that] furnished unlimited power for a tireless brain lusting for work."

Wilson Bissell, early in their partnership, also acknowledged this habit in Cleveland, remarking that he was "generally the first one in the office in the morning and the last one out of it at night." When preparing for a trial, "he would devote himself to the case absolutely and completely, whether it was large or small, whether with fee or without, and for a rich client or for a poor one. The noon hour was, for him, always an opportunity for further study and preparation—not for eating—and the hours of the night, not infrequently the whole night, a further opportunity." Many of these same traits would characterize Cleveland's handling of his executive duties in public office.[70]

As a prominent attorney who was held in high esteem by local lawyers, Cleveland was also an excellent negotiator, and local judges, recognizing his quality, often assigned him cases that could be settled out of court, where he could act as an arbiter. According to Buffalo Judge Joseph V. Seaver, other "lawyers sought his appointment as referee. They knew they would get sound law and a square deal." To journalist William Allen White, he had "an ox-like honesty," was "straightforward, trustworthy, true. Probably he never willfully deceived a human being in his life." In addition to his sound qualities as a man, judges also knew Cleveland did not mind sifting through the mountainous material usually associated with such cases, mainly relating to business and financial matters, which other lawyers detested, and that he would apply a strict interpretation of the laws in question. His concept of the office of president would be remarkably similar, as historian Lewis L. Gould has observed, approaching his White House duties "as the Buffalo, New York, attorney he had been before he entered politics in the early 1880s."[71]

Cleveland loved being a private lawyer and did not desire a steady position in the employ of another. He enjoyed the independence of his own practice, taking only those cases he wanted while remaining at home in Buffalo. In 1881 Chauncey Depew, the head of the New York Central Railroad, offered Cleveland the job of general council for the company because of his "character and ability," with a salary of $15,000 a year, compared to his annual income of $7,000, which he could also continue to receive. But money did not mean that much to him, and his thrifty ways kept his bank accounts relatively full, so he turned down the job. "No amount of money whatever," he told Depew, "would tempt me to add to or increase my present work." He also enjoyed his freedom, and taking the position with the railroad would have required him to be on duty often and would necessitate travel to other parts of the state. Furthermore, his decision not to accept the offer would pay political dividends in the future, as he could never be linked to the corrupt and hated railroads. His decision astonished Depew. "I doubt if there were many lawyers in the United States who had that philosophy or control of their ambitions."[72]

But while he engaged intensely on his law practice, politics did not stray far from his mind. Even as a lawyer engaged in nonpolitical court battles, he held tightly and passionately to his Jeffersonian principles.

This strongly held belief in Democratic ideals was apparently the main cause of a street fight with one Mike Falvey in 1873. Falvey evidently called Cleveland a liar, and before he knew it Grover knocked him into a ditch on Seneca Street. The melee continued over to Swan Street before mutual friends broke it up, inducing the combatants to a nearby saloon to cool down. Such was the rough and tumble world of nineteenth-century American politics, and Cleveland, a man of honor, would not back down from a challenge.[73]

Oscar Folsom, in addition to being his one-time law partner, would remain a close friend and steadfast political supporter. Like Cleveland, Folsom was a fervent Democrat and faithfully supported the party and its candidates, including his friend Grover. Folsom was so passionate about the Democratic Party that on election night in 1872, while reading vote results to the crowd at the Buffalo Young Men's Association, he threw up his hands in exacerbation. "Grant's elected," he exclaimed, "and the country's gone to hell!"[74] Ardent supporters like Folsom and Bissell greatly aided Cleveland's climb up the political ladder.

Cleveland had often considered a career in politics, despite its unpleasantness, but never dreamed it would take him as far as it eventually did; a local judgeship, a spot on the state Supreme Court, or perhaps a congressional seat had been the limit of his political ambitions. And when he did finally make a permanent foray into politics, his law partners were "loath to lose him" because they relied on "his great strength and ability as a lawyer."[75]

After his brief stints in the district attorney's office and as sheriff, Cleveland settled back into what he thought would be a quiet life as a successful attorney, never dreaming that his political career was about to surge with speed almost unmatched in American political history. Grover Cleveland, not unlike President Barack Obama, had a meteoric rise in politics, a climb historian Richard Hofstadter called "rapid and freakish." The remarkable ascent, wrote Henry Jones Ford, was "without a parallel in the records of American statesmanship."[76] In the spring of 1881, at the age of forty-four, he was a simple, largely unknown attorney in Buffalo, New York; four years later, in the spring of 1885, at the age of forty-eight, he was inaugurated as the twenty-second president of the United States. The precipitous rise surprised even him. After being in the White House just a few weeks, he spoke to Henry Watterson of the *Louisville Courier-Journal* about the sheer shock of it all. "Sometimes I wake at night and rub my eyes and wonder if it is not all a dream."[77]

In the years between his time as a lawyer and his inauguration as president, his only political experience consisted of a one-year stint as mayor of Buffalo in 1882 and two years of a three-year term as governor of New York, from 1883 to 1885. And in both instances, party leaders and concerned citizens sought his candidacy. In the fall of 1881, prominent townsmen of Buffalo approached him about the possibility of running for mayor, mainly because of his established reputation as a reformer and a no-nonsense officeholder. He took the opportunity, albeit reluctantly. When he did, he unwittingly set a course for the White House.

As mayor, he set out after the corruption in the city council with such fervor that it attracted the notice of the state Democratic Party. He vetoed numerous wasteful spending measures and took such tough stands against dishonesty in government that he emerged as a serious candidate for governor. He captured the nomination in the summer of 1882 and won election that fall by the largest majority in state history up to that time.

His fierce opposition to corruption and waste continued when he entered the governor's mansion in Albany in January 1883. But a year and a half into his term at the statehouse, he was approached yet again about seeking higher office. When asked to be a candidate for president of the United States in 1884, his political experience was far less than even that of Sarah Palin, and he faced the same questions as to his readiness for high office. But once elected, he proved to be an excellent president, though historians continue to place him in the realm of mediocrity.

HIS AGE

Grover Cleveland emerged during a period in US history not generally known for its outstanding presidents but for its outstanding transformations. Cleveland's America experienced monumental changes during what has come to be commonly called the Gilded Age, a period from 1877 and the end of Reconstruction, to 1901 and the beginning of Teddy Roosevelt's Progressive America. The term itself is derived from Mark Twain's novel of the same name. Emerging from a bloody civil war and a harsh phase of reconstruction, the nation began an era of rapid and extensive transformation, converting from a largely agricultural-based economy to one dominated by manufacturing and big business, growing from a second-rate economic power in 1860 to the world's leading economy by 1900 as the Industrial Revolution swept the land. Economic historian John Steele Gordon has written that during this period, the "American economy changed more profoundly, grew more quickly, and became more diversified than at any earlier fifty-year period in the nation's history."[78] Or any fifty-year period after it, for that matter.

Political leaders of the era also recognized the nation's phenomenal ascendancy. "We lead all nations in agriculture, we lead all nations in mining, we lead all nations in manufacturing," boasted William McKinley in the House of Representatives in 1890.[79] Indeed, economic data conclusively demonstrates that the United States sat atop the world in economic output, soaring past Great Britain and Germany by the turn of the century. Industrialization, manufacturing output, and agricultural production grew by astonishing rates. Between the Civil War and the turn of the century, gross national product (GNP) quadrupled, from $9 billion to $37 billion, while exports increased from $234 million to $1.5 billion, greatly surpassing imports.

The production of steel grew from 77,000 tons in 1870 to 11.2 million tons in 1900. The production of steel rails grew by 523 percent and railway track mileage by 567 percent. In 1861, there were 35,000 miles of railroad track in the country; by 1900 there were more than 200,000 miles of track. Coal production rose by 800 percent, and wheat yields increased by 256 percent.[80]

In 1880 Great Britain led the world in world manufacturing output with 22.9 percent of all industrial production. The United States came in second with 14.7 percent and Germany third at 8.5. However, by the beginning of the twentieth century the situation had changed dramatically. The United States had grown to control nearly one-third of world manufacturing output with 32 percent. Comparing the United States and Great Britain between 1870 and 1913, American industrial production rose 4.7 percent annually, more than twice as much as the United Kingdom, which enjoyed a 2.1 percent growth rate. In 1860, the United States produced half the amount of goods as Great Britain, but by 1914 the United States had more than twice as much production. That year, America produced twice as much steel as Germany, and four times as much as Britain. Gross domestic product (GDP) rose from $80 billion (1996 dollars) in 1865 to $319 billion in 1900, a 400 percent increase. Such rapid growth in industrial production led steel magnate Andrew Carnegie to call the era "the golden age of the Republic."[81]

The population of the United States also rose dramatically in the late-nineteenth century. In 1860, at the start of the Civil War, 31 million people resided in the North America States; by 1865, at the war's end, 35 million called themselves Americans, an increase that also takes into account the 620,000 soldiers killed during the conflict, as well as the 50,000 civilians. By 1900 the population had more than doubled, rising to 76 million. Immigration played a central role in this increase, accounting for 25 percent. More than 11 million foreigners entered the United States between 1865 and 1900, with the decade of the 1880s seeing the largest increase, as nearly 5 million immigrants came to the New World from 1880–90. The astonishing population growth, as well as the steady migration to the West, led to the formation of ten new states from 1867 to 1896.[82]

Politically, the nation was undergoing great change as well. With the country's great expansion came new national issues and revitalized political parties. For the first time since the fall of the Whigs in 1852, the nation had what could be considered "a working national party system," in the words of historian H. Wayne Morgan, which consisted of two parties with national, rather than simply sectional, appeal.[83] Today, pundits on both the right and the left have argued that the two parties are virtually the same; "not a dime's worth of difference between the two," to borrow a phrase from George Wallace.

But during the Gilded Age, there was no argument about it— Republicans and Democrats were as different as night and day on most issues. To prevent any confusion, as has been noted previously, the Democratic Party, in the nineteenth and early twentieth centuries, was the conservative party. Many right-wing Republicans today, though it may be hard to fathom, would have been Democrats in Cleveland's day, while most left-wing Democrats would have probably felt more at home in the Party of Lincoln. The two parties have, over time, switched ideological positions, particularly on economic issues, the Democrats shifted left beginning with William Jennings Bryan and Woodrow Wilson, while the Republicans moved to the right with Warren Harding and Calvin Coolidge.

In the nineteenth century, the GOP, ideological heirs to Alexander Hamilton and Henry Clay, believed in a more energetic national government; loose construction of the Constitution; activist judges; federally-administered civil rights and governmental assistance for former slaves; high protective tariffs; a national banking system; a national debt; government paternalism; subsidies to business; economic regulation; an inflationary monetary policy; and, at the end of the nineteenth century, foreign adventurism. The party was made up of eastern industrialists and bankers, Union army veterans, Western farmers, federal officeholders, and African Americans.

In stark contrast, their Democratic counterparts maintained their hold on the Jeffersonian values of smaller government; strict construction of the Constitution; respect for the states; low taxes and tariffs; no debt; laissez faire economic policy; a sound currency; and a non-interventionist foreign policy. Elements making up the Party of Jefferson and Jackson included the commercial element of the Northeast, urban workers, and Southern farmers.

Both parties were lenient on civil service reform and generally agreed on maintaining their respective political machines, though they both gave lip service to that important political issue. "Republicans," writes period scholar H. Wayne Morgan, "believed in federal economic subsidy and a workable amount of regulation for the national interest. Democrats, however, clung doggedly to ancient ideals of local rule—negative government that protected alleged individualism—and never understood the changes that covered America after the Civil War," which is a way of saying they were not "progressive."[84]

Until Cleveland came along, the Democrats faced what seemed like an insurmountable uphill battle in the quest to end Republican rule in the White House and throughout the federal government. The party had suffered mightily since the secession movement in 1860. The ensuing war had been a political disaster, particularly for Northern Democrats, as half the party walked out with the disunion of the Southern states. Before the war, Democrats dominated Washington, led by its strong Southern wing. Afterward, Northern Republicans mastered the art of "waving the bloody shirt," a campaign tactic employed to remind Northern voters just how destructive Democrats and their Southern base had been, thereby successfully branding all Democrats as rebels and traitors, destroying their political hopes. In the late 1860s and early 1870s, it seemed the Democratic Party barely had a pulse and remained nearly comatose for a decade after Lee's surrender. The Party of Lincoln maintained the trust of the majority of the American people for a greater part of the period. "To be Democrats in those days," wrote Newton D. Baker, Secretary of War to Woodrow Wilson, "was to be a member of a faithful band fighting a hopeless battle for a faith as old as the Republic."[85]

But the faith remained strong, despite the huge disadvantage, and Democrats managed to remain competitive, keeping the parties relatively even. Though they lost every presidential election from 1860 to 1880,

Democrats fought hard for every vote and were close to victory in 1876 and 1880. They were also viable in state and local races as well. In 1874, nine years after Lee's surrender to Grant, Democrats gained control of the US House of Representatives and controlled it during every Congress, with the exception of two, over the next two decades. The Senate remained firmly in Republican hands, aside from two Congresses, but the majority was always very close and the race in 1880 even resulted in a tie. Presidential contests tightened after Grant's landslide victories in 1868 and 1872. The disputed election of 1876 between Rutherford B. Hayes and Samuel J. Tilden was as close as any race in American history, with Hayes losing the popular vote by 3 percent but winning the electoral vote by one ballot after a compromise. Four years later James Garfield defeated Winfield Scott Hancock by just 0.09 percent of the national vote. It was obvious that Democrats were gaining on Republicans nationally and beginning to shed the "party of rebellion" image.[86]

The politics of the Gilded Age were dynamic, much more vibrant than has been portrayed. Before the Civil War, debates over slavery and state sovereignty dominated the political discourse, with economic issues, namely the tariff, taking a backseat, save a few testy years in the 1830s. After the war and Reconstruction, economic issues, such as trade and the currency, overshadowed all others, even civil rights, with civil service reform coming in a close second. These issues, though different than their antebellum counterparts, were as hotly debated and divisive as those that tore the nation in two in the early 1860s. The battle over the tariff in 1894, wrote one veteran Washington reporter, "literally set the country on fire."[87] The nation also nearly went to war over the disputed presidential election in 1876. So it cannot be argued that there was anything passive about the politics of the Gilded Age.

Throughout the entirety of the nineteenth century, politics was the nation's pastime, if ever there was one. The American people loved politics, almost as if it were a national sport. Large gatherings could be found in every town on the day of elections, a ritual that generally coincided with market day. The mood was festive, not gloomy, as citizens met, talked, ate, drank, and were generally as jovial as modern Americans might be at a college football game. Most presidential elections saw heavy voter turnout, with an average of 70 percent throughout the Gilded Age. Turnout jumped to 80 percent for the crucial election of 1896, with five states reporting 95 percent or more of its eligible voters going to the polls, a feat nearly impossible to imagine today.[88]

Such participation is even more astonishing when the number of elections is considered. Many states divided its political contests into four or five separate days over the course of a year, holding votes for state-wide offices, such as the governorship on one day and then another for local jobs, which might also be divided into city and county races. State legislative contests would also be held on a different day. New York, for instance, elected its legislature every year during the late-nineteenth century, while all offices in Massachusetts were one-year terms, requiring a yearly election. Voting for Congress was most often held in October, and the presidential election would always be in November, as the Constitution prescribes. Even with this multitudinous electoral arrangement, the American people fully participated in the political system.

Along with the nation's rapid growth and the American love of politics came the politicians, most not necessarily being of the finest stock. The Gilded Age was one of rampant corruption and narcissism, a time of great wealth and tycoons—the infamous "robber barons"—as well as a time of great dishonesty and exploitation. Famed historian Henry Adams, grandson of John Quincy Adams and great-grandson of John Adams, criticized the political depravity of the era in his memoirs. "One might search the whole list of Congress, judiciary, and executive, during the twenty-five years 1870 to 1895 and find little but damaged reputation. The period was poor in purpose and barren in results. No period so thoroughly ordinary had been known in American politics since Christopher Columbus first disturbed the balance of American society."[89]

Modern historians have characterized the period as consisting of unexceptional and unfamiliar chief executives, contemptuously called "postage stamp presidents." But in the midst of the mediocrity, Grover Cleveland stands out as the most underestimated of all, largely forgotten by the American public and having received scant attention by scholars, who, when they do write of him, are often less than sympathetic. As Dr. Henry Graff, professor emeritus of history at Columbia University writes in his biography for the American Presidents Series, Cleveland was "the best unknown president."[90] But his legacy should be far from unknown, for he did much to preserve America's limited form of government.

The United States nearly lost its constitutional republic during the Civil War and Reconstruction. "The war," wrote Governor Richard Yates of Illinois in 1865, "has tended, more than any other event in the history of the country, to militate against the Jeffersonian idea, that 'the best government is that which governs least.' The war has not only, of necessity, given more power to, but has led to a more intimate prevision of the government over every material interest of society." When Confederate General Richard Taylor, son of former President Zachary Taylor, returned home to his Louisiana plantation in 1865, he found that "society has been completely changed by the war. The [French] revolution of '89 did not produce a greater change in the 'Ancien Régime' [the corrupt, party-driven reign of Louis XVI and Marie Antoinette that led to the French Revolution] than has this in our social life."[91] In short, the war destroyed the Age of Jefferson.

Historians, even those who lived through the conflict, understood the profound changes the war brought. George Ticknor wrote in 1869 that the war had left a "great gulf between what happened before it in our century and what has happened since, or what is likely to happen thereafter. It does not seem to me as if I were living in the country in which I was born."[92]

Modern scholars have also made note of this fact. As James M. McPherson points out in *Abraham Lincoln and the Second American Revolution*, after the war "the old decentralized federal republic became a new national polity that taxed the people directly, created an internal revenue bureau to collect these taxes, expanded the jurisdiction of federal courts, established a national currency and a national banking structure. The United States went to war in 1861 to preserve the Union; it emerged from war in 1865 having created a nation. Before 1861 the two words 'United States' were generally used as a plural noun: 'The United States are a republic.' After 1865 the United States became a singular noun. The loose union of states became a nation."[93] And all of this at the hands of the Party of Lincoln, which hoped to dominate the "new nation" as no other political entity had.

Other scholars have also noted how great the Republican War had altered the nation. "Republicans," writes historian Heather Cox Richardson, "transformed the United States." Before the war the "national government did little more than deliver the mail, collect tariffs, and oversee foreign affairs. By the time of Appomattox, the United States had changed." Wartime Republicans constructed "a newly active national government designed to promote" a worldview of an industrialized America, with Washington playing an increasingly interventionist role. "A strong central government dominated the postwar nation," she continued. "It boasted a military of a million men; it carried a national debt of $2.5 billion; and it collected an array of new internal taxes, provided a national currency, distributed public lands, chartered corporations, and enforced the freedom of former slaves within state borders."[94] Each of these developments flew in the face of Jeffersonian Democracy.

As a conservative, Cleveland saw himself as one who could, as president, put the spilled milk, or at least some of it, back inside the bottle. He believed himself to be in the mold of the nation's founders, namely Jefferson, who could reverse the destruction of political institutions the war and Reconstruction had wrought, just as the Sage of Monticello turned back the destructive Federalist tide in 1800. This is why Republicans fought so hard against his election as president. Cleveland stands out as the lone Jeffersonian among all presidents, from Lincoln to the present, and held as tight to classical liberalism as any president in American history. For that, progressives of the era loathed him.

In many ways he was able to turn the nation back to the notions of the Founders, what he often referred to as "good government." Journalist H. L. Mencken wrote favorably of him as "the last of the Romans."[95] Congressman Samuel Cox, who also served as Cleveland's ambassador to the Ottoman Empire, wrote passionately of a president he admired greatly, comparing him to a Roman statesman who'd battled Caesar. "Rome never needed a Cato more than America needed a man of similar qualities, to free her from the gives of corrupt politics," he wrote in his memoirs. "This nation has such a man for president. While others may falter in duty, he will stand firm and true to the principles of the platform on which he was elected, and observe and carry out his pledges of reform in letter and spirit. His need was so exigent that we may well stand appalled at the danger we have escaped, and which threatened our free institutions. It needed a statesman as courageous as Caesar and as honest as Cato to save our liberties from a decadence worse than death."[96] American had its "Cato" in Grover Cleveland.

II

GROVER THE GOOD: CLEVELAND'S REMARKABLE PUBLIC CHARACTER

In many respects ... Mr. Cleveland made the country a good president. He was of absolute integrity, honest and faithful in the discharge of his official duties, and would not tolerate graft, fraud, or corruption in public places or among government officials.
—*O. O. Stealey, Louisville Courier-Journal*[97]

Today we are inundated with political scandal, dishonesty, and incompetence from the courthouse to the White House. Scarcely a day passes that we can turn on the television without hearing of more corruption out of Washington and our state capitals. But as more and more politicians promise to clean out the pigpen, it seems more and more manage to fall into it. It has become a story without end throughout our history.

CAMPAIGN CONDUCT

The comportment of a candidate in a political campaign is a good indicator of how a person will behave once in office. As Senator John C. Calhoun once said, "We may rest assured that those who will play false to get power will play false to retain it."[98] The ugliness of campaigns in our own time, as well as the subsequent scandals, is a testament to his irrefutable wisdom.

Yet nineteenth-century campaigns were as nasty and bitter as they are today, and some historians might even say they were worse. By 1884, Cleveland's first run at the presidency, Republicans had possessed the White House for twenty-four successive years and had no intention of ever giving it up to an opposition party they considered synonymous with rebellion. The Civil War had all but destroyed the Democratic Party, painted as it was with the brush of treason. Like Germany after World War One, Democrats received all the blame for the bloody conflict. If any Democrat, North or South, tried to gain political power in any branch of the federal government, Republicans quickly brandished their "bloody shirt" campaign in retaliation, reminding voters who was at fault for more than 600,000 battlefield deaths and the sundering of the Union.

When seeking a candidate for president in 1884, Democrats, after six consecutive presidential defeats, decided to try someone new, a reform candidate not tied to the Washington crowd. They reached out to Grover Cleveland, the sitting governor of New York, specifically because of his personal character and conduct in office. During his service as mayor in Buffalo and governor of New York, he led crusades against public corruption, and his honest, straight-talk campaigns impressed members of both parties, as well as independents. In every race he ran, Cleveland gained votes from the opposing party, winning record-breaking majorities in his mayoral and gubernatorial contests. Just as the 1980s saw the emergence of Reagan Democrats, the 1880s beheld Cleveland Republicans. And since the "bloody shirt" card finally seemed to be losing steam by the mid-1880s, Cleveland's reform credentials and his vote-getting ability made him an attractive candidate who might be the one to finally take down the Grand Old Party.

The campaign, as usual, would prove a nasty affair. Republicans depicted their Democratic counterpart as the "town drunk," a "debaucher," a "lecherous beast," a "hangman," an "obese nincompoop," and a "drunken sot."[99] But Grover Cleveland would not play their dirty game. He had character, such that even those who loathed him had to acknowledge it. His great character came from his strong Christian upbringing, being raised in a spiritual home with a father and older brother who were both pastors in the Presbyterian Church and a mother who was equally grounded in the faith. Cleveland believed in the power of prayer, feeling "so much safer" with his mother's invocations, which he believed "had so much to do with my success."[100] Even his career in the great game of politics did not cause him to abandon his personal conduct.

When placed on the Democratic ticket in 1884, he had every reason to toss ethics to the wind and conduct a mudslinging campaign in order to win. He would face the quintessential establishment candidate in James G. Blaine of Maine, the GOP nominee. Blaine had been in politics his entire adult life it seemed, and, what's more, he was good at it. As a young man he served in the Maine state legislature, including a stint as speaker, and then in the US House, where he again sat in the Speaker's chair. He also served as a US Senator and finally as Secretary of State under James Garfield. He was, without question, the most popular Republican in the country. When his name was announced at the Republican National Convention that summer, pandemonium ensued from the self-professed "Blainiacs."

But with such distinguished service came the inevitable scandals. In short, Blaine was notoriously corrupt, a man who, in the words of reformer Carl Schurz, "wallowed in the spoils like a rhinoceros in an African pool." In his worst scandal, while serving as House Speaker, Blaine, in shades of the Clintons' Whitewater scam, got involved in a crooked Arkansas land deal. In exchange for company stock, Blaine ensured that a rail line received a land grant from the government. The situation only grew worse when Blaine's letters surfaced discussing the arrangement. At the end of each post, he instructed the recipient to "burn this letter." But his correspondent did not, and the letters became public, though Blaine was never convicted of any crimes or censured for his conduct. In politics, however, the scam stuck to him like glue, denying him the presidential nomination in both 1876 and 1880. He finally won out in 1884 only because it was "his turn," an affliction that seems to inculcate the GOP every few presidential election cycles.[101]

With Blaine's potential troubles, and a public fed up with corruption, Cleveland could coast into the White House, provided the Democrats ran a smooth campaign free of mud thrown in their direction. But scandal soon struck Cleveland in a personal way. Opponents alleged that while residing in Buffalo as a young man he had fathered a child out of wedlock more than a decade before. Such news terrified his campaign managers, who tried to coax him to lie to save his chance at the presidency. But Cleveland refused, sending an instructive telegram to Charles Goodyear, one of his supporters. "Whatever you do, tell the truth," he told him.[102]

To this day it has never been conclusively proven whether Cleveland fathered the child. The woman in question, Maria Halpin, named the baby Oscar Folsom Cleveland, supposedly after his father. But complicating the matter was the fact that Oscar Folsom, a law partner and good friend of Cleveland's, might also have had a dalliance with Miss Halpin. So to whom did the boy belong? One likely explanation may lie with another certain fact: Folsom was married and Cleveland was not. It is quite possible that Cleveland simply took the blame for the child rather than see one of his closest friends fall from grace with a shameful divorce. Cleveland paid child support for the first year of the boy's life, and finally, with the help of a local judge, placed him in an orphanage because Halpin had become an alcoholic. Folsom died in a carriage accident in 1875, a year after the child's birth, and could not come to his friend's defense. Cleveland himself remained silent on the matter.[103]

Charles McCune, a reporter for the *Buffalo Courier*, a politically friendly newspaper, wrote a story alleging that Cleveland had, in fact, been protecting the good name of his dear friend Folsom. Given this opportunity, Cleveland could have done what many politicians would have jumped at: throw his friend under the bus to protect his campaign. Folsom had been dead nearly a decade, so hurting him personally would not be a factor. But after seeing the newspaper story, Cleveland angrily wrote a friend about the allegation. "Now is [McCune] crazy, or does he want to ruin anybody? Is he fool enough to suppose for a moment that if such was the truth (which it is not, so far as the motive for silence is concerned) that I would permit my dead friend's memory to suffer for my sake?"[104] He would not tarnish the reputation of his friend to win the White House. He would continue to take responsibility for it, election be damned. In the end, though, it did not hurt Cleveland's reputation with the American public.

Now contrast Cleveland's character with that of Barack Obama. In 2008, candidate Obama ran into numerous problems with his personal conduct, namely his associations with persons of dubious character—including the "terrorist" Bill Ayers, hate-filled preacher Reverend Jeremiah Wright, race-baiter Father Michael Pfleger, and slumlord Tony Rezko. Obama ran away from every one of those relationships, claiming ridiculously on his Ayers ties that, "Oh, he was just someone from the neighborhood," even though he began his political career in Ayers's living room, and regarding Wright, he said "I wasn't in church the day those sermons were preached," even though he was married by him, his daughters were baptized by him, and he spent twenty years attending his church. But perhaps his most shameful display is the day Grandma—an elderly white woman who raised him after his father split and his mother was too busy with her career to care for him—was thrown under the bus. Obama labeled her a "typical white person" for her racist language, which essentially threw every Caucasian under the bus with her. He did this even though she was in the last few months of her life. Anything to win high office for today's politicians.

Having embarrassing mud slung at you generally begets retaliation. Cleveland's campaign managers found some serious personal dirt on Blaine they sought to use to smear the Republican nominee, perhaps as payback for the Halpin scandal. But if the information were leaked to the press, it would have been deeply embarrassing for Blaine's wife, Harriet. In short, the allegation was that the Blaines had not been legally married when their firstborn son arrived, an appalling disgrace in those days. Aides brought a man into the governor's office who claimed to have documentation of the alleged infidelity. Cleveland paid him for the evidence and then dismissed him. He then asked his assistants if all facts of the scandal were now in his possession. When they affirmed that he had all in existence, Cleveland shredded the documents and threw the pieces into the fire. "The other side can have a monopoly of all the dirt in this campaign," he said, and ordered the matter dropped. There would never be an "October Surprise" in any campaign Cleveland was involved with.[105]

It was very common, if not expected, in the nineteenth century for campaign managers to make promises to state leaders in order to gain their support for the presidential nomination and in the general election. Party leaders who made significant contributions to a victorious presidential campaign held it their sacred right to suggest nominees for cabinet officers and other high-ranking officials or even claim a top spot for themselves. The notion that campaign managers made deals to win support had pervaded American presidential politics from the beginning, since it was unfashionable for candidates to actively campaign for the White House. With the candidates absent from both the convention and the campaign trail, managers generally took it upon themselves to make promises, keeping the candidate in the dark. Once elected to the presidency, the White House's new occupant then discovered that the top spots in their new administration had largely been filled.

Even Lincoln himself, who instructed his managers to "make no contracts [that] bind me," found that promises had been made in order to gain enough support for him in 1860. Later, after discovering the deals, Lincoln angrily said his managers had "gambled me all around, bought and sold me a hundred times." After his retirement, President Benjamin Harrison told Teddy Roosevelt that when he won the presidency in 1888, he "found out that the party managers had taken it all to themselves. I could not even name my own cabinet. They had sold out every place to pay election expenses."[106]

In rare instances, some nominees made the secret deals themselves to assure support. James Garfield, who belonged to the "Half-Breed" faction of the Republican Party, desperately needed the support of Stalwart leader Roscoe Conkling in New York to overcome opposition from Tammany Hall. Garfield promised Conkling control of the state's patronage at a meeting with Conkling's surrogates at a Fifth Avenue hotel in August 1880, just before the kickoff of the fall campaign. Most often, however, such assurances were generally made on the candidate's behalf at closed-door meetings in smoke-filled backrooms away from the prying ears of newspaper reporters. In most instances, the public never knew any deal had been cut.[107]

But in Cleveland's day this was how the system worked. Corruption was simply part of the political equation in late-nineteenth-century America. As muckraking journalist Lincoln Steffens observed in *The Shame of the Cities*, politics in England is a sport, in Germany a profession, but in the United States, "politics is business." Large corporations had their hand in politics on every level, both legally and illegally, working hand-in-hand with political machines. After Harrison's close victory in 1888, a race in which he lost the popular vote, the president-elect remarked to friends, "Providence has given us the victory." But such high-minded rhetoric did not amuse Pennsylvania Boss Matt Quay. "Think of the man," he said. "He ought to know that providence hadn't a damn thing to do with it." Harrison, Quay noted, never knew "how close a number of men were compelled to approach the gates of the penitentiary to make him president."[108]

Cleveland, however, would not tolerate any deal making. "I will make no pledges. I will consent to none made for me," he told his campaign managers. "If I cannot go into the White House unpledged, I will not go at all." He also let it be known that if any pledges were made in his name, without his consent, he would disregard them. With such tough talk, Cleveland had stepped onto new ground. It was through "a series of improbabilities," writes Richard Hofstadter, "that a man of Cleveland's caliber became president in the Gilded Age." And when he became president, he vowed to clean up the corrupt system—and did, unlike his predecessors. He made good on his threat, ignoring any deal and promise made on his behalf.[109]

Cleveland also showed remarkable character when it came to the political issues facing the people. Time and again he stood on principle no matter the political consequences. He would rather lose an election than sacrifice his values, he often told his aides. He hated political expediency, which is doing things for purely electoral reasons, and loathed anyone who stooped to that level.

He absolutely would not triangulate on policy matters, the practice of taking up an opponent's issue to rob him of it, much like Bill Clinton did throughout his presidency. Cleveland faced a strong third-party candidate in his first White House run in 1884, Ben Butler of the Greenback Party, who bid for some of the same support, especially from Tammany Hall, run by John Kelly. To undercut Butler, campaign managers floated the idea that Cleveland could co-opt several issues from him, most importantly the imposition of inflationary currency to help debtors, and then kowtow to Kelly in order to keep Tammany off his back. But Cleveland did not think or act in such a politically calculated manner. Not in the slightest. He stuck to his Democratic principles no matter the political cost. To Daniel Lamont, his close personal aide and one of the campaign's managers, he wrote that he had no intention of bowing to either Butler or Kelly. "Now this is for you privately. I want to tell you how I feel. I had rather be beaten in this race than to truckle to Butler or Kelly. I don't want any pledge made for me that will violate my profession or betray and deceive the good people who believe in me." Tammany eventually supported Cleveland, albeit reluctantly, which had the effect of undercutting Butler's candidacy, making it a non-factor.[110]

While president in 1887, Cleveland decided to make his stand on the tariff issue, one of the hottest political topics of the era, to uphold the promises he made on the campaign trail to reduce rates. In December of that year, he sent Congress his annual State of the Union message centered solely on the tariff, an unheard of tactic. He wanted to focus the nation's attention on the reduction of duties and then push through a tax cut bill in the spring of 1888. Coming as it did in an election year, his aides tried to persuade him to tone down his effort for the campaign. But he would hear none of it. "I would stultify myself if I failed to let the message go forward from any fear that it might affect my election," he told them. "What's the use of being reelected unless you stand for something?"[111] Later in the year, the bill was defeated in the Senate, and Cleveland was defeated in November. But he stood his ground and remained true to his principles.

WORK ETHIC

Today, in our modern-media age, presidents work hard to show the American people that they are, in fact, working hard. In one of the best stories, according to Secret Service agents, President Jimmy Carter often rose before sunrise and headed to the Oval Office so the White House press corps, always on the job early, would see him hard at work. But once inside, Carter routinely closed the curtains to outside view and went back to sleep on the couch. It was a classic case of political showmanship, so often the case in the Carter Administration.[112]

But Cleveland's work ethic was not showmanship; it was legendary. White House staff, politicians from both parties, reporters, and friends marveled at how hard he labored each and every day. He often worked in his upstairs office until 2:00 a.m. or later and was usually back at it by 8:00 a.m. It was not unusual for him to spend "fifteen to eighteen hours out of the twenty-four" hard at work, wrote O. O. Stealy, the Washington correspondent for the *Louisville Courier-Journal*. Walter H. Page, a reporter from North Carolina, noted that the president "rises early and works late and does not waste his time—all because his time is now not his own but the Republic's, whose most honored servant he is." Often after finishing a long day of laborious work, he would shove back from his desk and tell his private secretary, Dan Lamont, "Well, I guess we'll quit and call it half a day." According to Allan Nevins, Cleveland "probably worked longer hours, day after day, than any other President since James K. Polk, who had worked himself to death."[113]

He had complete faith in the people and believed it his solemn duty to work hard on their behalf. His speeches and writings are littered with references to the people—how he did not want to disappoint them and hoped he could serve them effectively. Thomas F. Pendel, who served as doorkeeper at the White House in every administration from Abraham Lincoln to Theodore Roosevelt, remarked in his memoir that Cleveland "was a very hard worker—the hardest working president I ever saw in my life." White House usher Ike Hoover arrived to observe Cleveland's work ethic during his second term. Hoover served every administration from Benjamin Harrison to Franklin Roosevelt and wrote that Cleveland was "the most laborious of all the presidents under whom I have served."[114]

As a chief executive, one aspect of duty is to decide which bills to approve and which to reject. While we are accustomed to our modern-day presidents and politicians not reading bills before voting on or signing them, usually passing off laborious work to aides, Cleveland, citing duty, took on the load himself. And he was meticulous in his detail. If bills had been sloppily written (or, God forbid, had never been read by Congress before voting on it), he would not sign them. As governor he once angered a young legislator named Theodore Roosevelt for threatening to veto his set of municipal reform bills because they were carelessly drafted. Upon hearing of the threatened vetoes, Roosevelt demanded a meeting with Cleveland, and when he arrived in the governor's office burst out, "You must not veto those bills. You cannot. You shall not ... I won't have it!" Cleveland, slamming his fist down on his desk, shot back, "Mr. Roosevelt, I am going to veto those bills!" And he did. Once a bill had been passed and sent to him, observed David S. Barry, a political reporter and one-time sergeant-at-arms for the US Senate, Cleveland "took off his coat, hung it on the back of a chair, and sat down to burn the midnight oil in reading the bills and personally setting forth his endorsement or his opposition thereto."[115]

Other than the occasional vacation, which never lasted more than a week, Cleveland rarely enjoyed leisure activities. Professional baseball was an up–and-coming sport in the late-nineteenth century, and he was very fond of it. He once hosted the Chicago White Stockings (now the Chicago Cubs) at the White House. When invited to the ballpark to watch an upcoming game, Cleveland respectfully declined. "No, thank you," he told manager Cap Anson. "What do you think the American people would think of me if I wasted my time going to a ball game?"[116]

Cleveland also sought to change the decorum of the presidency, as Thomas Jefferson had when he entered the White House in 1801. In Jefferson's opinion the office had already taken on the style of a monarch. His predecessor, John Adams, had even wanted to give the president an title befitting that of a king: "His Highness the President of the United States and Defender of the Rights of the Same." Adams loved the trappings of high office. Wearing an expensive suit that included an elegant sword he'd arrived at his inaugural ceremony in a fancy carriage pulled by a fine team of six white horses. By contrast, Jefferson had worn a simple suit with shoes that laced rather than buckled—which he felt was too aristocratic—and walked to the Capitol for his inauguration rather than in a horse-drawn carriage. Residing in the mansion, he opened the door himself when someone knocked, even in his sleep attire, and removed the large rectangular dining table in favor of a circular one so that everyone present would be considered equal. He also served his guests personally, rather than have a servant do it.

Like Jefferson, Cleveland also had a lavish predecessor in Chester A. Arthur, who at the time would have been called a "dandy." Arthur loved the finer things in life, like fancy clothes, fine furniture, silver utensils, and the most expensive wines. Upon winning the vice presidency in 1880, he went on a shopping spree at Brooks Brothers, purchasing more than $700 worth of new clothes, about $15,000 in 2011 dollars. After becoming president with the tragic assassination of James A. Garfield, he completely redecorated the White House because he felt it had become too drab and dreary. He filled it with butlers, personal servants, valets, and even a French chef. When Mrs. James G. Blaine dined one evening with President Arthur, she wrote later that the "dinner was extremely elegant," with "hardly a trace of the old White House taint being perceptible anywhere." The "flowers, the silver, the attendants, all showing the latest style and an abandon in expense and taste."[117]

Cleveland followed in Jefferson's footsteps. He did not like the pomp and pageantry of any public position, what he once termed the "purely ornamental part of the office." The White House paymaster, Colonel W. H. Crook, wrote that Cleveland "was a plain, simple man, who had no desire to make himself prominent" with lavish events. He spent the "better part of each night over his desk" and generally kept himself "so deeply occupied that he could not see any one except on official business." From his first days in the White House, Crook noted that he "felt that the glitter of official life was distasteful to Mr. Cleveland. He was a man who believed that he had work to accomplish, and that work was a serious matter which must be attended to, and with which nothing must interfere." Cleveland was married during his first term, in a ceremony in the White House, and according to Crook, Cleveland worked "as hard as he ever did in his life" on the day of his wedding. He "worked harder, and kept longer hours than any other president we have ever had."[118]

The presidency had been greatly strengthened under Lincoln, and Cleveland also opposed its evolution into that of a monarchy, particularly where appearance was concerned. He dispensed with as much luxury as possible, dismissing all of Arthur's servants, even the fancy French chef. Ike Hoover witnessed Cleveland's cuts to the White House staff. The president dismissed "practically all of the domestic help; had a cyclone struck this portion of the establishment, it could not have been swept cleaner." Hoover noted that more "changes were made during the first two or three days of this administration than at any other time the oldest employee can remember."[119]

Even though he loved to fish on his days off, Cleveland refused to use the presidential yacht, the *Dispatch*. His executive staff was reduced to an almost nonexistent level, consisting of just a handful of men. If an aide were not available, Cleveland answered the recently installed White House telephone himself. To pay White House bills, he personally wrote out the checks.

President Carter also tried to craft a new image of the presidency, making it seem as though he was a "Regular Joe," but it was, once again, a case of political smoke and mirrors. When traveling, Carter could often be seen carrying his own luggage from Air Force One, an attempt to show the American public that he was not above anyone else. Secret Service agents, however, have revealed that bags carried by the president were empty. Crewmembers of Air Force One carried his real luggage.[120]

President Obama has made no attempt to refashion the image of the presidency in any meaningful way, even though Michelle Obama made sure cameras caught her shopping at a local Target store. But in contrast to Cleveland, the Obamas have taken White House entertainment and presidential trips and vacations to new heights. He "takes more vacations than any human being I've ever seen," Donald Trump said on Greta Van Sustren's show on Fox News, as Obama was about to embark on yet another expensive trip, this time an eleven-day getaway at Martha's Vineyard as the nation's economic woes continued, a junket where he and Michelle arrived on separate jets just four hours apart. He flew to New York City to take his wife to a Broadway show, traveled to Europe to lobby for Chicago as the host city for the 2016 Olympic games, and took a family trip to Hawaii every Christmas, one that lasted seventeen days, and included separate, and more costly, jet service for the First Couple.[121]

Michelle Obama also enjoys luxury courtesy of the American people. She spent $10 million in taxpayers' money on vacations in one year, including a four-day skiing trip to Vail, Colorado, a very expensive family jaunt to South Africa and Botswana for a safari where the flights alone cost more than $400,000, and a luxurious excursion to Spain with forty close friends, an outing that occupied sixty to seventy rooms at an expensive seaside resort. That's more than one-third of the entire hotel, with each room costing taxpayers $2,500 per night. What's more, some seventy Secret Service personnel accompanied the entourage. And maybe if you happen to be in an area that President Obama and his family are visiting, and perhaps you would like to get a glimpse of them leaving a bookstore or ice cream shop (an Obama favorite), then you must be swept by security, as law enforcement personnel walk through the crowds. If you don't want to be bothered, then you must move on and cannot remain in the area. Like it or not, the modern office has taken on the aura of a king.[122]

Presidents and their families have all enjoyed the trappings of the office, but it seems as though this is all the Obamas are interested in. To gain the presidency, Obama spent lavishly and raised a record $745 million, all the while laying plans for a $1 billion reelection campaign in 2012. This is more than obscene; it's downright repulsive. Anyone who would spend that kind of money has no business occupying the nation's highest and noblest office. With all those campaign IOUs, how can he govern efficiently and effectively?

While serving as president, Obama has also spent extravagantly on fancy parties and gatherings, as he said at one event, "We never need an excuse for a good party." His inauguration alone cost $170 million. Within three weeks of entering the White House, Obama threw an expensive cocktail party and served Wagyu steak, a Japanese variety and one of the most expensive cuts in the world, priced at $125 per pound, which had to be flown in from Japan. Entertainers, such as Jennifer Lopez, Stevie Wonder, Tony Bennett, Martina McBride, Alison Kraus, Brad Paisley, Charley Pride, Seal, Sheryl Crow, Smokey Robinson, and John Legend, just to name a few, have performed for the First Couple. The Obamas also threw what has been billed as a secret, "over-the-top" Alice-in-Wonderland-themed event, complete with Tim Burton and Johnny Depp and with punch served in "blood vials" that worried the administration so much that it was covered up. The White House has also put on a Fiesta Latina night to honor Hispanic artists and at least two lavish Super Bowl parties, serving the kind of food that First Lady Michelle Obama has preached that we the people should not eat—bratwurst, cheeseburgers, deep dish pizza, buffalo wings, twice-baked potatoes, ice cream, and beer, all at one bash.[123]

Obama also broke the record for a first-year president in foreign travel, visiting twenty nations. By the end of his second year, he had spent a total of fifty-eight days in thirty-three foreign countries, another record. With the nation in an economic crisis, as well as in wars in the Middle East, Obama played scores of golf games, and by his second year had already played more than the entire eight years of George W. Bush, who took a beating in the media for any trips to the links. Bush gave up his golf game because, with Americans at war, it "just sends the wrong message," he said. No so with Obama. It was also reported in the press that the Obamas fly in a personal trainer from Chicago every week to keep the family in top shape. And all of this on the taxpayers' dime while the unemployment rate climbed above 10 percent. According to Nile Gardiner of the *London Telegraph*, the Obama administration "resembles a modern Ancien Régime," the corrupt, party-driven reign of Louis XVI and Marie Antoinette that led to the French Revolution.[124]

But we need no such revolution, only the return of a little Jeffersonian simplicity in the White House. All future presidents should be more concerned about the great problems facing the nation and a little less concerned with entertaining himself and his family. We need a Cleveland, a true man of the people, not a king.

CLEAN GOVERNMENT

Though most Americans might try to dispute it, nineteenth-century politics was a dirty affair, much more so than today; it was an era full of scandal and corruption on a scale that is hard to fathom. Dens of corruption, known as rings, littered the cities of the great industrial North. Perhaps the most infamous, the Tweed Ring of New York City, stole an incalculable amount of public money, with some estimates as high as $200 million. The Tweed Ring and the superfluous corruption are very accurately portrayed in the Martin Scorsese film *Gangs of New York*.

One of the worst Tweed scandals concerned the construction of a new county courthouse in New York City, originally budgeted at $250,000, a mighty sum in 1862, but by the time it was finished a decade later, taxpayers had been bilked for $14 million, most of it finding its way into the pockets of the Tweed Ring. The amount of money skimmed by the Ring on the courthouse construction, according to scholars Edwin Burrows and Mike Wallace, equaled "four times as much as the Houses of Parliament and twice the price of Alaska." All for one building.[125]

Roy Morris Jr., in *Fraud of the Century: Rutherford B. Hayes, Samuel Tilden, and the Stolen Election of 1876*, relates a story about how Tweed's corruption actually worked. An electrician, who wanted to install fire alarms in the new courthouse building, submitted a high bid for the sum of $60,000. Boss Tweed responded to his request by asking, "If we get you a contract for $450,000, will you give us $225,000?" This was the Tweed machine in action, with surcharges to the city ranging from 10 to 85 percent.[126] Money stolen from public treasuries was then used to fund the political machine; to pay its members; to bribe politicians; to hire workers; to buy votes; and, ultimately, to stay in power, thereby allowing the ring to maintain its position and the theft to continue. The cycle continued in perpetuity, it seemed. Very few public officials dared take on the rings for fear of being ground down by their power and might. Many just went along and reaped the rotten, though eventually welcomed, rewards.

Cleveland's own hometown of Buffalo was no island oasis in this vast sea of theft. Being in the hands of Republicans a majority of the time, it was as corrupt and inefficient as any city in America. But Democrats were by no means immune to scandal. The municipal government had come under the influence of an "aldermanic ring," led by dishonest, thieving politicians from both parties. Mayors, regardless of party, were generally "yes men" who allowed the various city departments to grow tremendously, likely due to graft and corruption, but most probably because the mayor was also part of the gang. Many of the town's citizens, particularly the more affluent who paid the highest taxes, wanted the ring cleaned up and asked Grover Cleveland to run for mayor in 1881.[127]

That autumn, he accepted the nomination and spoke to an assembly of Democrats to outline the philosophy that would govern his administration, placing a strong emphasis on fiscal conservatism. "I believe that much can be done to relieve our citizens from their present load of taxation, and that a more rigid scrutiny of all public expenditures will result in a great savings to the community. I also believe that some extravagance in our city government may be corrected without injury to the public service." Government officials should treat the people's money as honestly as they did their own, he contended. "There is, or there should be, no reason why the affairs of our city should not be managed with the same care and the same economy as private interests. And when we consider that public officials are the trustees of the people, and hold their places and exercise their powers for the benefit of the people, there should be no higher inducement to a faithful and honest discharge of public duty."[128]

Throughout the brief fall campaign he echoed similar themes, vowing to clean up the corruption and bring fiscal sanity to City Hall. He spoke to people wherever he found them, even in bars, where he addressed them standing atop tables. "We believe in the principle of economy of the people's money," he told one crowd, "and that when a man in office lays out a dollar in extravagance, he acts immorally by the people." There would be no waste, fraud, abuse, or special earmarks when he ran the mayor's office. "A Democratic thief is as bad as a Republican thief," he told another group.

"Why shouldn't public interests be conducted in the same excellent manner as private interests?" He also echoed Thomas Jefferson's famous "tree of liberty" theme. "It is a good thing for the people now and then to rise up and let the officeholders know they are responsible to the masses."[129]

The people enthusiastically responded to his message and gave him an overwhelming victory at the polls. Wasting no time, on his first day in office he sent a written message to the city's Common Council, one that concentrated heavily on fiscal responsibility. "We hold the money of the people in our hands to be used for their purposes and to further their interests as members of the municipality," he told the members. When "any part of the funds which the taxpayers have thus entrusted to us is diverted to other purposes, or when, by design or neglect, we allow a greater sum to be applied to any municipal purpose than is necessary, we have, to that extent, violated our duty." To the new mayor, there could be "no difference in his duties and obligations, whether a person is entrusted with the money of one man or many. And yet it sometimes appears as though the officeholder assumes that a different rule of fidelity prevails between him and the taxpayers than that which should regulate his conduct when, as an individual, he holds the money of his neighbor."[130]

Mayor Cleveland took on the ring when no one else would. In his boldest move, he vetoed a street sweeping contract rife with corruption and kickbacks. The issue concerned a five-year agreement the city had awarded to a company to clean the streets. The business in question, owned by George Talbot, had previously done business with the city and submitted a bid of $422,500 for the contract. The council approved it by a vote of fifteen to eleven, even though the bid was $100,000 more than the lowest proposal. In fact, *five* companies submitted lower bids. Furthermore, the council's appropriation was $50,000 *higher* than the original bid. Cleveland quickly suspected that palms had been greased. The extra funds had to be a kickback.[131]

Cleveland immediately vetoed the bill and ripped into the members for such outrageous behavior. "This is a time for plain speech," he told the council in his veto message. The bill was nothing more than the "culmination of a most barefaced, impudent, and shameless scheme to betray the interests of the people and worse … to squander the public money." He warned the members that "there are influences, both in and about your honorable body, which it behooves every honest man to watch and avoid with the greatest care." When it came to being good public stewards, there could be "no middle ground. Those who are not for the people either in or out of your honorable body are against them and should be treated accordingly." The corrupt council vowed to override the veto, especially after Cleveland's tongue-lashing message hit the press. The override attempt failed.

Talbot and Cleveland were actually acquaintances, as the former had been a client in the mayor's old law firm. But that didn't matter to Mayor Cleveland. Afterward, he explained the matter to Talbot. "This is neither a personal nor a legal matter. While I was your attorney I was loyal to your interests. Now the people are my clients, and I must be loyal to them." He would not award personal friends out of the public treasury, which was commonplace in the North at that time. He served the people and no one else. "I only did my public duty," he told fellow Buffalonian Arthur S. Bissell after the veto. The following day, the *Courier* ran the headline "A Victory for the People." As for the present council, noted the paper, "Mayor Cleveland has turned out the lights and torn off all disguises."[132]

During his one year in office he saved the citizens of Buffalo more than a million dollars, big money in those days. By tackling corruption head-on and dressing down members of the City Council for tolerating it, Cleveland impressed party officials across the state. The boldness of his crusade enthralled western New Yorkers and launched his successful campaign for governor in 1882.

As governor he took on Tammany Hall, the great Democratic political machine, and, as a former home of the Tweed Ring, a major and efficient engine of corruption. No one in New York City politics in the late-nineteenth century dared trifle with Tammany, but Cleveland possessed no fear. He dismissed corrupt officials connected to the machine, signed reform bills, cut the size of government, and publicly exposed Tammany's vice. From the first moment he arrived in Albany, "Tammany hated Cleveland with a sleepless vindictiveness," noted biographer Allan Nevins.[133]

In his capacity as New York's chief executive officer, Cleveland was responsible for upholding and maintaining the state's election laws. He had campaigned on a pledge to preserve clean elections, leaving them "uncontaminated and fairly conducted." In November 1883, just before the annual legislative elections, he issued a proclamation for state and local officials to enforce "laws relating to bribery and corruption at elections." A clean electoral process, he reminded public officials, "is absolutely the foundation upon which our institutions rest." Elections "should be fairly expressed and honestly regarded. Without this, our system is a sham and a contrivance, which it is brazen effrontery to call a republican form of government." So the governor called on "all district attorneys within this state, and all sheriffs and peace officers and others having in charge the execution of the laws to exercise the utmost diligence in the discovery and punishment of violations of the statutes referred to, and they are admonished that neglect of duty in this regard will be promptly dealt with."[134] Despite the dirtiness of the era's politics, Cleveland believed the electoral process, as importantly as political offices, should be free from corruption. And he vowed to hold accountable public servants who failed to do their duty.

Because he worked hard on behalf of the people and was honest to a fault, Cleveland expected those serving under him in the government to do likewise. He loathed lazy, incompetent bureaucrats and vowed to fire anyone who did not give the taxpayers an honest day's work for an honest day's wage. As mayor, Cleveland criticized the practice of city offices closing "at the early hour in the day, which seems now to be regarded as the limit of a day's work." The taxpayers paid the salaries and wages of city employees and were entitled "to a fair day's work."[135]

He also did not want government employees involved in politics, which was the custom of the time. During his first presidential campaign, he vowed that "public departments will not be filled with those who conceive it to be their first duty to aid the party to which they owe their places, instead of rendering patient and honest return to the people." When he became president, he did not change his mind or his stance, as many modern presidents do. "I insist upon officeholders ... attending to the duties of their offices and not interfering improperly with the political actions of others," he wrote to a friend during his first presidential term.[136] Today the Hatch Act, a law passed in 1939, prohibits executive branch bureaucrats from participating in politics. But in the nineteenth century no such law existed, so the political party holding office routinely mobilized the entirety of the governmental workforce to participate in a variety of campaign activities, such as public speaking, distributing pamphlets, and raising funds. In the pre–civil service days, most federal workers owed their jobs to presidential appointment, so bureaucrats had a stake in the outcome of the election. If the other party prevailed, they would find themselves out of a job.

Cleveland ended that practice, just as he'd promised voters he would, with an executive order on July 14, 1886, to "warn all subordinates" in the federal government "against the use of their official positions in attempts to control political movements in their localities." Public officials "are the agents of the people, not their masters" and should avoid any "display of obtrusive partisanship." Those who hold public office have no right to "dictate the political action of their party associates or to throttle freedom of action within party lines." Furthermore, they could not engage in the "manipulation of political primary meetings and nominating conventions." However, their rights as voting citizens would not be infringed upon. Two officials decided to test his resolve; both were fired.[137]

In his day, before the completion of civil service reform, presidents appointed tens of thousands of people to offices across the country, even down to the local postmasters in the smallest towns. When the opposing party won the White House, the entire government changed hands, so the new president faced a barrage of office seekers who filled the White House halls, as well as the lawn, hoping to get an interview. He also relied on members of Congress and others—party members, friends, and friends of friends—to recommend appointees, as the president could not hope to know enough qualified people in every state in America. And if that appointment did not turn out to be sound, Cleveland's wrath would most assuredly be felt.

One poor fellow felt the full brunt of Cleveland's hostility by recommending someone for appointment who turned out to be unsound. After writing a letter to the president confessing the error of his recommendation, Cleveland responded by accusing him of committing an unpardonable crime, and even treason, which should be punished with a jail sentence:

> I have read your letter … with amazement and indignation. There is but one mitigation to the perfidy which your letter discloses and that is found in the fact that you confess your share in it. I don't know whether you are a Democrat or not; but if you are, the crime which you confess is the more unpardonable. The idea that this Administration, pledged to give the people better government and better officers, and engaged in a hand-to-hand fight with the base elements of both parties, should be betrayed by those who ought to be worthy of implicit trust, is atrocious; and such treason to the people and the party ought to be punished by imprisonment.

> Your confession comes too late to be of immediate use to the public service; and I can only say that while this is not the first time I have been deceived and tricked by lying and treacherous representations, you are the first one that has so frankly owned his grievous fault. If any comfort is to be extracted from this assurance you are welcome to it.[138]

All throughout his presidency, unworthy officials were removed from service regardless of party affiliation, while vice and corruption was stamped out. Cleveland earned praise from the *New York World* newspaper for the "destroyed nests of corruption in the Navy Department, the Treasury, the Indian Bureau, the Land Office, the Coast Survey, and the War Department."[139]

The American people, fed up with all the corruption in government, wanted a strong president with the character to clean it up. When he endorsed Cleveland for president in 1884, Joseph Pulitzer, in his *New York World* paper, did so for four reasons: "1. He is an honest man. 2. He is an honest man. 3. He is an honest man. 4. He is an honest man."[140] Cleveland had pledged to the people he would provide good government, and he worked hard each and every day to see they had it.

OPENESS AND TRANSPARENCY

In his life of public service, Cleveland maintained one of the most open governments in history. As president, Cleveland made himself available to the general public. He held open houses two days a week, allowing citizens to walk in and shake his hand, as well as discuss political matters with him. He once told George F. Parker, his secretary, that it was "one of the characteristic features of our institutions that any person, young or old, rich or poor, white or black, known or obscure, could, if even decently clad, not only see the man who, for the time, was the head of his country's management, but that he could speak to him upon any question in which he had a peculiar interest."[141]

Even in the White House, if one knocked on the front door it was not unusual to be received by Cleveland himself, the last president to do so. During Cleveland's residence, fences did not surround the executive mansion, nor were there any guard shacks, Secret Service agents trolling about, or security at the entrances to the building. All one had to do was walk up to the White House and knock on the door to see the president, who would generally listen to concerns or desires, if he had the time.[142] Obviously such an arrangement would be impractical now, but presidents have certainly taken on an aura of aloofness with respect to the people.

As governor, Cleveland also had a very open, transparent, and accessible government. In a manner strikingly Jacksonian, his first official act was to open the mansion to all visitors. His executive offices at the state capitol were also open to any who desired to call upon him "without the intermediary services of a secretary or a clerk," noted his aide William Hudson. Lt. Governor David B. Hill remarked that the policy resembled "a town meeting. The governor might just as well place his desk on the grass in front of the Capitol." Hill hated the idea, believing it a "waste of energy" that "must be stopped." Cleveland later altered the policy when he saw how much time he needed to conduct the state's business but while governor, wrote Hudson, "access to him was easy." A reporter from the *New York Herald* also acknowledged the difference in accessibility. "The formalities surrounding a visit to the governor, so annoying under former administrations, are entirely absent now. Little trouble is experienced by the humblest citizen in having an interview with the governor of the state."[143]

Cleveland had just one instance of real governmental secrecy. In 1893, while battling a severe economic depression, a calamity perhaps second only to the Great Depression in severity, he hid cancer surgery from the public. After finding a rough spot on the roof of his mouth, Cleveland had doctors examine him. Their determination was that it was a cancerous growth that needed to be removed as soon as possible, along with part of his upper jaw, in order to ensure his future health.

Normally, having an operation of that magnitude would be public knowledge. However, the economic situation was precarious. The problem concerned the nation's monetary policy and a possible presidential succession. Cleveland believed in maintaining the gold standard at all costs, which at the time was under threat, while his vice president, Adlai Stevenson, favored the free and unlimited coinage of silver. The president feared that if he died during the medical procedure, or the fear surfaced that he might die, a situation that would leave the nation's economic fate in the hands of the Silverite Stevenson, panic might grip the business community and the markets. The nation's fragile economic situation, which he was in the process of trying to stabilize, might collapse. Fortunately, Cleveland survived the surgery and had no further bouts with cancer. Yet while the true story hit the press, the White House denied it, telling reporters that the president had had some dental work done. Though it might have gone against his Jeffersonian instincts, Cleveland felt that the nation's economic well being, and with it that of the people, was more important.[144]

Running for president in 2008, Barack Obama promised the American people that his administration would be the most open in history, while bashing George W. Bush for presiding over the most secretive. Yet the Obama Administration has denied more Freedom of Information Act requests, a full one-third of applications, than Bush did. Obama also promised when seeking to take over the nation's health-care system that any negotiations would be televised live on C-SPAN. But White House negotiations were held behind closed doors, and those on Capitol Hill were conducted in secrecy, with only Democrats privy to the discussions. He further pledged that any bill passed by Congress would be available online for the American people to read themselves for a full five days before he took action on it. That has not happened either. Despite his dismal record, Obama received a "transparency award" from five open government organizations at a ceremony in the White House—with no press allowed.[145]

RETIREMENT

It has been estimated that modern presidents stand to earn as much as $100 million once leaving office. Some, if young enough, may make even more. The most recent presidential retiree who has had time to accumulate great wealth is Bill Clinton, who clears $191,000 per year in pension funds while receiving $96,000 for his staff. Rent for office space, equipment, phone bills, travel expenses, and a Secret Service detail that also includes protection for every former first lady, are all covered by taxpayers. Each president also receives money to run his lavish presidential library, which collectively cost taxpayers another $46 million per year. In addition to his pension, Clinton makes $100,000 per speech, as well as income from consulting and other endeavors. His net worth has been estimated at $111 million as of 2009, and he is not nearly done.[146]

Ex-presidents did not earn pensions and perks until Harry Truman. For six years after he left the White House in 1953, Truman survived on a World War One pension of $112 a month, not even enough to answer his personal mail. He had opportunities to make money during retirement but refused. "I could never lend myself to any transaction, however respectable, that would commercialize on the prestige and dignity of the office of the presidency." After hearing of his troubles, Congress granted him a presidential pension of $25,000 per year and a sum for a small staff of assistants.[147]

Truman originally took a page from Cleveland, who refused to sit on corporate boards after his retirement from politics, and he had many offers to do, as so many nineteenth-century presidents did. Such jobs paid well but required little. To him, such an enterprise would have violated a cardinal principle of American government—the office should never be used to enrich oneself, even after retirement. "He wouldn't do that because he didn't think you were supposed to benefit from public service," surviving grandson George Cleveland said recently. "Some people say that's why we're Clevelands and not Kennedys," he joked.[148] Cleveland saved as much of his salary as he could, and once out of office, pursued honest, moneymaking jobs like everyone else. He spent most of his latter days serving on the board of trustees at Princeton University.

After he retired, Cleveland did not like to campaign for Democratic candidates. Modern presidents spend an inordinate amount of time campaigning—for themselves, to win a second term, and for other party candidates around the nation, raising money and taking to the stump. In retirement many just can't let go and often make the rounds to help the party. Bill Clinton can't seem to keep his nose out of politics, even though he has been out of office for more than a decade. Cleveland refused on many occasions to take part.

As the only living Democratic president, many party members looked to Cleveland for leadership, especially during his first retirement in 1889. Though he was out of power, he still remained the top Democrat in the country. The former president found himself bombarded with letters from across the country for advice about how best to defend party principles and attack the Republicans. "I find it very hard to shake off the results of my official incumbency," he wrote his friend William Vilas. "It takes much of my time to answer letters of all sorts, and it really seems sometimes as though the people did not appreciate that I was no longer president. Everybody is very kind to me, but the pressing invitations to go to all sorts of places embarrass me a good deal, for I feel that I must work or be ready to work as it comes along. I am very pleasantly situated professionally and think I shall gradually get on."[149]

During his retirement, the popular former president was asked to speak on behalf of Democratic candidates. But he was simply not up to the task, mostly because such an undertaking would take up time he wanted to devote to work and family—not to mention the fact that he did not particularly like making public speeches. His letters of regret were usually lighthearted. "There are very few things I would not do for you and the others for whom you speak," he wrote to Governor William E. Russell of Massachusetts. "I want to avoid all the speechmaking possible, for in the first place I do not think I am very good at it, and secondly, during my vacation I am such a vagabond and lazy good-for-nothing that I find any mental exercise a great effort." To another friend he wrote that he was "in a miserable condition," a "private citizen without political ambition trying to do private work and yet pulled and hauled and importuned daily and hourly to do things in a public and semi-public way which are hard and distasteful to me." The flood of requests was "as wearing and perplexing as it was to refuse applications for office at Washington."[150] To him, ex-presidents were simply private citizens and should remain as such.

THE MODERN SWAMP

Corruption and scandal have rocked the nation's capital since it has been on the Potomac. But we need not travel back too far in time, not even as far back as Watergate, to discover plenty of it. Recent decades have seen some pretty hefty indignities in Washington. The savings and loan scandal of the 1980s involved five senators, including the legendary John Glenn and 2008 Republican presidential nominee John McCain, all of whom intervened on behalf of Charles Keating, head of the Lincoln Savings and Loan Association, which was under federal investigation. In 1992 the House banking scandal emerged, as members were allowed to overdraw on their checking accounts, with dozens of hot checks totaling hundreds of thousands of dollars that remained in overdraft for months, even years. The congressional post office scandal ensnared Dan Rostenkowski of Illinois, who chaired the House Ways and Means Committee, and Joe Kolter of Pennsylvania, both of whom went to prison.

Bill Clinton's administration had more "gates" than any in history—Troopergate, Monicagate, Whitewatergate, Chinagate, Filegate, Pardongate, to name a few. In more contemporary times, one sitting member of Congress, Republican Randy "Duke" Cunningham, who took $2.4 million in bribes from a defense contractor, was recently sent to prison, while a newly defeated one, Louisiana Democrat William Jefferson, joined him after it was found he took a bribe and had $90,000 in cash hidden in his freezer. Long-time Republican Senator Ted Stevens of Alaska lost his bid for another term when scandal loomed and he was convicted of bribery, though the charge was later dismissed. The Jack Abramoff scandal revealed just how corrupt many members of Congress actually were, with both parties pocketing millions in contributions, as well as special favors, though Republicans received all the blame. As part of the Abramoff scam, Congressman Tom Delay, known in Washington as "The Hammer," was convicted of money laundering in 2011, to the delight of Democrats.

Such incidents only served to further sicken people, which Democrats took full advantage of by blaming everything on the majority Republicans. Campaigning for a Democratic majority in 2006, and with it the speakership, Congresswoman Nancy Pelosi promised to clean up what had become a Republican "culture of corruption" in Washington and to "drain the swamp." But when Democrats arrived, the swamp only got muddier and deeper. The 2008 mortgage crisis revealed that Democratic senators Chris Dodd and Kent Conrad received sweetheart mortgage deals from Countrywide Mortgage. Dodd, as chair of the Senate Banking Committee, made sure the financial sector received sweetheart legislation in return—like, say, billion-dollar bailouts. Rod Blagojevich, the governor of Illinois, was impeached and sent to jail for trying to sell Barack Obama's former Senate seat, while New York's Governor Elliot Spitzer resigned after being caught with an expensive call girl, even though he had once crusaded against prostitution rings. Congressman Anthony Weiner resigned his seat after he was caught exposing his … well, wiener, to a young girl online. Charlie Rangel, the chairman of the House Ways and Means Committee, decided he wouldn't pay taxes on rental property he owned in the Dominican Republic. The excuse from the nation's top tax law writer: he didn't realize he was supposed to.

President Obama, who once told high school students that ethics was not his favorite subject, does not escape scrutiny, at least as far as his appointments to office are concerned, naming several tax cheats to the cabinet, crimes which, if committed by a member of the taxpaying public, would have resulted at the very least in interest payments and a hefty fine, if not outright imprisonment. Yet Tim Geitner, tapped to head the Treasury Department, and with it the IRS, made no mention of fines or interest when he revealed during his Senate confirmation hearing that his delinquent taxes, some $34,000, had been recently paid, just before being named to the nation's top economic post. If he can be believed, his mistake was only just then discovered, upon which he made immediate recompense. It was chalked up to a slight mistake on the part of the president of the

Federal Reserve Bank of New York. Tom Daschle, picked by President Obama to head the Department of Health and Human Services, also decided which taxes he would pay and those he would not. When the heat got too bad he withdrew, only to be replaced by Governor Kathleen Sebelius of Kansas, who also had tax problems. US Trade Representative appointee Ron Kirk, a former Dallas mayor, had issues too. All this from a party that believes everyone should pay higher taxes but never seems to want to pay their own.[151]

When not busy stealing and cheating, our presidents and politicians can usually be found lying, making promises they never intended to keep. As Nancy Pelosi said when questioned about certain issues not being brought to the House floor, "There are a number of things said on the campaign trail," she laughingly reminded the press.[152] Many, like Obama, simply told people what they wanted to hear, and then, once in office, did what he wanted to do all along. And then we are treated with the usual litany of excuses, such as one used by both Bill Clinton and Barack Obama - *Oh, I didn't realize how bad things were until I got into office* - which, to my ears, is an admission of stupidity.[153]

Political offices have become very lucrative, with money, power, and prestige. Though married to a rich real estate mogul, Nancy Pelosi saw her wealth rise an astonishing 62 percent in one year, from a minimum of $21.7 million in 2009 to a minimum of $35.2 million the very next year.[154] Defenders will argue that such gains result from smart investing, but those same liberals will not allow the American people to invest their own money for a better retirement than government-run Social Security. Even mentioning privatizing part of the program is an unspeakable heresy. The people are simply not smart enough to do that, in liberal eyes.

As a result of all the money flowing into the pockets of politicians, campaigns have remained nasty, carried on by the unscrupulousness of those who ambitiously seek public office for no other reason than the personal prestige, privilege, and wealth that inevitably come with it. Such vicious mudslinging does nothing for the process and only serves to drive (or scare) good people away from wanting to serve the public. Yet this is what the establishment wants. "I learned long ago, never to wrestle with a pig," George Bernard Shaw once said. "You get dirty, and besides, the pig likes it." And the pigs in Washington will fight to keep it that way. I would dare say that the vast majority of those serving in Congress are only there for themselves. They do not have the public's best interests in mind. If they did, problems would get solved rather than get worse. And when the great public career is finally over, whether from retirement or indictment, the gravy train is still on the move with rewarding pensions and perks. This is why Grover Cleveland's story can be so refreshing to modern-day Americans, just as it was to those in the late-nineteenth century who sought him for president.

Grover Cleveland had the most honest and ethical administration in history. Whether during his stint as mayor, governor, or president, he was never called upon to explain scandals to the public, which have plagued so many recent administrations, because there were none. He prided himself in selecting the most competent public officials. He was a good judge of character and made sound appointments. And those who proved to be otherwise were summarily dismissed from service. He kept his pledge to provide the people with good government.

III

BUSINESSMAN'S PRESIDENT OR CHAMPION OF THE TAXPAYER?

In long-range perspective Grover Cleveland stands out as one of the great figures of our political history. It was not only his eight years of conscientious service as president but also the tenacity with which he stuck to his principles and the vigor with which he fought for them that made him preeminent.
—*Robert Lincoln O'Brien, President Cleveland's Personal Secretary*[155]

Throughout the vast historical literature of the Gilded Age, scholars have repeatedly, and unfairly, branded Grover Cleveland an exclusive champion of the business interest. They say he was in the pockets of Wall Street and the big banks and that he did not hold the lower classes in high regard. Such attacks are not unlike the condemnation conservatives receive from the left today. But these attacks are one of the most erroneous ascertains in academia, as well as in political punditry. Cleveland did not believe in government assistance to any group, rich or poor, for such aid from Washington would only have built dependence on government and unjustly robbed taxpayers of the fruit of their labor, a violation of his cherished Jeffersonian ideology.

GOVERNMENT PATERNALISM

A basic question that has been asked throughout American political and constitutional history: What role does the government play in the lives of ordinary citizens? There have been numerous answers.

For liberals, the government should play a vital role, from cradle to grave, in the lives of the people. They especially love to portray themselves as the defender and guardian of the "little guy." Progressives have always hailed it a virtue to be paternalistic when it comes to the common man. But what the left really means is that people can't take care of themselves, that government must do it for them. Perhaps Nancy Pelosi said it best in 2011: "I am a mom and a grandmother. I view my work in politics as an extension of my role as a mom. There are things we want to do for our children that are simply beyond us" as individuals.[156] So for Democrats, government must step in and take on the role of caretaker.

For true conservatives, the issue is a simple one: government has no business getting involved in areas outside its limited, constitutional role and should never take a position as a custodian. The people are free to pursue their own dreams without government interference, to rise as high and as far as their God-given talent, abilities, and determination will carry them. And, yes, to make as much money as they wish.

Though the media elites and scholars of every conceivable stripe portray conservatives, like Cleveland, as the enemy of the workingman and the "little guy," liberals are seen as their protectors and saviors. In truth, however, conservatives are much better for the lower classes. As a society, whether under Democrats or Republicans, we've used a liberal philosophy for more than half a century and are still dealing with the same issues, the only difference being we are trillions of dollars in debt as a result. None of the problems of poverty or wealth inequality have ever been solved using government, and most never will be. That's because conservatives rightly understand that there will always be a certain percentage of people in poverty, a certain number who will never pull their own weight, who will always want something for nothing. It has been that way since the beginning of time, and no government program will ever correct it.

But in their misguided attempt to fix what they contend is a serious national issue and provide a little "fairness" to the system, liberals believe in redistributing society's wealth, a scheme of robbing Peter to pay Paul, with higher taxes on the wealthy. As Barack Obama told Joe the Plumber during the 2008 presidential campaign, spreading wealth around, or taking from one to give to another, is "good for everybody." This is how liberals define compassion, by "how many are on the government dole," to paraphrase the late Jack Kemp. But conservatives, Kemp often noted, define it by how many of our fellow citizens no longer need any help from the government. Conservatives seek to spread opportunity, not handouts. As the old saying goes, "Give a man a fish and feed him for a day. Teach a man to fish and feed him for a lifetime." In truth, spreading opportunity is good for everybody. The poor and working classes will only rise up the social ladder with true conservative leadership, principles, and ideals. But with the litany of dumb liberal notions, it looks to many as if they don't want the lower classes to rise but to keep them mired in poverty and, more importantly, keep them voting for Democrats. In truth, that's exactly what they want.

Aside from the poor, liberals, in their hypocritical and contradictory nature, also believe in government paternalism for the rich, even though they attack the wealthy for political purposes. During the intense debate over the financial bailouts in the fall of 2008, it was true conservatives who strongly opposed the multibillion-dollar package, while liberals were among its strongest advocates. Conservatives most often argued to let the big financial institutions crash and burn, while liberals wanted them propped up with public funds. Many Democrats, including Speaker Pelosi, wanted even more money pumped in than was originally allocated to save the collapsing financial institutions, while many Republicans tried in vain to block it.

And let us not forget the infamous Kelo decision in 2005 by the US Supreme Court, when the most liberal members of the court sided with an "evil" pharmaceutical company, Pfizer, and against the "little guy," a homeowner in New London, Connecticut, who wanted to keep her house. The court's liberals allowed the city to eminent domain private property and give it to a big business, one liberals supposedly hate, while the conservative justices sided with the homeowner. One of the left's greatest literary engines, the *New York Times*, praised the decision as defining "the limits of property rights."[157] But the lesson should be both simple and obvious—liberals will *always* side with government, on any level, and against the interests of the all people, common or not, despite their heart-wrenching campaign rhetoric, which is nothing more than a ploy for sympathetic votes.

Liberal members of the Senate pressed Chief Justice-nominee John Roberts during his 2005 committee hearings on his willingness to stand up for the "little guy" at all times, as they do every conservative nominee to the court. But Roberts replied with one of the best answers ever given in testimony for a seat on the prestigious High Court: "If the Constitution says that the little guy should win, the little guy is going to win in court before me. But if the Constitution says that the big guy should win, well, then, the big guy is going to win, because my obligation is to the

Constitution."[158] But the left has no obligation to the Constitution or anything else, only their hold on power.

The result of this paternalistic attitude run amok is that now the government has taken up the role of parents to its children, the children being we the people. Socialistic-minded politicians and bureaucrats in Washington believe we are helpless without them, that they must make life's difficult decisions for us, lest we make the wrong ones. They seek the right to tell us how to live, what to eat, what to drink, and how we spend our hard-earned dollars. Amazingly, they now tell us what kind of light bulbs we can have in our homes and how much water is flushed in our toilets. As Bill Clinton once told us, the government could give the people more of their own money and "hope you spend it right." Such talk should have angered every freedom-loving American.

The new target is now our food. The Obama Administration, through the Interagency Working Group on Food Marketed to Children, has ordered producers of children's cereal to change their recipes or stop advertising their products to kids. First Lady Michelle Obama has even instituted a campaign for Americans to eat healthier, seeking government mandates on diets and the proper foods, yet her regimen is as bad as anyone in the country. The Obamas never miss a chance to stop at an ice cream parlor, rib shack, or burger stand. In typical liberal fashion, it's "do as I say, not as I do."[159]

But as bad as our current paternalistic government is now, the nineteenth century was not much different, at least in terms of the growing liberal attitude. Cleveland, as a strong conservative, rightly understood that the government should never interfere in the free market nor meddle in the lives of the people. By keeping Washington out, the people could easily ascend the social ladder with desire, determination, discipline, hard work, and thrift, just as he had done. Handouts and the subsequent laziness would only result in entrapment at the bottom and breeding more dependence on the government. It was a cycle that would never be broken, and history has proven him right.

President Cleveland would not allow the government to assume the role of parent for either the rich or the poor. In the latter part of the nineteenth century, paternalistic ideas, though rare, were slowly beginning to emerge and become more prevalent, mainly from the mouths of Republicans.

James A. Garfield, elected president in 1880, was described by the *Boston Herald* as the representative of the "liberal and progressive wing of the party,"[160] though we have no way of knowing if he would have governed that way or not, since he served but two hundred days in office before being assassinated by Charles Guiteau.

President Rutherford B. Hayes sought federal aid for public education, and after leaving office he became what amounted to a socialist, pondering "how to secure a more equal distribution of property among the people." He advocated crippling inheritance taxes and government support for the elderly. Hayes's plan called for inheritance to be capped at $500,000. All inherited wealth of more than half a million dollars would be confiscated by the government to distribute to those less fortunate.[161]

The famous Republican "Billion-Dollar Congress" in 1890 tried to spend money on everything, including a public education bill. Jacob Coxey, a wealthy businessman who led an "army" of unemployed men from Ohio to Washington DC during the Panic of 1893 lobbied Congress to issue $500 million in new paper currency to spend on the construction of public roads, a precursor to the New Deal. At the time, the entire federal budget was less than $500 million. The conservative Democratic Congress never seriously considered it.[162]

No such ideas or notions would ever be heard from Grover Cleveland. "It is the duty of those serving the people in public place to closely limit public expenditures to the actual needs of the government economically administered," he said in his first inaugural address in 1885, and "our system of revenue shall be so adjusted as to relieve the people of unnecessary taxation … preventing the accumulation of a surplus in the Treasury to tempt extravagance and waste." Upon winning the 1892 nomination for a second attempt at another presidential term, Cleveland wrote in his letter of acceptance, "Paternalism in government finds no approval in the creed of Democracy. It is a symptom of misrule, whether it is manifested in unauthorized gifts or by an unwarranted control of personal and family affairs." There would be no handouts or government intrusion of any kind under his leadership.[163]

COMBATING HANDOUTS TO THE POOR

When Congress decided to get generous with other people's money, Cleveland struck it down with his veto pen. During the late 1880s, a severe drought struck Texas. No such organization as the notoriously inept, incompetent, and corrupt FEMA existed in those days, so Congress sought to help in its own way. In February 1887 legislators appropriated $10,000 to buy seed to distribute to suffering farmers. President Cleveland, without hesitation, vetoed the bill, returning it to Congress with one of his most famous declarations:

> I can find no warrant for such an appropriation in the Constitution, and I do not believe that the power and duty of the general government ought to be extended to the relief of individual suffering, which is in no manner properly related to the public service or benefit. A prevalent tendency to disregard the limited mission of this power and duty should, I think, be steadfastly resisted, to the end that the lesson should be constantly enforced that though the people support the government the government should not support the people.

> The friendliness and charity of our countrymen can always be relied upon to relieve their fellow-citizens in misfortune. This has been repeatedly and quite lately demonstrated. Federal aid in such cases encourages the expectation of paternal care on the part of the government and weakens the sturdiness of our national character, while it prevents the indulgence among our people of that kindly sentiment and conduct which strengthens the bonds of a common brotherhood.[164]

Jeffersonian Democrats across the country applauded Cleveland's veto. Texans, as exhibited in two of the state's major newspapers, also praised the president's action against the seed bill, even though his decision directly affected their state. The *Houston Daily Post* called it "a very proper veto" of a bill that was "clearly unconstitutional." Crops fail in all parts of the country, noted the *Post*, and "it will not do to expect Uncle Sam to repair the damages wrought by nature." The *Dallas Morning News* noted that, although the veto might be "abrupt and ungracious" to some, it was "a truly exemplary act." The "Texas Democracy should look with peculiar pride and satisfaction upon an executive act indicating that the official head of the Democratic party of the country is disposed to assist a principle which they have so long cherished by laboring to redeem the national government, if possible, from the vice of paternalistic prodigality." Congress or the president should never "dream of thrusting the hand of government in the pockets of the people for either charity or robbery."[165]

By contrast, historians have used this particular veto as evidence that Cleveland did not support farmers and the lower classes because of his favor toward the interests of business. But he supported the Constitution first and foremost, over the interests of individual interest groups. He believed, as did all Jeffersonians, in "equal and exact justice to all men," that the government should see all people in the same way and should not divide them into classes. Furthermore, private charities and the goodness of the American people would be sufficient to take care of any needs among the populace. Government aid would only invite more government aid.

Historians, however, generally never bother to point out the end result of Cleveland's veto and request for private charitable help for Texas farmers. Some of the nation's leading newspapers issued calls for donations, as did Clara Barton, the president of the American Red Cross. In all, people across the nation raised money in excess of $100,000 for drought-stricken farmers in Texas, more than ten times what Congress sought to appropriate. Despite liberal rhetoric to the contrary, private charities work.[166]

President Cleveland also weakened government paternalism in the area of pensions for Union soldiers, which had come to be what one scholar called the "first large-scale federal welfare system." To receive a pension, the aged Union veterans of the great sectional conflict applied at the Federal Bureau of Pensions, which could either accept or reject the application. If the bureau rejected the application, the veteran or his dependent could appeal to representatives in Congress, who would then place a private pension bill on the floor to override the bureau's recommendation. This scheme had been in operation since the end of the Civil War and was popular enough that Congress had to set aside time each week, known as "pension day," to handle the barrage of bills. The situation was so bad that in the Forty-Ninth Congress, which sat during Cleveland's first two years as president from 1885 to 1887, 40 percent of the bills passed by the House and 55 percent enacted in the Senate were private pension acts. The pension system had become just another way for Congress to dole out favors, pay campaign debts, and buy votes.[167]

As with our current welfare and disability programs, the pension system was rife with fraud and abuse, which Cleveland had no patience for. He often displayed his distain in sarcastic veto messages. For example, in June 1886 he received a private pension bill for the relief of William Bishop, who was enrolled as a substitute soldier on March 25, 1865, just days before the war ended. During the next month he contracted the measles and was admitted to a hospital in Indianapolis. He did not return to duty until May

8 and was then mustered out of service on May 11. Cleveland pounced on the apparent giveaway. Despite Mr. Bishop's "brilliant service and terrific encounter with the measles," the president noted, the claim should be rejected, just as the pension bureau had recommended.[168]

In addition to measles, President Cleveland rejected pension claims by an applicant who "spent the most of his term of enlistment in desertion or in imprisonment as a punishment of that offense" and another who claimed "sore eyes among the results of diarrhea." Such shenanigans aggravated the president as much as anything. He continually lashed out at these repeated attempts to steal public funds. As he stated in one veto message, "I believe this claim for pension to be a fraud from beginning to end, and the effrontery with which it has been pushed shows the necessity of a careful examination of these cases," an investigation the hardworking president was always eager to conduct. After rejecting a widow's claim, submitted because her husband had died after falling off the roof in 1881, Cleveland summed up his feeling toward those pensions he believed were without merit. "It is not a pleasant thing to interfere in such a case," he wrote Congress in his veto message, "but we are dealing with pensions and not with gratuities." Cleveland showed courage and did what other presidents did not dare do: veto any payments to the multitude of soldiers who "saved the Union." In all, he killed 228 of these private and mostly fraudulent pension acts.[169]

In an attempt to get around the president's persistence, and play politics with a favored group, Congress, in early 1887, decided to pass a general pension law called the Dependent Pension Bill, which, unlike previous laws, established the precedent for providing pensions without regard to service-incurred disability. In other words, if a person had a disability and was unable to work, regardless of the cause of the handicap, and had served at least ninety days in the Union army, that person was entitled to a federal pension of $12 a month. The proposal would also cover the veterans' dependents. But the bill was so bad and so obviously full of potential fraud that the *New York Times* referred to it as the "pauper pension bill."[170]

Cleveland, unhappy with the liberal requirements, summarily vetoed the bill as a raid on the treasury, stating that the pension list would cease to be "a roll of honor" but would include those "willing to be objects of simple charity." It was unfair to equate someone disabled by war to one who suffered from an unrelated disease, a farm accident, or the bottle. Those who incurred disabilities in any manner other than the war did not deserve a pension and would not receive one as long as Grover Cleveland was president.[171]

Though it is easy to see otherwise, Cleveland believed he was simply doing his duty in upholding his constitutional oath of office. Historians, however, have derided him for such acts they consider a callous disregard for the poor and working classes. Such criticism is so pervasive that it has come to define Cleveland in historical circles. Basic lectures in most survey courses in American history say that Cleveland was in the pockets of Wall Street, the large corporations, and big banks, displaying a heartless disdain toward those who had not received as fair of a shake from society's tree. But the real reason these scholars scorn Cleveland is because he was not a wealth redistributionist progressive.

Scholars use a variety of unconstructive words to describe the man and his public career: lucky, stubborn, stolid, negative, inflexible, uncompromising, and unimaginative, the latter being a nicer way of saying he was stupid, which is a favorite liberal attack against conservatives. But they save their best venom for his attitude in regard to the lower classes - farmers, artisans, laborers, pensioners, small shop owners, and minorities. One of his fiercest critics, Vincent De Santis of Notre Dame, wrote that Cleveland's policies "appealed to the conservative businessmen" and "provided little consolation to the masses of the people. Cleveland fought the idea of the social service state." He "was an extreme conservative, and the people's quest for social justice" did not advance under Cleveland's administrations. He had "little understanding of the broader and more positive role that government could play."[172] So this is the real beef historians have with Grover Cleveland, that he did not believe in advancing social justice or using government as a positive force in the lives of the common man to provide social services. He simply believed in the principles of the Declaration of Independence and the Constitution as crafted by the Founders. But for leftwing historians, any president who believes in original intent and does not consider government a positive force is an anachronism worthy of the title "failure."

TAKING ON THE WEALTHY

Where we make a great mistake is assuming that paternalism is a one-way enterprise, encompassing government programs aimed at helping the poor and the downtrodden. But there is another side to the coin. The rich have had their hand stuck out in Washington, benefiting from large bailouts, tax deductions, subsidies and corporate welfare, and favorable trade deals. And although the left often portrays the modern-day Republican Party as the engine for Big Business, in reality both parties are equally tied to corporations, banks, and industries. Both have their hand in the same cookie jar, but liberals actually have their hand much deeper than conservatives. The left is just dishonest about it and uses rightwing ties to Wall Street as a populist battering ram to smash conservatives.

In truth, major Wall Street banks and investment houses, such as Bank of America, Citigroup, Goldman Sachs, and Merrill Lynch, donated more to liberal Democrats than conservative Republicans in recent times. According to Charles Gasparino, in his book *Bought and Paid For: The Unholy Alliance between Barack Obama and Wall Street*, from January 2007 to June 2010 Wall Street firms and executives donated more than $20 million to Democrats but just $13 million to Republicans. At the height of the 2008 financial panic, in the month of September, Goldman Sachs gave nearly $600,000 to Democrats, including the party's presidential nominee, Barack Obama, a sum that was nearly eight times what they gave Republicans. J. P. Morgan Chase contributed $230,000, two-and-a-half times what they gave the GOP.[173]

As a result of all the heavy donations, Democrats voted in favor of the massive TARP financial bailout package that month. But that is not to say that conservatives opposed the bailout package because they received less money. They received less money because they do not believe in aiding corporations as much as Democrats do. And the liberal support to the financial industry has paid off, as major Wall Street firms gained profits of $83 billion during the first two-and-a-half years of the Obama presidency, despite a severe and deepening recession, while earning just $77 billion in profits during George W. Bush's entire eight-year administration. I guess it's much easier to gain large profits with a $700 billion check from the government. For its part, the financial sector reciprocated the generosity. For the 2012 national campaign, Wall Street, by the fall of 2011, had donated some $15.6 million to both Obama's reelection effort and the DNC, more than all Republican presidential candidates combined.[174]

In Cleveland's day, the very wealthy in America donated to both parties, but it was the more liberal Republicans who gained the most and had Wall Street's ear, for which the rich gained plenty of protection and influence from the GOP-administered government. Despite disapproving of help for the lower class, Cleveland aggressively combated paternalism toward the wealthy. He had no problem with wealth but, believing as he did in a strong work ethic, one should become rich the old-fashioned way; that is, with innovative ideas and by the sweat of one's brow. Gaining wealth with the aid and influence of Washington, and the taxpayers, was not the American way, nor was it "fair." So he cannot be regarded as a businessman's chief executive. A simple analysis of major accomplishments during Cleveland's tenure as governor of New York and president of the United States would quickly determine that he approved laws for the benefit of the common man, which went against the business interests, far more than he did for the commercial and moneyed elite.

As governor, he signed a law to regulate the cigar-making industry, a legislative proposal by Assemblyman Theodore Roosevelt. Despite disagreements on other concerns, Cleveland worked closely with Roosevelt on a number of important reform issues. Sitting on a three-member state assembly committee, the future trustbuster and regulator took aim at the horrid conditions of the cigar industry in New York City, all at the behest of the cigar-makers' union headed by Samuel Gompers. Much of the industry's work was done in private, one-room homes rather than in a factory setting, with most of the workers being comprised of poor immigrants and their children. Conditions within these establishments were unsanitary and unhealthy, to put it mildly. Seeing the conditions firsthand, Roosevelt supported a bill to place regulations on the industry. Before it passed, the young TR strolled down to Cleveland's office and, "acting as a spokesman for the battered undersized foreigners," hoped to persuade a "reluctant" Cleveland to sign it, even though "it was contrary to the principles of political economy of the laissez faire kind," the young assemblyman noted. The governor signed the bill, for he always did what he could for the most pitiful among us.[175]

Governor Cleveland, on a number of occasions, pointed to the "injustice and discrimination" in New York's tax laws, which should receive the utmost "care and attention," he wrote to the legislature. He sought "to preserve the honor of the state in its dealings with the citizen, to prevent the rich, by shirking taxation, from adding to the burdens of the poor, and to relieve the landholder from unjust discrimination." Historians who routinely attack Cleveland as an ardent supporter of the business and financial interests over those of farmers and the poor conveniently forget this important goal he had for a fair tax system. He believed government should be on the side of everyone, not to actively aid any individual group, but, rather, by staying out of the way, providing equal and exact justice to all. Taxes could be kept low for every group if the legislature could "furnish the people a good government at the least possible cost."[176]

As a "most valuable protection to the people," Governor Cleveland also sought laws that would require large corporations to report their financial conditions to a state agency, much as railroad corporations had to report to the state Railroad Commission each year. Cleveland scolded the corrupt practices of big business, including the practice of lobbying. His message to the legislature could have been made during the 2008 financial panic.

> While the stockholders are the owners of the corporate property, notoriously they are oftentimes completely in the power of the directors and managers, who acquire a majority of the stock and by this means perpetuate their control, using the corporate property and franchise for their benefit and profit, regardless of the interests and rights of the minority of stockholders. Immense salaries are paid to officers; transactions are consummated by which the directors make money, while the rank and file among the stockholders lose it; the honest investor waits for dividends and the directors grow rich. It is suspected, too, that large sums are spent under various disguises in efforts to influence legislation.[177]

This is yet another example that shows Cleveland was not in the back pocket of the nation's largest businesses but sought to make sure they acted with honesty and integrity, though the legislature did not act on this recommendation.

As president, he took on some of the most entrenched special interests in Washington. The government, under the administration of Republicans, had been very beneficent toward the railroads, the largest industry in America during the late-nineteenth century, akin to the denigrated Big Oil today. A key part of the GOP economic program was corporate subsidies, which, in truth, was nothing more than "crony capitalism." In building the transcontinental railroads, the government lavished those corporations with handouts in the form of massive loans and enormous land grants. Like Obama's crooked loan deals to "green energy" companies like Solyndra and SunPower, where big donor corporations received nearly $2 billion in taxpayer guaranteed money, most of the railroad loans were never repaid because many rail companies went bankrupt. Though some of the money was repaid, in all railroad corporations made off with more than $350 million in government funds and 150 million acres of land over a period of thirty years. These programs of "bounties and subsidies," Cleveland said in his second inaugural address in 1893, "burden the labor and thrift of a portion of our citizens to aid ill-advised or languishing enterprises in which they have no concern."[178]

There would be no such enterprises in his administration. He struck back against the railroads and seized 80 million acres of land for the public, mainly because the railroads did not live up to their end of the bargain. Those railroad tycoons, such as James J. Hill, who backed Cleveland for president, thought they might receive favors in return for their support but found out just how wrong they were. When Hill desired a government right-of-way to take his Great Northern railroad through an Indian reservation and sent a telegram to the president for permission, Cleveland told him no. The venture would only proceed when the government negotiated with the Indians and made sure they were not the victims of fraud, so often the case throughout American history. He also signed legislation creating the Interstate Commerce Commission, which began regulating railroads and preventing them from continuing to employ what many considered discriminatory practices, while others considered it just good business.[179]

Though the Interstate Commerce Commission might have been seen as necessary to many in Washington, it represented a potential threat of government encroachment into the free market, particularly under a more progressive administration. In the words of Professor Thomas DiLorenzo, the commission "soon created a bureaucratic monstrosity that attempted to micromanage all aspects of the railroad business, hampering its efficiency even further."[180]

To Independent Institute scholar Ivan Eland, the law set "a precedent for federal regulation of private economic behavior, which would expand dramatically over the next century. Cleveland thus provided the underpinning for the progressive movement, which would, in the name of progress, advocate further usurpation of individual economic and political rights—to the detriment of those it was trying to help."[181] Though Eland's assessment may be a bit harsh, the creation of the Interstate Commerce Commission was not Cleveland's finest Jeffersonian moment and did cause major harm to laissez faire capitalism for future generations.

Cleveland, though, never intended the ICC to be a monstrous federal agency. To George F. Parker, he confided that, after "a careful study of the question, and in spite of reservations, I signed the bill." In what would later come to be called "presidential signing statements," he desired, upon approving the measure, to "file a memorandum setting forth my doubts on constitutional points, and explaining my conception of its limitations." Deciding against that course of action, he determined that it was better to "assume responsibility and then to see that the new system started under the most favorable auspices" and made sure that its commissioners, as well as the rules governing it "were instituted on safe and conservative lines." The original commission "did not clash with the powers of the states; it was not partisan, either in organization or direction; and did not meddle or assert authority not comprehended in its enactment or inconsistent with the theory and workings of our institutions. It did not check enterprise or initiative, nor was it used by one interest against another."[182] Sadly, it did not long remain that way, as progressive administrations would expand its use.

President Obama, like all liberals before him, believes the government can be a great impetus for prosperity and an engine for growth and has even used the railroads as his proof. In his first address to Congress on February 24, 2009, the president challenged the nation "to act boldly and wisely—to not only revive this economy but to build a new foundation for lasting prosperity." Obama rejected the view "that says our problems will simply take care of themselves, that says government has no role in laying the foundation for our common prosperity. For history tells a different story. History reminds us that at every moment of economic upheaval and transformation, this nation has responded with bold action and big ideas." Among his examples were the transcontinental railroads. "In the midst of civil war, we laid railroad tracks from one coast to another that spurred commerce and industry." The federal government "didn't supplant private enterprise" in this instance, Obama said, "it catalyzed private enterprise. It created the conditions for thousands of entrepreneurs and new businesses to adapt and to thrive."[183]

But history tells no such story. The great continental railroad system was a colossal economic failure. During the late-nineteenth century, five lines were constructed to connect the east coast to the west. The first four operated under the government's paternalistic system, receiving the outrageous amounts of cash and land. The results were inefficiency, cost overruns, corruption, and insolvency. All four lines went bankrupt, some more than once. The fifth, constructed by Cleveland supporter James J. Hill, used private sources to buy land and construct the entire line from Minneapolis to Seattle. It took a bit longer, but the company remained efficient, prosperous, and free of corruption, never once going broke, not even during the Panic of 1893, which took down several competitors. Government paternalism toward business simply does not work and will only lead to corruption and inefficiency, something Cleveland and earlier Americans knew and understood, while modern presidents, like Obama, do not.[184]

Though the railroads had a great relationship with Washington, that subsidized program paled in comparison to another. The largest single form of government paternalism to any social class during the late-nineteenth century was the high protective tariff, an early form of corporate welfare aimed at aiding those at the very top of society's ladder, notably the major industrialists. The tariff was the heart of the Republican Party's platform. Cut it out and the party was as good as dead. They planted their flag on the hill of high protection and would not budge from that position.

From the enactment of the Morrill Tariff in 1861 until 1885, Republicans controlled the government and with it tariff rates, keeping them at a very high level, near 50 percent. No Democrat occupied the White House until Cleveland, so low tariff proponents had no chance to cut taxes during their twenty-five-year period in the political wilderness. In addition to the high tariffs, Republicans expanded federal excise taxes and inflated the currency with fiat money to fund their spending schemes, like the subsidies to railroads and generous pensions to military veterans. The steady stream of revenue led to the accumulation of large surpluses, excess money the Republican Congress was all too eager to spend.

Once in office, Cleveland took on the Republican sacred cow head-on. Seeing there was no need to continue piling up these huge surpluses, aside from providing Congress with ample reason to splurge, he advocated a lower tariff rate, sufficient to gain only enough revenue to fund the essentials of the federal government, applying such taxes, including excises, to luxury items while removing them from raw materials and goods deemed essential for day-to-day living, which would benefit domestic industry and the working classes. Furthermore, in the late-nineteenth century, American industry was "no longer infantile," the president believed. It stood on its own two feet and needed no further protection. American products dominated the domestic market, as well as that of most foreign nations. No other country, not even the British, threatened American manufacturing supremacy. So protective tariffs, in this case, were simply political payoffs to mercantilist fat cats who bankrolled the GOP.[185]

In 1886, a tariff reform bill authored by Democratic Congressman William R. Morrison met defeat in the House by a vote of 157 to 140. But despite the setback, Cleveland wanted to focus intensely on his economic program and began gearing up for a major fight. In June 1887, he wrote to Tammany Hall on his tariff position. "Our government belongs to the people. They have decreed its purposes, and it is their clear right to demand that its cost shall be limited by frugality and that its burden of expenses shall be limited by its actual needs." The surplus, continually piling up in the treasury, is nothing more than "extortion on the part of the government." It was over-taxation, pure and simple. His plan would return money to the taxpayers and help everyone equally, even those at the bottom of society's rungs. Yet the opponents of tariff reform "attempt to disturb our workingmen with the cry that their wages and their employment are threatened," but they "advocate the system [that] benefits certain classes of our citizens at the expense of every householder in the land—a system [that] breeds discontentment because it permits the duplication of wealth without corresponding additional recompense to labor." A high tariff "enhances the cost of living beyond the laborers' hard-earned wages." Politicians then attempt "to divert the attention of the people from the evils of such a scheme of taxation by branding those who seek to correct these evils as free traders and enemies of our workingmen and our industrial enterprises. That is so far from the truth that there can be no chance for such deception to succeed."[186]

In December that year, Cleveland decided to get tough and took the unprecedented step of sending Congress his annual State of the Union message on only one subject, the tariff. Gilded Age historian H. Wayne Morgan argues that Cleveland did this only because he needed a winning issue in order to gain a second term in the White House, as tariff reform "would cover the party's weaknesses" in the 1888 presidential election. Cleveland scholar Richard E. Welch Jr., author of *The Presidencies of Grover Cleveland*, concurs with Morgan and contends that by the time of the 1887 message, Cleveland had already decided to seek reelection and sought "to distract the attention of the Democratic party from the divisive issue of free silver."[187] But the silver issue was not nearly as disruptive as it would be during the 1890s. Cleveland also did not need a signature issue and certainly had no thought of politics when he decided to be bold with his message. In fact, his aides and political friends advised him *not* to send the message for fear it would hurt his reelection chances. But Cleveland would not be moved by political expediency. He sought tariff reform for philosophical and economic reasons, crafting a message that was a brilliant tribute to Jeffersonian political economy.

In the nineteenth century, federal taxes essentially arrived as two types—tariffs and excise taxes, both a direct and indirect form. The tariff was the main source, accounting for 56.1 percent of federal revenue in 1885.[188] But Cleveland believed current tariff rates were "the vicious, inequitable, and illogical source of unnecessary taxation," he told Congress in his message, and "ought to be at once revised and amended." And by "revised and amended," he meant downward, to ease the burden on the backs of the people who bought manufactured goods, products that rose in price with high tariffs. He also wanted excise taxes to remain on expensive items, those bought by the rich and not deemed necessary for one to depend upon, and reduced on the essentials for everyday living. "The taxation of luxuries presents no features of hardship; but the necessaries of life used and consumed by all the people, the duty upon which adds to the cost of living in every home, should be greatly cheapened." With the president squarely behind the effort with his tariff message, a second attempt, the Mills Bill, survived a House vote in the spring of 1888 but met defeat in the Senate, where all tariff reduction proposals went to die in those days.

But 1888 was a presidential election year. Republicans vowed to return to the White House, and now they had an issue to use against the popular president. Cleveland's supporters had been right, that to maximize an effort on a tariff reform bill would damage him politically. To help carry their counterargument, Republicans engaged in a very aggressive fundraising campaign, hitting up large corporations for big donations. This was necessary, since being out of power deprived Republicans of the aid of federal officeholders for campaign purposes. Their fundraising tactic, applied mainly to the manufacturing interest, was simple and unveiled. If businesses desired tariff protection, they must contribute to the GOP cause. This technique became known as "frying the fat" out of corporations and was nothing more than a shakedown. In all, the Republican Party raised millions for its battle against Cleveland. The campaign tactic worked, as the president went down to defeat against Benjamin Harrison, though Cleveland won the most popular votes. But having lost the election, he felt no regret in having pushed an issue he'd felt strongly about.[189]

THE CLASS CARD

Even though Democrats are in the same bed with Wall Street and the very rich, one of their favorite political tactics is to pull out the "class card," a scheme they use as often as the "race card," in order to pit one economic group of citizens against another in a shameless bid for power. Liberals, like their socialistic forbears, see the history of the world much the same way Marx did, as a division between the haves and the have-nots. Those who are wealthy, no matter how they got that way, have done so simply because they were lucky, or, as Dick Gephardt famously remarked, were "winners of life's lottery." The poorer classes were simply dealt an unlucky hand through no fault of their own.

The use of the class card is essential for guarding one of the left's greatest strongholds, the Supreme Court, as John Roberts's testimony before the Senate Judiciary Committee attests. When Cleveland appointed Mississippian Lucius Quintus Cincinnatus Lamar to the Supreme Court in 1888, the liberal press blasted the nominee with nearly identical rhetoric. The *San Francisco Chronicle* did not believe Lamar would show any sympathy for the "little guy," for he leaned "naturally and spontaneously to the side of the strong against the weak. He is a friend of monopolies."[190] Substitute Lamar for justices Roberts or Alito, and no one would know the difference. It seems liberal tactics never change.

With their socialistic mindset, the left has forever tried to pit the poor against the rich on the issue of taxes by whining incessantly about the wealthy not paying their fair share. This was the driving force behind the "Occupy Wall Street" protests that sprang up in the fall of 2011, most likely orchestrated from inside the Obama White House itself.

To be fair, some of what the authentic protesters decry carries some weight. The top 1 percent, those making more than $500,000 a year, owns a great portion of the nation's wealth, and it has grown exponentially. According to the Congressional Budget Office in a 2011 report, the income of the top 1 percent grew by 275 percent from 1979 to 2007, while the income for everyone else grew at just 18 percent. To many in the Occupy Wall Street crowd, as well as many in the Tea Party, the wealthy class continues to receive favored status from the government, just as they did in Cleveland's day. In fact, today seven out of ten Americans believe that the government and the largest businesses are in cahoots against the people, a main reason why their riches continue to grow far more than the middle class's.[191]

But there is another side of the coin, one the left never addresses, as most of the facts don't support their misguided notions. The much-maligned top 1 percent, facing the full brunt of protesters' anger, pays nearly 40 percent of the total tax bill, while the top 10 percent contributes nearly 70 percent.

The bottom 50 percent pays less than 3 percent; the bottom 47 percent of wage earners pay nothing at all yet receive an enormous amount of benefits from those who do.[192] But to a warped liberal mind, this is simply not fair. The rich should pay more, they say, a lot more.

Barack Obama campaigned in 2008 pledging that he could "bring us together" as a nation, but his policies, as well as his rhetoric, has done the opposite. He has sought to capitalize on the growing divide in his reelection effort, which has only driven us further apart. This seems to be his real intention, to shamelessly play the class card in order to ensure a second term because he cannot run on his abysmal record. Class warfare seems to be the new order of the day. United States Supreme Court Justice Stephen J. Field prophesied about these future days of class warfare in a harsh concurring opinion that struck down the nation's first peacetime income tax law in 1895, a proposal enacted with wealth redistribution in mind. He saw the real danger in such a tax. "The present assault on capital is but the beginning," he wrote. "It will be but the stepping stone to others, larger and more sweeping, till our political contests will become a war of the poor against the rich; a war constantly growing in intensity and bitterness."[193] President Obama has done nothing but make it more intense and bitter. Yet our government was never supposed to regard citizens based on any classification but to uphold equality before the law. Our justice system is blind; our Constitution is blind—blind to race, sex, wealth, and every other conceivable factor.

Cleveland dealt with the same issue. Before his departure from the White House after his defeat at the hands of the Republicans, Cleveland used his final State of the Union message to Congress, in December 1888, to discuss economic troubles he saw in the land, namely the great disparity of wealth. "Upon more careful inspection we find the wealth and luxury of our cities mingled with poverty and wretchedness and unremunerative toil," he wrote. Because of government action in prior administrations, the vast "fortunes realized by our manufacturers are no longer solely the reward of sturdy industry and enlightened foresight, but ... the discriminating favor of the government and are largely built upon undue exactions from the masses of our people." As a result, the "gulf between employers and the employed is constantly widening, and classes are rapidly forming, one comprising the very rich and powerful, while in another are found the toiling poor." The wealthy existed under "trusts, combinations, and monopolies, while the citizen is struggling far in the rear or is trampled to death beneath an iron heel. Corporations, which should be the carefully restrained creatures of the law and the servants of the people, are fast becoming the people's masters." This arrangement was simply unfair to the average taxpayer and, what's more, it would produce an unstable class-based society, that "when fully realized, will surely arouse irritation and discontent." He could clearly see the potential political use of the infamous class card.[194]

Cleveland believed, as he had long advocated, that most of these problems could be corrected—not by any program on the part of the government to redistribute wealth but by a fairer system of taxation. Though he had just recently lost reelection while arguing that very cause, he continued to pound on the tariff and tax issues and the unjust inequality he found in the current system. "Instead of limiting the tribute drawn from our citizens to the necessities of its economical administration," he told Congress, "the government persists in exacting from the substance of the people millions which, unapplied and useless, lie dormant in its Treasury" in the form of a surplus. The present system "is not equality before the law."

The result of such an unjust system might result in a variety of Communism, which, to Cleveland, was "a hateful thing and a menace to peace and organized government." However, it would not be the traditional form advocated in Europe but "the communism of combined wealth and capital, the outgrowth of overweening cupidity and selfishness, which insidiously undermines the justice and integrity of free institutions." This form "is not less dangerous than the communism of oppressed poverty and toil, which, exasperated by injustice and discontent, attacks with wild disorder the citadel of rule." As Cleveland biographer Alyn Brodsky has noted, "No other president before (or since) had spoken so radically on the disparity between the haves and the have-nots."[195]

But Brodsky's analysis of Cleveland's remark is not accurate, as he insinuated that President Cleveland was "prepared … to see the imposition of stringent curbs upon wealth."[196] No program to limit the accumulation of wealth was ever enunciated by Cleveland. He believed that the disparity of wealth, with its possible communistic outcome, resulted in those at the bottom of the socioeconomic spectrum, the very ones Grover Cleveland supposedly detested, not deriving the same benefits from the government as those at the top. The government, mainly through the tariff and burdensome taxation, aided the rich in gaining more wealth. America's farmers and other laborers, who were "struggling in the race of life with the hardest and most unremitting toil, will not fail to see, in spite of misrepresentations and misleading fallacies … that without compensating favor they are forced by the action of the government to pay for the benefit of others such enhanced prices for the things they need that the scanty returns of their labor fail to furnish their support or leave no margin for accumulation."[197] Only an equitable tax system and an end to government paternalism would fix the situation, growing the nation's wealth for all.

Cleveland's economic policy sought to return to "the principles of true Democracy because they are founded in patriotism and upon justice and fairness toward all interests," he wrote in a letter to Mississippi Congressman Thomas C. Catchings. He sought a system that favored no one and a government that treated everyone fairly and equally. This alone would ensure an equitable system, the very structure crafted by the Founding Fathers. That was Grover Cleveland's only goal, and it should be ours as well.

MAN OF THE PEOPLE

Grover Cleveland rose to the presidency from modest means, just as Lincoln had, with hard work and determination, not through privileges or handouts. He possessed very little formal education, receiving most of his instruction from his father in a home-school setting. And because of his circumstances, a college education proved beyond his reach. But he labored to make something of himself and believed everyone could do likewise. He believed that the government should take no side, not for big business or small business, nor for the farmer or the laborer. The government should treat everyone equally. That is precisely why he hated the protective tariff system, because it sided with the business class over the working class.

For Cleveland, the government existed for a certain purpose as outlined in the Constitution and nothing more. The government should see all citizens in the same light, regardless of class or race or any other distinction. He believed in equality before the law. The government was there to see that the economy ran smoothly, that commerce flowed freely, that the money supply was stable, that foreign affairs were appropriately handled, and, above all others, that individual liberty was always protected. It did not exist to enrich one class of citizens at the expense of another. If the government handled its constitutional duties, the people could take care of their own lives.

And the plain folks throughout the country praised him for his principled stand as a man of the people. A *New York Times* reporter visited

Kentucky in the spring of 1891, when it was rumored Cleveland might seek a second presidential term, and described his support as very strong, noting that "it would take a search warrant to discover a Democrat opposed to the re-nomination of Cleveland." Speaking with an old Kentucky farmer, who was a well-read and educated man, the reporter learned just how strongly in regard the common man in the Bluegrass State held him. "Cleveland is the man; he is the third link of the Democratic chain: Jefferson, Jackson, Cleveland," the farmer said. The plain people, he continued, will not "permit that New York crowd of traders to dictate to us."[198] The people wanted one of their own as their president, not a candidate of Wall Street. They trusted Cleveland to look out for their interests.

John Goode of Virginia, who served in the US House from 1875 to 1881 and then later as Cleveland's solicitor general, also discovered the working class affinity for Cleveland first hand. Questioning an "old Democrat from the county of Grayson" at the Virginia state Democratic convention, Goode inquired as to which Democrat the plain people, those "who live in log cabins on the mountainside" in the Old Dominion, supported for president. "Why, they are all for Cleveland," the old gentleman responded. "Every time any of the speakers made reference to Mr. Cleveland, the applause of the people was so great that it seemed to me they would take the roof off the courthouse," he continued. Intrigued, Goode then asked why such enthusiastic support for Cleveland. The old Democrat promptly listed three reasons. "In the first place, they say he is honest; in the second place, they say he is the poor man's friend; and in the third place, they say he is the boss dog in the tan yard," meaning he stood up to the special interests in Washington.[199] The plain folk were with Cleveland and he with them.

When he accepted the Democratic nomination in 1892 for a second term, the New Orleans *Daily Picayune* praised him in an editorial. Cleveland's principles bring him "close to the people. No man, in manner and utterance, is further from being a demagogue. No man seems to cater less to the demand for cheap notoriety, but when he talks on great public questions he seems to be talking to the people and for the people," noted the editors. Cleveland's "constant expression of interest for their welfare … brings him so near to the popular heart. No man in the country today is more beloved by the masses of the people, and the secret of it is that they believe he is their friend."[200]

Liberals simply can't understand the mentality of earlier Americans, like the farmers in Kentucky and Virginia in Cleveland's time, conservatives who did not seek, nor desire, government assistance. Nor do liberals understand conservatives today. For Jack Beatty, a senior editor of the *Atlantic Monthly*, an analyst on NPR, and author of *The Age of Betrayal: The Triumph of Money in America, 1865–1900*, Cleveland's refusal of simple aid, such as seed to help farmers, raised important questions: "Why did the people support a government that on principle refused to support them, that wouldn't spend pennies to save farmers from ruin?" he asked. "Why return to office politicians like Cleveland, who vetoed three times as many bills in one term as all his predecessors combined? What had gone wrong with the Republican experiment in positive government for the country to settle for negative government?"[201]

Like most leftists, Beatty believes not in the conservative principles of Thomas Jefferson but those of the more liberal Abraham Lincoln, a philosophy that is an antithesis of Cleveland's. As president, Lincoln had broken the old Jeffersonian mold and provided a new view of the role of government in the everyday lives of the people, once saying, as Beatty approvingly reminds us, "The legitimate object of government is to do for a community of people, whatever they need to have done, but cannot do, at all, or cannot so well do, for themselves—in their separate and individual capacities."[202] Which begs other questions: Who decides what the people can or cannot do for themselves? Or if they can ever do it good enough to suit the government?

Ultimately the people themselves rejected the Lincoln line of thinking in favor of Cleveland Conservatism, at least for a while. Nineteenth century Americans and their early twentieth century brethren did not believe in an active, or positive, government. The American Revolution, contrary to Beatty's thinking, was not about creating an energetic government. Our forebears held true to the Jeffersonian admonition, "That government is best which governs least." They had faith in God, in themselves, and in their families and fellow citizens. They had no faith in government. People in those days had honor and pride, believing they could handle their own problems. And to tell a man he needed assistance from Washington was to insult him to the highest degree. It would have been better to spit in his face, for to tell him he needed help from the government was to tell him he was not a man.

The Constitution, earlier Americans correctly understood, does not contain any language that allows the government to spend money for public assistance, not even the general welfare clause authorizes such acts. James Madison, the father of the Constitution, explained on numerous occasions that the general welfare clause, so often cited by today's liberals, was not a grant of power. "If Congress can do whatever in their *discretion* can be *done by money*, and will promote the *general welfare*, the government is no longer a limited one possessing enumerated powers but an indefinite one subject to particular expressions," he wrote in 1792 [Emphasis in the original]. In other words, the federal government could do as it pleased under the general welfare clause had it been intended as a separate allocation of authority. But that was not what the founders intended at all.[203]

"It would be absurd," Madison said in a speech on the floor of the US House in 1792, "to say ... that Congress may do what they please" under the general welfare clause. He continued in a declaration that is eerily prophetic to our current situation of government run amok:

> If Congress can apply money indefinitely to the general welfare and are the sole and supreme judges of the general welfare, they may take the care of religion into their own hands, they may establish teachers in every state, county, and parish, and pay them out of the public treasury; they may take into their own hands the education of children, establishing in like manner schools throughout the union; they may assume the provision for the poor; they may undertake the regulation of all roads other than post roads; in short, every thing, from the highest object of state legislation, down to the most minute object of police, would be thrown under the power of Congress; for every object I have mentioned would admit the application of money, and might be called, if Congress pleased, provisions for the general welfare.[204]

Madison had it exactly right. In those bygone days it was always held to be unconstitutional, and even immoral, to tax one group of citizens and give it to another. As Senator John C. Calhoun once said, "Why should the government pay the expenses of one class of citizens rather than another?"[205] The answer was obvious to earlier generations: they shouldn't.

The Jeffersonian view of hard work and thrift carried into the early twentieth century. In 1927, the Mississippi River overflowed its banks in one of the worst floods in the nation's history. Herbert Hoover, a great engineer and Commerce Secretary under President Calvin Coolidge, traveled to the South to offer his assistance. But unlike the situation in

New Orleans eight decades later with Hurricane Katrina, stories abound of many local people wanting Hoover to leave, particularly in places like Mississippi. They did not trust the federal government and did not want out-of-town bureaucrats sticking their noses in local affairs. There were no shouts of "help" from stranded citizens who suffered from the severe flooding, as we saw around the Superdome. They understood that with government aid came government rules, regulation, oversight, and control. Once the government got in, it might be next to impossible to get them out. Cleveland, as a student of Madison and the Constitution, understood this perfectly, and this is the reason he was so steadfast in his opposition to government handouts.

THE MODERN PATERNALISTIC WELFARE STATE

When Cleveland returned to the presidency in 1893, after the splurging "Billion-Dollar Congress," he spoke out harshly against paternalism in his second inaugural address. He wanted to stamp out what he feared would soon become an entrenched dependence on government handouts. "The lessons of paternalism ought to be unlearned, and the better lesson taught that while the people should patriotically and cheerfully support their government its functions do not include the support of the people," he told his fellow citizens. "Every thoughtful American must realize the importance of checking at its beginning any tendency in public or private station to regard frugality and economy as virtues we may safely outgrow. The toleration of this idea results in the waste of the people's money by their chosen servants and encourages prodigality and extravagance in the home life of our countrymen."[206]

Liberals today would argue that such talk is "extreme" and "mean-spirited," yet Cleveland believed, as did all Jeffersonians, that the Constitution did not allow the federal government to spend money on public charity, and if Washington started down the road of paternalism, where would it end? And because of Cleveland's presidency, those paternalistic lessons were "unlearned" and early Jeffersonian principles held true, for the most part, for more than thirty years after Cleveland left the White House for the final time in 1897.

Yet attitudes were slowly but surely changing. As a Texas progressive said in 1910, more people were coming to believe the government was created "for the protection of the weak against the encroachments of the strong" and existed to referee "the contest between strong and weak, the powerful and the helpless, the many and the few, between the general and the special interests."[207] But it was not until the horrible period of the Great Depression in the 1930s, when the economy nearly imploded, that most Americans, for the first time, began to look to government for everyday things. FDR used massive government aid to help those affected by the depression, the first direct assistance in US history. From that point on, a dependence on government grew within the American people and has continued to increase. Americans have evolved from a freedom-loving people that looked to themselves for their own livelihood to one believing that government has, at the very least, some positive role to play in society.

But what began as small, seemingly insignificant programs aimed at giving a helping hand to those down on their luck has evolved into a massive transfer of wealth from one class to another, to the tune of trillions of dollars, and has done very little to alleviate the problem of poverty. This is precisely why the Founders did not give the government the authority to create a social safety net. Though the idea of a helping hand might have been a good one, it never ends there when dealing with government.

About the only thing that might be said positively about FDR's New Deal programs, should anyone really desire to do so, is that at least they provided jobs and not direct cash handouts. As he said in his 1935 State of the Union message to Congress, "Work must be found for able-bodied but destitute workers." But after Roosevelt's first step into large-scale government paternalism with the New Deal in 1933, Lyndon Johnson launched a "Great Society" program in 1964, putting the effort into high gear by declaring "an unconditional war on poverty" with the enactment of direct assistance programs. LBJ declared poverty to be a national problem requiring national solutions, and he called for greatly expanding government services. The Eighty-Ninth Congress, in session from 1965–67, enacted sixty new laws touching almost every aspect of American life, "the most productive law-making record in American history," one Johnson biographer wrote approvingly. Despite all the growth in government, and an unpopular war raging in Southeast Asia, Johnson, like a typical liberal, promised to cut the deficit in half and maintain a "frugal" administration. He was nowhere close, as the budget deficit grew and grew throughout his administration.[208]

Subsequent presidents followed his lead, if not expanding programs, at least keeping them in place. Today, the bottom 50 percent of Americans pay less than 3 percent of federal income taxes but gain more than a trillion dollars in welfare benefits and income tax credits. This paternalistic nature of Washington has been on going for nearly eight decades, causing many to wonder if such lessons can ever again be "unlearned." Conservatives may howl that welfare programs have failed, yet for modern Democrats they have worked exactly as they were intended, not by pulling people out of poverty but by creating a dependent class and a vast liberal voting bloc, forever reliant on leftist Democrats for their very lives, and forever trapped, to use Star Parker's wonderful phrase, on "Uncle Sam's Plantation."[209]

Cleveland's assessment of government efforts at paternalism has been proven exactly right, as the current situation shows. It was reported in 2011 that government handouts equal 35 percent of all wages in the United States. In 1960 the figure was just 10 percent. Nearly half the population lives in a household that receives some type of government benefit. Forty-six million Americans were considered living at the poverty level in 2010, including 22 percent of all children, while more than 45 million are now on food stamps, making the United States a "food stamp nation," an increase of 74 percent in just four years, to the tune of $68 billion a year. Fifty million receive Medicaid, which has nearly bankrupted the states. Today a majority of all government spending, 58 percent, is on entitlement programs, not defense and foreign wars, as many erroneously believe.[210]

According to reports by the Heritage Foundation in 2010 and 2011, federal welfare spending is thirteen times what it was in the 1960s, which is about four times what it would cost to pull every poor family above the poverty line. In 2008, the final year of the Bush administration, federal antipoverty programs cost taxpayers around $550 billion.

But the handout system has skyrocketed under liberal Democrats. In his budget request for fiscal year 2011, President Obama asked for $953 billion for welfare programs, an increase of 42 percent in three years. Direct cash payments have skyrocketed by 32 percent, rising by $600 billion in just three years, while scheduled to climb another half a trillion by 2016. As of 2012, taxpayers are paying $2.5 billion a day on welfare, more than is spent yearly on national defense and a full one-third more than what George W. Bush spent on Iraq throughout his entire administration, even though Obama lambasted him for irresponsible war spending that would bankrupt the nation.[211]

Welfare now encompasses more than seventy federal programs spread over thirteen government agencies that include cash payments, food stamps, Medicaid to provide medical care, disability, and rent subsidies and housing. The federal housing program, however well intentioned, has been a titanic bust. Why should America's workers provide housing to the poor? Howard Husock, the director of public policy case studies at Harvard's John F. Kennedy School of Government, has called it "a trillion dollar mistake—that, like so many other misguided antipoverty programs, has harmed those it set out to help and has caused serious, and continuing, collateral damage to our cities."[212]

And it's only going to get worse. Over the next decade, welfare spending is projected to cost the American people $10.3 trillion. If not reined in, according to the Heritage Foundation, it "will drive the United States into bankruptcy if allowed to continue unreformed." But despite the massive spending, some $16 trillion in wealth transfers since the 1960s, federal poverty rates remain unchanged while other problems have steadily increased. When LBJ declared war on poverty in 1964, just 7 percent of the nation's children were born out of wedlock. In 2010, that rate was 40 percent, while the birthrate for illegitimate blacks was an astonishing 70 percent. According to the USDA, 49 percent of all children born in the United States are in families who receive food subsidies. The enormous spending has done virtually nothing.[213] Nothing, that is, except destroy families, breed illegitimacy, and wreck cities. Welfare "queens" have more and more babies out of wedlock and get paid more for doing so, in addition to receiving food stamps, cash payments, free housing and other goodies, including taxpayer payments for the hospital bills for bringing the kid into this world.

But as enormous as that problem is, one socialist member of Congress, Representative Rosa DeLauro of the Socialist Republic of California, wanted to go further. She authored a bill in 2011 to distribute free diapers to poor mothers.[214] It's not enough that we have to pay for the child and its care, now we are supposed to give them diapers too. Which begs the question: Can those on public assistance do anything on their own? Not to the paternalistic leftist.

But the government also has a major hand in making a bad situation worse—if it can, in fact, get worse. If single mothers who receive welfare benefits want to keep all of their assistance, they are prohibited from finding a job or even getting married. As a result, 60 percent of children grow up in a home with a single parent. Who could have designed a better way to destroy the family unit and build a dependent class? A government handout does not pull the poor out of poverty but encourages laziness. These programs have made our once proud inner cities little more than dilapidated war zones. But the left got what it wanted. Johnson's war on poverty "represented the crowning triumph of the liberal vision of society," writes economist Thomas Sowell, "and of government programs as the solution to social programs." But it has only led to "disastrous consequences."[215]

But it's not just the poor who have benefited from Uncle Sam's generosity since the 1960s. The wealthy have been loyal recipients as well. The 2008 bailout package passed by Congress handed $700 billion to the banks and financial institutions on Wall Street to keep them from crashing, or so we were told. The Federal Reserve kicked in billions more in loans. Flush with taxpayer cash, these monstrous economic giants paid record salaries and bonuses to their top officers to the tune of $145 billion in 2009, with no regard for the public, particularly the middle class, who worked so hard to provide it.[216] Without the millions to lobby a corrupt Congress, the common middle class taxpayer doesn't stand a chance, and if they crash, there's no one to bail them out.

Any citizen with any semblance of common sense knows this insanity must end. Even FDR knew that public assistance could not go on forever. Echoing Cleveland, he said in his 1935 State of the Union address, "The lessons of history, confirmed by the evidence immediately before me, show conclusively that continued dependence upon relief induces a spiritual and moral disintegration fundamentally destructive to the national fiber. To dole out relief in this way is to administer a narcotic, a subtle destroyer of the human spirit. It is inimical to the dictates of sound policy. It is in violation of the traditions of America."[217] Yet despite his rhetoric, FDR never made any attempts at retrenchment the way Cleveland did. He even planned the enlargement of the social service state he had created. In October 1944, as the war was beginning to wind down and worry grew about the return of the depression, he laid out plans for a vast expansion of the state, including new federal initiatives for housing and medical care, areas the federal government had never before ventured. But Congress, for once, stood up and said no, if only for a while.[218]

Just as Cleveland warned it would, once the government started down the paternalistic road it would grow and grow, possibly without end. He did not favor government handouts for anyone, not for rich or poor, the business class or the lower class. He championed not the businessman, not the common man, but all the American people. He saw himself as a champion of the taxpayer, the ones who had to work to pay the bills, and so should we. But without major cuts and efforts to end the handouts, the current welfare state will eventually sink our once prosperous republic.

IV

How Cleveland Used Capitalism to End the Panic of 1893

As chief executive, Cleveland was strong-minded and forceful and adhered to his views on public questions with a remarkable degree of tenacity, utterly regardless of his party.
—*Republican Senator Shelby Cullom of Illinois[219]*

In the fall of 2008, the United States found itself slipping into a severe economic recession, perhaps even worse. Financial experts warned that without major government action, another Great Depression might be on the horizon. Though the economy had been slowing since 2007, the panic struck when major financial institutions, such as Lehman Brothers and AIG, began collapsing. The government's response was what we have sadly come to expect for the past eighty years, to rush in with guns blazing—or, should I say, with money blazing.

EARLY AMERICAN DEPRESSIONS

On December 11, 2011, in an appearance on the CBS news show *60 Minutes*, President Obama discussed the nation's continued economic woes and remarked that the situation was so bad that it was going to "take more than one term. Probably takes more than one president" to fix it.[220] Yet that doesn't square with history. Throughout the nineteenth and early twentieth centuries, economic depressions, called panics in those days, occurred in approximate twenty-year intervals—1819, 1837, 1857, 1873, 1893, and 1907. Prior to the market crash in 1929, the federal government did not intervene in economic downturns. Politicians stayed out of it, allowing the market to remain free and correct itself. Because of laissez faire or "hands off" economic policy, none of those downturns lasted nearly as long as the Great Depression of the 1930s did, when the government engaged in a massive intervention to "save capitalism." In most cases they lasted less than a presidential term and never more than multiple administrations.

Most of the depressions in our history have been caused by monetary policy, namely imbalances in the currency. Too much cheap money and lax credit have been the chief faults in causing many economic storms, including the Panic of 2008. Easy money and easy credit, brought on by misguided government policies, cause reckless speculation, which leads to overexpansion and overvaluation. The economy can only take so much and eventually the bubble will burst, as it did in the fall of 2008 with land and home values, causing millions of people to go under.

A panic similar to the one in 2008 occurred in 1837, the first year of Martin Van Buren's presidency, and can also be attributed to imbalances in the currency. Van Buren's predecessor, Andrew Jackson, had waged war on the Bank of the United States, a forerunner to the Federal Reserve, and vowed to kill the bank's charter. To keep that from happening, the bank's president, Nicholas Biddle, began a campaign of currency manipulation in an attempt to cause a boom in the economy. With an economy humming, calls for the end of the bank would stop, and Biddle would keep his fiefdom. But regardless of Biddle's actions, President Jackson made good on his promise to end the bank's charter by vetoing a re-charter bill in 1832. The bank's charter, though, did not end until 1836. So to further weaken the bank, President Jackson withdrew the government's deposits, placing them in smaller state banks, called "pet banks." Biddle's policies, however, were already in full force.

The state banks operated under the unstable fractional reserve system, where institutions hold only a fraction of its deposits and lend out the rest to customers. Flush with substantial amounts of Biddle's cash, banks began loaning to businesses and individuals as fast as possible. All the new money, a tidal wave of paper currency, along with cheap and easy credit led to wild land speculation and business overinvestment, which initially caused an economic boom. But with land values soaring and consumer prices and interest rates on the rise because of the bank's unstable policies, President Jackson grew worried about the speculative boom and issued an executive order, known as the Specie Circular that directed all federal land purchases be made with hard money, that is gold or silver, and not with paper money.

He hoped this monetary restriction would slowly cool down the economy, less it become overheated and bring on too much inflation.[221]

But in the end the bank's speculative bubble popped in 1837. A restoration of sound money after a period of inflation always causes a time of adjustment, oftentimes painful, and the American economy crashed as Van Buren settled into office. The new president faced mounting pressure, mainly from his Whig opponents, to raise tariffs and taxes, assume state debts, and increase federal spending, particularly for internal improvements projects like road and harbor construction. Henry Clay and his Whig allies also sought the creation of a new national bank to regulate the economy. President Van Buren resisted and took the opposite approach. In a message to Congress, which he called into special session in September 1837, Van Buren reminded the members of their obligations and duties. "Those who look to the action of this government for specific aid to the citizen ... lose sight of the ends for which it was created and the powers with which it was clothed." The federal government was not "established to confer special favors on individuals or on any classes of them," he lectured Congress. "All communities are apt to look to government for too much. Even in our own country, where its powers and duties are so strictly limited, we are prone to do so, especially at periods of sudden embarrassment and distress. But this ought not to be." The framers well understood "that the less government interferes with private pursuits the better for the general prosperity." Instead of tax hikes and a massive government infusion of cash, Van Buren cut expenditures by 21 percent in four years, from $30.9 million to $24.3 million.[222]

Rather than increase government regulation, particularly with a national bank, the president embarked on a bank reform plan, to separate federal deposits from the banking system and create an Independent Treasury System. The new deregulated structure would house all federal tax receipts, and all bank notes would be redeemable in gold or silver. This crucial step finally completed the long, sought-after goal of disassembling Alexander Hamilton's centralized financial apparatus. The economy recovered, though not quite in time to save Van Buren's reelection, as he and his party received all the blame for the calamity. But his economic policies, writes Jeffrey Rogers Hummel, "thwarted all attempts to use economic depression as an excuse for expanding government's role,"[223] a justification our current government is all too ready to employ.

THE PANIC OF 1893

During his second term, President Cleveland faced a situation very similar to that of Van Buren and later for George W. Bush and Barack Obama—a speculative boom and bust caused by an imbalance in the nation's credit and currency. Upon taking office on March 4, 1893, the realization that things were not right in the economy soon came to fruition as major financial houses and railroads began to fail. Though many historians argue otherwise, President Cleveland, who chose the road taken by Van Buren, ended the Panic of 1893 quickly, and he did so, not with a massive infusion of government like Bush and Obama employed but with free-market principles.

The currency issue occupied much of President Cleveland's time in the White House during both of his administrations. The monetary system in the late-nineteenth century was vastly different from our present structure. Before the days of the infamous Federal Reserve, Congress made decisions about inflating the currency. Every few years they passed laws to put more currency into circulation, which type would be used, and when it needed to be restricted. Whereas the United States currently circulates Federal Reserve Notes, backed by nothing but the confidence of the people, in Cleveland's day the United States operated under a system whereby both gold and silver coins circulated, as well as greenbacks, which had the backing of gold since the 1870s. Throughout his public career, Cleveland consistently advocated a sound monetary policy, steadfastly supporting the gold standard, and fought any attempt to over-inflate the currency with silver or paper dollars.

But first a little background on the nation's monetary policy and the conditions that caused the panic. The nation's currency had been backed by gold until the rise of Abraham Lincoln to the presidency in 1861. Though historically known as the gatekeepers of the gold standard, the Republican Party had inflationary ideas of their own that essentially ended gold's supremacy. In 1862, to help finance the war against the South, as well as their other spending schemes, Republicans, with the urging of Treasury Secretary Salmon P. Chase, passed the Legal Tender Act, an inflationary plan that allowed for the creation and circulation of a national paper currency, called greenbacks, that did not have the backing of gold, though the Constitution specifically gives Congress the authority to "coin money," not to print it. In all, Congress issued more than $450 million in paper dollars during the four-year conflict, producing ample inflation to double the cost of living. The United States had not seen that level of inflation since the days of the American Revolution with the old, worthless Continental dollar.[224]

In 1869, the United States Supreme Court ruled the Legal Tender Act unconstitutional in the case of *Hepburn v. Griswold*, preventing the issuance of paper dollars. The Chief Justice in that case, who sided with the majority, was none other than former Treasury Secretary Salmon P. Chase. The decision angered Republicans in Congress. Just a few years before, in a move to prevent Andrew Johnson from naming any justices to the Court, Congress, using its constitutional authority, had taken away two of the Court's seats when they became vacant, to keep the Southern-born president from naming any new justices. But with Republican Ulysses S. Grant in the White House at the time of the ruling, Congress raised the number of seats on the court to its present total of nine. President Grant then nominated two new Stalwart Republican justices in 1870 in an effort to "pack it," and the court reversed itself that year, in *Knox v. Lee*, allowing Congress the authority to issue paper currency.[225]

Republicans, however, returned the nation to the gold standard within a decade. In 1873, Congress, in an overwhelming vote by both houses, enacted the Coinage Act, which demonetized silver. Silverites, mostly Southern Democrats and Western Republicans, who represented poor farmers in need of inflationary measures, were livid and denounced the new law as the "Crime of '73." In 1875, Congress passed the Specie Resumption Act, which would redeem greenbacks with gold beginning January 1, 1879, thereby putting the United States back on a true gold standard.[226]

Democrats, more conservative than their GOP counterparts, were traditionally stronger supporters of a gold-backed, sound money policy than were the more liberal Republicans. As Yale Professor Ray B. Westerfield has written, "Every silver act that was passed—the Bland-Allison Act of 1878 and the Sherman Compulsory Silver Purchase Act of 1890—was passed during and by Republican administrations." Gold Democrats reigned supreme until the emergence of the "silver-tongued orator" William Jennings Bryan in 1896, when the party endorsed the free coinage of silver. But like Republicans, Democratic inflationary elements began emerging during the war years. Ohio Congressman George Pendleton, who received the party's vice presidential nomination in 1864, backed a plan called the Ohio Idea, a scheme to pay government bonds in greenbacks, not gold. The plan failed, but Pendleton, campaigning on inflation, attempted to gain the Democratic presidential nomination in 1868, but lost out to Governor Horatio Seymour, a sound moneyman from New York. At that time, the party of Jefferson and Jackson was not ready to give up its traditional support of sound currency. But with harder economic times in the South and West, brought on by deflation, Democrats, strongest in the South and heavily represented out in the western frontier, eventually became the main backers of the inflationary silver policy.[227]

The situation worsened with the Panic of 1873. Since 1861, Washington, along with state and local governments, began pumping hundreds of millions of dollars into railroad construction, creating an artificial bubble, which, like all government-inflated scams, finally burst in the fall of 1873. With Congress demonetizing silver months before, Democratic inflationists had a mighty weapon with which to attack the ruling Republicans, and they used it. In 1878, responding to rising public pressure and the discovery of new silver mines out West, Congress passed the Bland-Allison Act to begin the limited purchase and coinage of silver, in the hopes of alleviating the stresses of deflation.[228]

It was this new element of silver in the economy that Cleveland and other conservatives knew would eventually cause trouble. When he entered office in 1885, the US Treasury continued to purchase and coin silver, under Bland-Allison, at a congressionally mandated ratio of 16 to 1, meaning 16 ounces of silver equaled one ounce of gold at the US Mint. But the real ratio, at the bullion market, reached as high as 20 to 1. So silver was overvalued at the mint, requiring more silver to buy gold on the market. This being the case, 16 ounces of silver could be taken to the mint to exchange for gold, flooding the treasury with silver. The one ounce of gold purchased at the mint could then be taken to the bullion market and exchanged for 20 ounces of silver, a profit of 25 percent on each transaction. In addition to American citizens, foreigners contributed to this problem, bringing silver into the country to exchange for American gold. Either way, gold flowed out of the treasury while cheap silver flooded in. Cleveland had warned of this day throughout his first term, prophesying that silver could one day replace government gold in the treasury if the silver purchases were not stopped, but Congress paid little heed to his words.

As part of their big government scheme, the Billion-Dollar Congress in 1890 inflated the currency yet again with the Sherman Silver Purchase Act, buying all the nation's silver bullion and paying for it with new paper currency to the tune of $50 million per year. The government also continued to coin silver for circulation. This only worsened the inflation as ratios eventually reached 32 to 1.

Most scholars in various academic fields have always been in disagreement over what caused the downturn of the 1890s but generally agree that it resulted not from one source, like the level of money, but from a number of factors, such as an overexpansion of industry, overinvestment in railroads, declining farm prices, and falling incomes. "The depression had more fundamental causes than the volume of the nation's currency," writes Richard E. Welch Jr. "It was primarily the product of problems in international markets of trade and finance, the overexpansion of the agricultural and transportation sectors of the US economy, and a banking system that failed to provide a necessary measure of central authority and regional cooperation."[229] But most of these listed reasons cannot be considered the ultimate root of the problem, only symptoms of the Depression.

The source was something else entirely, namely too much cheap currency in circulation. "Uneasiness about the shift from gold to silver and the continuing free-silver agitation caused foreigners to lose further confidence in the US gold standard and to cause a drop in capital imports and severe gold outflows from the country," noted economist Murray Rothbard in his book *A History of Money and Banking in the United States*. "This loss of confidence exerted contractionist pressure on the American economy and reduced potential economic growth during the early 1890s."[230] It was this policy of currency expansion that led to speculation, providing for the overexpansion of industry and the overinvestment in railroads, mainly from government intervention, thereby causing an eventual drop in farm prices and declining incomes when the economy began to contract.

Many astute businessmen at the time were well aware that the inflationary scheme would cause major problems in the economy. Wealthy financier Henry Villard knew from the start that the Sherman silver law "would before long plunge the whole country into general disaster." He advised friends as early as 1891 to "abstain from all long engagements, and to keep their investments in the United States in as liquid a form as possible." The "blackest clouds were gathering fast and would burst before long and sweep like a devastating tornado over the whole land," he said. He advised all he spoke with "to put their houses in order, and especially to keep out of debt and new ventures, and prepare for the worst."[231]

Yet the average American, as well as many politicians, saw only prosperity as 1893 dawned. All the new cash injected into the economy initially acted as an impetus for rapid growth. Unemployment, which stood at 5.4 percent in 1891, dropped nearly 2.5 points to 3.0 in 1892, a remarkably low figure. The nation's exports rose by $150 million in the same year, a full percent of GNP. And despite the increased spending by the Harrison Administration, the national debt stood at just $961.432 million in 1893, its post–Civil War low point. By contrast, in 1885, Cleveland's first year as president, it had been more than $1.5 billion, which he cut to $1.2 billion. The nation seemed to be doing well, at least on the surface.[232]

Even President Harrison made note of the excellent economic growth in his final message to Congress on December 6, 1892. A "high degree of prosperity and so general a diffusion of the comforts of life were never before enjoyed by our people," he wrote. "There never has been a time in our history when work was so abundant or when wages were as high." Even agriculture, which always struggled in the late-nineteenth century, gained "a fair participation in the general prosperity." But the affluence, noted reformer Carl Schurz, "produced the usual effect of inciting recklessness in borrowing and lending, and of stimulating the spirit of venturesome enterprise." Harrison failed to see the clear warning signs, that the nation's financial success would be short-lived, as a speculative bubble had formed held up by a flurry of treasury notes and silver, all redeemable in gold.[233]

President Cleveland had yet to move into the White House on March 4, 1893, when the opening salvos of a major economic depression hit. The first signs that the speculative bubble had begun to burst came in late 1892. In the latter half of that year and into the beginning of 1893, prices for staples such as breadstuffs, cotton, and iron began a steady decline, cutting into the profits of farmers and manufacturers. Railroads, including the colossal transcontinentals began failing. Just days before the inauguration, the Philadelphia & Reading Railroad, whose stock plunged on news that its debt had climbed to a catastrophic $125 million, suddenly declared bankruptcy on February 26, and then the Erie in July, Jay Gould's Northern Pacific in August, the Union Pacific in October, and the Atchison in December. In all, 70 major railroad lines went into receivership, a full 25 percent of all US rails. The shock caused alarm on Wall Street, which began seeing record stock sales.[234]

The overexpansion of railroads is a great example of the economic chaos during the 1890s, just as it had been in the 1870s. With all the new money floating around, particularly the massive subsidy program from governments on every level, railroads constructed 74,000 miles of new track during the decade of the 1880s, a record-breaking increase. The spurious building continued into the 1890s, though not necessarily out of the need to keep pace with an expanding economy but to keep pace with competing rail companies. Each railroad company, writes Professor Harold Faulkner, "recklessly and hastily threw up lines that were not needed, through miles and miles of uninhabited wilderness, merely to ensure that another road would not claim the territory first." The expansion, brought on in large part because of government interference, was too much for the economy to take, causing railroads to fail. With railroads going down, other industries inevitably followed, such as the vital manufacturing of steel. Ripples were spreading across the American economy.[235]

In early May, a major trust, the National Cordage Company, failed when its stock plummeted from $140 a share to $70. But the panic had just begun, and it would grow into one of the worst depressions of the nineteenth century and one of the most severe in American history. Unemployment reached as high as 18.5 percent, caused by the failure of 15,242 businesses in 1893 alone, and another 13,905 in 1894, which was the highest rate since the downturn of the 1870s. In total, the panic saw the suspension, outright bankruptcy, or temporary closure of 575 banks, while the GNP fell 10 percent in two years.[236]

The situation was bad. Historian Henry Adams believed there was "nothing but universal bankruptcy before the world." He wrote that men "died like flies under the strain, and Boston grew suddenly old, haggard, and thin." Senator Shelby Cullom of Illinois noted, "The year 1893 closed with the prices of many products at the lowest ever known, with many workers seeking in vain for work, and with charity laboring to keep back suffering and starvation in all our cities." A young reporter in Chicago wrote home about what he saw in the Windy City. "There are thousands of homeless and starving men in the streets. I have seen more misery in this last week than I ever saw in my life before." The American correspondent for the *Bankers' Magazine* of London wrote that "ruin and disaster run riot over the land." The people of the United States were "in the throes of a fiasco unprecedented even in their broad experience." The country was on the verge of "a pronounced and serious panic."[237]

Though the economy was shrinking at an alarming rate, President Cleveland, who was supposedly in the pocket of Big Business, did nothing to help struggling companies and corporations with any direct government aid. He believed that everyone, individuals as well as businesses, should pull themselves up by their own bootstraps and not look to Washington for help. This was the commonly held economic view of his day, particularly for Jeffersonian Democrats. Congressman Michael D. Harter of Ohio reminded the nation that it was "not the business of the United States to raise prices, provide work, regulate wages, or in any way to interfere in the private business or personal affairs of the people." But some were beginning to believe the government could be a positive force in relieving people who were suffering through bad economic times. Senator James H. Berry of Arkansas was shocked that members wanted to "be more liberal in appropriating money," simply "because times are hard," he said. "That is not my theory of the Constitution. My idea is that each individual citizen of the United States should look to himself, and it is not the purpose of this government to give work to individuals throughout the United States by appropriating money that belongs to other people and does not belong to the Senate."[238]

COMBATING INFLATION AND SAVING THE GOLD STANDARD

Instead of increasing the money supply, or worse, increasing government spending as a solution, Cleveland focused on what he perceived as the real problem—the Sherman Silver Purchase Act of 1890, specifically its nefarious purchasing clause. He believed the only solution was for Congress to correct its mistake and rescind the bill. If not, Gresham's Law would come into play: "Bad money drives good money out of circulation." When too much cheap currency entered circulation, the nation's gold standard would be under threat, as people would hoard the more valuable coin, which is exactly what was happening. This would place the nation on a de facto silver standard, the monetary system of the poorer nations of the world.

Yet the small but growing liberal wing of Cleveland's Democratic Party, as well as those in the Republican Party, believed the problem stemmed from a scarcity of money. In other words, they contended that not enough currency in circulation is what caused the contraction. A policy of inflation would benefit the poor by cheapening the dollars in circulation and making it easier to pay debts over time. This would greatly aid the lower classes, especially farmers, just as today's liberals want to use more debt to fight too much debt, more spending to fight too much spending, and more borrowing to fight too much borrowing. As Ron Paul has said on numerous occasions, that's like saying you should use more disease to fight a disease. Or as we said in Vietnam, we must destroy the village to save it. It's a completely absurd notion that defies all logic.[239]

Cleveland saw the problem from the viewpoint of purchasing power, which would decrease as the currency increased. Every additional cheap dollar put into circulation caused the nation's money to lose value and caused the hoarding of gold. Should the nation continue to purchase 4.5 million ounces of silver a month, paying for it with treasury notes, and should the nation then enact a policy of free and unlimited coinage, coining the silver bullion and putting it into circulation, the results would have been disastrous. "I want a currency that is stable and safe in the hands of our people," Cleveland wrote to Governor W. J. Northern of Georgia, an advocate of free silver. "I will not knowingly be implicated in a condition that will make me in the least degree answerable to any laborer or farmer in the United States for a shrinkage in the purchasing power of the dollar he has received for a full dollar's worth of work or for a good dollar's worth of the product of his toil."[240]

In August 1893, Cleveland called Congress into special session to repeal the purchasing clause of the Sherman Silver Purchase Act. He sent a special message on the nation's financial situation and asked Congress to rescind the law. The "alarming and extraordinary business situation," wrote Cleveland, involves "the welfare and prosperity of all our people." The cause of the economic calamity was the continued "purchase and coinage of silver by the general government," a policy that has "made the depletion of our gold easy and have tempted other and more appreciative nations to add it to their stock." If the policy continued, the value of gold and silver "must part company" rather than remain in parity, which would cause the nation to lose its place "among nations of the first class" and deprive the people of "the best and safest money." Though he faced stiff resistance, on August 28, the House voted for repeal. The Senate followed suit but not until the end of October.[241]

Cleveland took overwhelming criticism for his leadership in seeking repeal, but stopping the inflation allowed the economy to begin to correct the imbalances within it. O. M. W. Sprague, who wrote a history of banking crises under the national banking system for the US Senate, noted that getting rid of the silver purchases "did much to restore confidence." Economist Murray Rothbard also believed that stopping the inflation helped bring an end to the panic by the end of 1893, as "foreign confidence rose with the Cleveland administration's successful repeal of the Sherman Silver Purchase Act," which saved the gold standard. Rothbard's analysis of the situation has been proven correct, as subsequent administrations held tightly to the gold standard and the economy eventually soared as a result.[242]

But Cleveland faced another problem, as gold left the treasury at an alarming rate. To maintain a gold standard, the federal government had to maintain a reserve of at least $100 million to back the amount of currency in circulation. That reserve was now under threat. In an epic effort to stop the drain on the gold reserves, the president decided to issue bonds, which could be purchased only in gold, in order to shore up the gold supply in the treasury. The president had the power to do this under law. In one bond sale, big banking tycoons headed by J. P. Morgan bought most of them and turned a major profit, which caused a flurry of protest, especially when it was discovered that Morgan had met with the president in the White House to discuss the merits of the plan. But Cleveland's deal, a use of the free-market financial system, helped save the gold standard and with it the American economy. Murray Rothbard, himself a libertarian of the Austrian school of economic thought, credited the "heroic" Cleveland-Morgan deal with restoring "confidence in the continuance of the gold standard."[243]

Though many wanted to keep the policy of inflation in place, and even increase the injection of silver into the economy to help the working classes, Cleveland stood strong against the tide. Critics hurled abuse at him daily. Henry Adams, an advocate for the poor and for free silver, even took to calling him "His Imperial Highness by God's Grace Grover the First." Many politicians in his own party shunned him. Progressive Democratic Governor John Altgeld of Illinois hurled a vicious attack at a Jefferson Day event. "To laud Clevelandism on Jefferson's birthday is to sing a Te Deum in honor of Judas Iscariot on a Christmas morning," he said. But none of the abuse bothered the president or kept him from doing what he knew to be the right thing, maintaining sound money at all costs. As biographer Allan Nevins has written, Cleveland's "greatest single service to the nation was ... his stubborn defense, against terrific assaults, of a sound financial system."[244]

These "terrific assaults" continued throughout the next century, and the inflationists eventually got their way. Though it took some time, the United States finally went off the gold standard completely in 1971 when Richard Nixon cut the last strings. And since that day, noted Charles Kadlec in 2011 in *Forbes* magazine, "the unemployment rate has averaged [more than] 6 percent, and we have suffered the three worst recessions since the end of World War II. The unemployment rate averaged 8.5 percent in 1975, almost 10 percent in 1982, and has been [more than] 8.8 percent for more than two years [2009-2011], with little evidence of any improvement ahead. This performance is horrendous compared to the post–World War II gold standard era, which lasted from 1947–70. During those [23] years of economic ups and downs, unemployment averaged less than 5 percent and *never* rose above 7 percent."[245] Cleveland was right on the gold standard.

CUTTING TAXES AND GOVERNMENT

After stopping the currency inflation and saving the gold standard, Cleveland turned his attention to the main source of federal revenue, the high protective tariff, operating at levels of 50 percent across the board, thanks to Bill McKinley's act in 1890. Taxes needed to be trimmed in order to help the economy recover, Cleveland believed, and he vowed to make it successful this time, especially with a Democratic Congress.

It wasn't just the maintenance of party strength or the desire to keep his campaign pledges that stirred Cleveland to enact tariff reform. He had always believed the Republican protective tariff, in operation since 1861, was simply too high and in most cases brought in more revenue than the government needed. But with the sky high McKinley Tariff, it began to reduce revenue, and with increased spending by the GOP, and a slowing economy, caused deficits. That level of protection, Cleveland believed, was no longer necessary. As Cleveland argued during his first term, American industrial products dominated the world, and the Treasury had enough revenue to pay Washington's expenses, though only if Congress maintained the principles of economy in government. The high tariffs, then, looked to Cleveland like political payoffs to the main Republican special interest—Big Business. Reformer Carl Schurz called the high tariff "the greatest engine of political corruption on a grand scale that this country has ever seen." The *New York Times* agreed, referring to the Republican tariff act as the "McKinley abomination," to which every "monopolist and tax eater in the land … has been pouring into the corruption fund of the Republican Party a part of the iniquitous tax he has been able to levy through Republican favor."[246]

Cleveland's main goal in tariff reform was to help the working classes receive lower prices on consumer goods. In the first annual message of his second term, sent to Congress on December 4, 1893, the president wrote that in order "to aid the people directly through tariff reform, one of its most obvious features should be a reduction in present tariff charges upon the necessaries of life. The benefits of such a reduction would be palpable and substantial, seen and felt by thousands who would be better fed and better clothed and better sheltered. These gifts should be the willing benefactions of a Government whose highest function is the promotion of the welfare of the people."[247]

On December 19, 1893, William L. Wilson, Chairman of the House Ways and Means Committee, rolled out a new tariff reform bill, which passed the House on February 1, 1894, by a significant margin, 204 to 140. Tariff duties were modestly cut by 15 percent. However, to make up for any projected loss of revenue, the final House version of the bill included a provision for an income tax. The young Democratic congressman from Nebraska, William Jennings Bryan, introduced the tax amendment and vigorously defended it. "There is no more just tax upon the statute books than the income tax," he told the House.[248]

Though not a new concept, a tax on income was first enacted in 1862 to help finance the Civil War, and despite the Constitution's prohibition against direct taxes, federal courts had left it alone as a war revenue measure. The original act created the Bureau of Internal Revenue, the forerunner to the IRS, to collect the tax. It covered all incomes of more than $600 a year at two graduated rates. Income greater than $600 and up to $10,000 was taxed at 3 percent, while everything greater than $10,000 was taxed at 5 percent. In 1864 the top rate was increased to 10 percent. When applicable, the federal government had actually withheld the tax from people's income, such as government salaries, dividends and interest from bank stocks and bonds, as well as directly from corporations, such as railroads. By the end of the war, some 15 percent of households were paying the tax. In 1872 the law expired, and Republicans were content to leave it dead, as the tariff was continually pouring money into the federal treasury, making additional taxes unnecessary.[249]

The income tax of 1894 established a rate of just 2 percent on incomes of $4,000 or more, effectively exempting more than 99 percent of the population. The 2 percent rate also applied to corporations, but those entities did not receive any exemption. So only the very rich would be affected by the new tax. With more than 12 million households across the nation, the tax would touch just 85,000 who had incomes of $4,000 or greater. This made the 1894 income tax much different in scope than its 1862 predecessor. "For the first time in American history," writes economic historian John Steele Gordon, "a tax was seemingly proposed on a particular class of citizens, a class defined by economic success." Critics used this feature to attack the tax proposal as "socialism." Cleveland's fellow New Yorker and longtime antagonist Senator David B. Hill blamed the tax on "little squads of anarchists, communists, and socialists" from Europe infecting America with foreign ideas.[250]

But supporters pointed to the massive concentration of wealth to make their case. "The tax proposed on incomes," wrote former Congressman Roger Q. Mills in its defense, "is but a light touch on the monumental piles of wealth, for the protection of which the government is standing guard." Mills argued that continued wealth accumulation might lead to "an upheaval" not unlike that of Revolutionary France in 1789 when the clergy and nobility "persistently refused to bear any burden of taxation to support the government."[251]

Thomas G. Shearman, a political economist and founder of the Shearman and Sterling Law Firm in New York City, conducted a study on the concentration of wealth in America, which he published in 1889 in *The Forum* under the title "The Owners of the United States of America." Shearman contended that just 70 persons owned a combined wealth of $2.7 billion. Some 50,000 families owned half the nation's wealth, while four-fifths of the people earned less than $500 a year. Although he represented such prominent American figures as Jay Gould, Henry Ford, and John D. Rockefeller and his Standard Oil giant, Shearman supported an income tax "upon rents and corporations having exclusive privileges." The tax burden, Shearman noted, was disproportionately placed upon the poor, who paid taxes equivalent to 75–80 percent of their savings while corporations and the wealthy paid only 8–10 percent. Federal taxes had increased six-fold since the Civil War, he maintained, while untaxed corporations saw their profits soar tenfold. This had to change, he contended.[252]

As a strong Jeffersonian, Cleveland had his own reservations. He had discussed the great disparity of wealth in his final State of the Union message in 1888, and had given his support for "a small tax upon incomes derived from certain corporate investments." His proposal was certainly not an income tax in the traditional sense and would, in no way, touch the lower classes but would resemble modern-day capital gains taxes, first instituted in 1913, and tax the massive corporations that paid almost no taxes yet stood protected behind an enormous tariff wall. But this proposal by Bryan was essentially wealth redistribution, something Cleveland would never support.[253]

The president also had another reason to look on the income tax with suspicion. Not only did it violate a fundamental principle of Jeffersonian economic thought, it gave Congress yet more funds to spend. "The income tax became the fuel for paternalism in government," writes tax historian Charles Adams, "just as excises and land and wealth taxes had done in Europe centuries before." Cleveland understood this and certainly did not want to see any more government paternalism. But many wanted to see a tariff reform act, any tariff reform act, become law. Even the *New York Times* wanted to see the bill passed, though it contained "the obnoxious income tax amendment."[254] With a complete Democratic government for the first time since James Buchanan's administration, this might be their only hope.

Chairman Wilson privately opposed inclusion of the tax, mainly because he feared it would upset Cleveland. In fact, the president wrote him that he "deprecated the incorporation in the proposed bill of the income tax feature," primarily because it was a major distraction from the real issue before Congress, that of tariff reform. According to Josephus Daniels, private secretary to the Interior Secretary Hoke Smith, it was "Bryan who forced the income tax provision in the Wilson Tariff Act. Mr. Cleveland, Mr. Carlisle [Treasury Secretary], and Mr. Wilson did not wish it incorporated in the tariff measure." In the end, however, Wilson relented to the pressure, and the income tax amendment passed by a vote of 182 to 48. The whole tax package was then sent to the Senate, where it faced an uncertain future in what many in the House considered an "aristocratic club of millionaires."[255]

As with the repeal of the Sherman Silver Purchase Act, the Senate dragged its feet on the tariff reform bill—not for the purpose of slowing down the process by procedure but in order to rewrite the entire bill. Cleveland was again aggravated by the actions of the Senate, calling their activities a "deadly blight of treason." Leading the effort to make the bill into the Senate's image was Maryland Democratic Senator Arthur Pue Gorman, joined by David B. Hill of New York and James Smith Jr. of New Jersey, along with three other Democrats who united with the opposition Republicans who would not tolerate any tampering with its signature policy.[256]

With Gorman leading the charge, no one in the administration could have a shred of confidence that things would turn out well. The bill "had the bad fortune to be in the hands of Senator Gorman," wrote Josephus Daniels. "He was one of the most astute men in public life, a straight party man, but he had no zeal for reform or righteousness." Every Senator "who wanted a little graft was accommodated." In the control of protectionists, the Upper Chamber considered the issue of tariff reform for five months, tacking on 634 amendments to the House bill that hiked tariff rates on a host of articles. Most senators wanted to protect the interests of their respective states. Louisiana's Senate delegation vowed not to support any deal unless a duty was placed on imported sugar from Cuba. Senator Stephen White of California sought duties on imported fruit. Senators from coal and iron ore states wanted those items taxed as well.[257]

Both sides—Cleveland and the reformers on one and Gorman and the protectionists on the other—dug in and battled throughout the spring. The years between the Civil War and the next conflict, the Spanish-American War of 1898 have been portrayed as relatively quiet. But one veteran Washington journalist, David S. Barry, noted that the fight over the Wilson Tariff Bill "literally set the country on fire," stirring "the people into a frenzy of political discussion." Because of his staunch silver stand, the animosity between Cleveland and many Senate Democrats was already strong; the tariff fight soured their already weakened relationship further. Senator John Morgan of Alabama professed to hate the very ground the president walked on. Not exactly the climate conducive to conducting the nation's business.[258]

Despite the rancor, the reform bill, now dubbed the Wilson-Gorman Tariff Bill, passed in the Senate on July 3 by a close vote of 39 to 34, with 12 senators abstaining from the vote. Raw materials on the free list dwindled to just two: wool and copper. Tariffs were raised on iron, wool and cotton products, glass, certain chemicals, and sugar, both raw and refined. The income tax amendment also remained. But because of the vast differences between the two proposals, it would be left up to a House-Senate conference committee to determine the final outcome.[259]

Cleveland had high hopes for a good bill emerging from the conference committee. It would "present the best, if not the only, hope of true Democracy," the president wrote Wilson in a letter read on the House floor, "and the redemption of Democratic promises to the people." The Senate bill "falls far short of the consummation for which we have long labored, for which we have suffered defeat without discouragement," and should the effort be abandoned, it would mean "party perfidy and party dishonor." The final bill, Cleveland insisted, must include the free importation of raw materials if it is to "bear a genuine Democratic badge" and be of any help to the people.[260]

But rather than work out a compromise, the House decided to accept the Senate's version, which included the income tax provision. On August 13, the House passed the Senate's bill by a vote of 182 to 105, despite Wilson's noble effort to prevent it. In the end the final bill lowered rates from 50 to 42 percent. Cleveland was so disgusted with the process that he allowed the bill to become law without his signature. He hated the income tax provision and detested the Senate's action on the original bill, but he did favor the small cut in taxes.

As he had in his 1888 message, he went after the wealthy and their influence over the proposed tariff legislation. It was "the trusts and combinations—the communism of pelf—whose machinations have prevented us from reaching the success we deserved," he wrote Mississippi Congressman Thomas C. Catchings. The tariff law, though flawed, "presents a vast improvement to existing conditions" and lightens "many tariff burdens that now rest heavily upon the people. It is not only a barrier against the return of mad protection, but it furnishes a vantage-ground from which must be waged further aggressive operations against protected monopoly and governmental favoritism." This bill was a step in the right direction, he contended, but because it had provisions "which are not in line with honest tariff reform," with "inconsistencies and crudities which ought not to appear in tariff laws or laws of any kind," like the income tax, he did not sign it.[261]

But Cleveland had good reason to believe the Supreme Court, in a time when the justices actually looked out for the Constitution, would not allow the income tax to remain in place. During his first term in 1888, he appointed Melville Fuller, a steadfast Jeffersonian, as chief justice. Fuller was quite possibly the best chief justice in American history, ruling on many serious constitutional questions, including the Sherman Antitrust Act, and always upholding the original intent of the Founders. Unsurprisingly, the Fuller Court struck down the income tax provision in 1895 in *Pollock v. Farmers' Loan & Trust Co* by a 5 to 4 vote.[262]

President Cleveland also cut spending during his second term. With liberals, it's a knee-jerk reaction to spend more money when the economy slows, but it was not possible with a true conservative president. He urged restraint. "At this time, when a depleted public Treasury confronts us," he told Congress, "when many of our people are engaged in a hard struggle for the necessities of life, and when enforced economy is pressing upon the great mass of our countrymen, I desire to urge with all the earnestness at my command that Congressional legislation be so limited by strict economy as to exhibit an appreciation of the condition of the Treasury and a sympathy with the straitened circumstances of our fellow citizens." When he took over for Harrison, the federal budget was at $383 million, which he trimmed to $352 million by 1896, his final full year in office.[263]

And what were the results of these free-market measures? After the loss of 10 percent of GDP in two years, the economy began to grow in 1895, making up the losses and gaining an additional 20 percent by 1897 from its low point in 1894. Unemployment was a bit more sluggish, dropping from 18.5 percent in 1894 to 14.5 by 1897, but by 1900 it was at just 5 percent.[264] The quick turnaround has caused economists and historians to erroneously categorize it as no worse than a minor recession, but the Panic of 1893 had the potential to be the worst economic calamity in American history. And because Cleveland used free-market principles instead of socialistic intervention, the crisis was short-lived. It is an economic record that should not be shunned by conservative scholars.

LIBERAL "BLAME GAME"

The panic did have an unfortunate consequence: quickly ending Grover Cleveland's second Jeffersonian interlude. With the depression striking just as conservative Democrats took power, they received all the blame, even though they had nothing to do with the policies that had caused it. Beginning in 1888, with the election of Harrison, Republicans held the government until 1893 and put into place their policies of inflation and increased spending, fiscal programs that caused the downturn by making an already bad financial bubble much worse. Like meteorological storms, an economic recession or depression is an economic tempest or a "correction" in the economy as the free market corrects the imbalances within it, just as atmospheric storms correct the imbalances in the stratosphere. In this case, the economy was correcting a disproportionate amount of inflation from both the Sherman Silver Purchase Act and the ramped-up expenditures.

Just as President Obama and liberal Democrats in Congress have blamed everything and everyone for the bad economy—George W. Bush, the Tea Party, ATM and kiosk fees, business automation, the Japanese tsunami, the Arab spring—liberal Republicans did likewise to Cleveland. In his memoirs, Senator John Sherman, a former Treasury Secretary and younger brother of the famous Union general, held Cleveland responsible for the depression, even though he had not been in power for four years when the downturn struck. Nevertheless, Sherman argued that the *anticipation* of more conservative policies caused the crash. For Senator Sherman, whose name graced the silver purchase law, it was Cleveland's election that "created the disturbances that followed it. The fear of radical changes in the tariff law was the basis of them." Sherman even claimed that he only loaned his name to the bill, which he maintained was only a compromise hatched in order to prevent the free and unlimited coinage of silver. He objected to the silver purchases and to the issuance of the new treasury notes, stating that he "had foreseen this inevitable result" of economic depression. Cleveland had been saying the same thing all throughout his first term but received no credit for it. In addition to Sherman, other Republicans made similar assertions blaming Cleveland, most just as ridiculous. Sherman's position would be like blaming the fire department for the fire that burned the house down, even though they rushed over to put it out. Cleveland tried to clean up the economic mess made by others.[265]

Despite the persistent criticism, President Cleveland did receive some praise from members of the opposition party. He did what he believed was right to correct the economic depression that struck the nation in 1893 and demonstrated, according to Republican Chauncey M. Depew, "an extraordinary degree of courage and steadfastness." Senator William B. Allison, an Iowa Republican and the coauthor of the Bland-Allison Silver Act of 1878, also credited Cleveland for having the audacity to repeal the Sherman Act. It was God's mercy that Cleveland was elected in 1892, Allison told Horace White of the *New York Evening Post*, for no Republican "could have procured the repeal … however strongly he might have tried." No Democrat other than Cleveland could have been successful either, and had the president failed to get the bill repealed, "we should now be a ruined people." This was quite a compliment coming from a man who was so knowledgeable on economic matters that two presidents, Chester Arthur and Benjamin Harrison, asked him to serve as Secretary of the Treasury, offers he declined.[266]

Liberals in both parties had sown the seeds of depression, but unfortunately, Cleveland Democrats reaped the rotten fruit. Naturally the public laid the blame at the feet of those in power. In the midterm elections in 1894, Cleveland's party was decimated, losing control of both houses of Congress. Two years later, in 1896, they lost the presidency to William McKinley, even though the economy was finally beginning to rebound. The economy had suffered through three years of depression, which was not Cleveland's fault. He put in place the policies to get the nation moving again but the seemingly never-ending agitation over free silver held down economic growth. With the business community not knowing what type of monetary policy the nation would have, it caused what economists like to call "regime uncertainty," which is exactly what the nation has faced with Obama. The great economic growth enjoyed by President McKinley had little to do with his legislative program, save his market-calming adherence to the gold standard, but had more to do with the free market economic policies put into action by Grover Cleveland.

MODERN-DAY DEPRESSIONS

Every depression before 1929 had been fought using the "Grover Cleveland approach," lessons taken from America's founding generation, historically known as laissez faire economics. The government simply kept their "hands off" the economy and allowed the free market, or Adam Smith's "invisible hand," to work. As a result, those downturns did not digress into a depression of more than fifteen years like the one in 1929 did.

It all changed, first with Herbert Hoover, not FDR. "No president before had ever believed there was a government responsibility in such cases," wrote Hoover in his 1952 memoirs, defending his approach to the Great Depression. "No matter what the urging on previous occasions, presidents steadfastly had maintained that the federal government was apart from such eruptions; they had always been left to blow themselves out. Presidents Van Buren, Grant, Cleveland, and Theodore Roosevelt had all remained aloof." Government solutions changed with the onset of the Panic in 1929. Understanding that Washington had to "pioneer a new field," first Hoover and then his successor, Franklin Delano Roosevelt, intervened in the economy in the hopes of alleviating the depression, a policy approach that has remained in place ever since, despite its failure.[267]

President Hoover oversaw a massive infusion of government into the free-market economy. Though many might note that Hoover's intervention seemed paltry, that's only because it was dwarfed by FDR's, yet no administration before 1929 had ever spent so much money—or any money for that matter—trying to end a depression. Hoover spent a whopping $500 million on public works projects, a full 13 percent of the federal budget while insisting that state governments also increase their spending. In 1932 he injected another $2.3 billion into the same projects with the Emergency and Relief Construction Act. That same year the budget deficit hit $2 billion. Hoover's solution to the budget gap? Raise taxes. The Revenue Act of 1932 hiked income taxes at the top rate to 63 percent from Coolidge's 25 percent. He also raised tariffs to one of the highest rates in history with the Smoot-Hawley Tariff Act of 1930. These interventionist policies quickly turned a small recession into a major depression, which he handed off to FDR.[268]

Hoover's great-granddaughter, Margaret Hoover, has written in her book *American Individualism* that her great-grandfather was at a distinct disadvantage. "Circumstances beyond Hoover's control greatly complicated his efforts to revive the economy," she writes. "He was trying to cope with a global depression in a modern industrial economy without the benefit of some of the core theories of modern economics. Most major theories of macroeconomics were developed, in fact, by studying what happened during the Great Depression. John Maynard Keynes, Friedrich von Hayek, Milton Friedman, and other prominent economists emerged from that period with critical theories about monetary and fiscal policy, trade, and the interrelationship of taxes and the economy as well as the value of countercyclical policies. But none of this expertise was available to Hoover in 1930."[269] That may be so, but the governing laws of economics never change, nor had the nation's economic history, a history Hoover had obviously studied, given the statements in his own memoirs.

In 1933, FDR followed in Herbert Hoover's footsteps and employed Keynesian economic theories, formulated by the British economist John Maynard Keynes, which is the infusion of government spending to pull the economy out of a slump, though Roosevelt expanded it to a much higher level. FDR and his team believed they had to aggressively fight a downturn that had begun four years before, but as a result of the intervention, the depression worsened and lasted until the late 1940s. FDR, like his predecessor, raised income taxes to their highest levels in history, with the top rate peaking at 94 percent on incomes of more than $200,000, which cut federal revenue in half. He also raised corporate taxes, added new ones, such as Social Security, employed wage and price controls, and spent heavily on programs designed to relieve the nation of the depression with his "alphabet soup" of new government agencies, many of which are still in existence today.

The situation was so bad that after a massive, government-funded "shovel-ready" jobs program artificially lowered the unemployment rate to 14 percent, the economy crashed again in 1937, a "depression within a depression," pushing the rate back up to near 20 percent. *New York Times* columnist and economist Paul Krugman, as well as most liberal academics, contend that when FDR tried to cut spending and balance the budget in 1937 it sent the economy into another tailspin. Had FDR not listened to conservatives and done such an unspeakable thing as cutting spending, the depression would have ended sooner. If this is the case, why did the economy not crash again under Van Buren or Cleveland when they slashed expenditures? Why did it not crash in 1921 when the Harding-Coolidge Administration cut taxes and reduced spending by 40 percent? In the case of the 1920s, massively slashing spending and cutting income taxes produced a lasting economic boom the likes of which we have not seen since.

Despite leftwing drivel to the contrary, FDR's solutions failed. As his Treasury Secretary Henry Morgenthau testified before Congress in 1939, the New Deal flopped.

> We have tried spending money. We are spending more than we have ever spent before and it does not work. And I have just one interest, and if I am wrong ... somebody else can have my job. I want to see this country prosperous. I want to see the people get a job. I want to see people get enough to eat. We have never made good on our promises.... I say after eight years of this administration we have just as much unemployment as when we started ... and an enormous debt to boot! We are just sitting here and fiddling, and I am just wearing myself out and getting sick. Because why? I can't see any daylight.[270]

In fact, as Professor Burton Folsom has pointed out, the Great Depression did not abate until after the war. In 1945 Congress cut personal and corporate taxes and discontinued price controls in 1946. Congress also reduced spending by two-thirds, from $98.4 billion in 1945 to $33 billion by 1948. The economy did not crash as a result of retrenchment; it soared. True economic growth began producing surpluses, which had not happened since 1930, and brought unemployment down to less than 4 percent.[271] Laissez faire economic policy works.

When reports began surfacing that the US financial sector might be in a heap of trouble in the fall of 2008, the federal government sprang into action. The Bush Treasury Department, headed by Hank Paulson, a former Wall Street titan as CEO of Goldman Sachs, proposed a $700 billion bailout package known as TARP—Troubled Asset Relief Program. Even though Democratic strategist James Carville once labeled the conservative opposition "Wall Street-protecting Republicans," in reality it was economic interventionist Democrats on Capitol Hill who jumped at the chance to bail out their friends in the financial world. The first shot at passage in the House failed miserably, by a vote of 205 in favor and 228 against. Democrats supported the measure 140–95, while free-market Republicans did not, by a vote of 133–65. With that the Dow Jones, badly wanting Uncle Sam's money, dropped 777 points. The Senate swiftly passed a revised version, 74–25, with fifteen Republicans voting no. The House then passed the Senate bill 263–171, with Democrats again supporting it 172–63, while Republicans again did not, by a count of 108–91. President Bush supported the plan and quickly signed the bill, remarking in Lincolnian fashion that he had to "abandon the free-market system to save the free-market system." The expensive "abandonment" bill would stop the market slide, the nation was told, but the Dow continued to plunge, as did the nation's economy. Flush with new cash, Wall Street paid out record salaries and bonuses; Main Street got a big fat bill for a splurge they were not allowed to partake in.[272]

When he entered the White House in January 2009, Obama and his economic team continued employing the Keynesian model. The new president immediately began pushing for an economic stimulus package that would stop the plunge, as job losses for the month of January hit 600,000. Liberals in Congress wanted something in the neighborhood of $1 trillion in new spending. In the end, they settled for $787 billion, but with interest it would top $1 trillion in new debt. Obama promised that unemployment would not rise above 8 percent if Congress passed his stimulus plan. So they did, but the unemployment rate rose above 10 percent. After huge midterm election losses, and a public souring on "hope and change," Obama's solution to the downturn was—you guessed it—more stimulus spending, although with the added bonus of higher taxes. Like all Keynesian stimulus packages before it, the massive money binge did nothing to pull the nation out of the recession nor aid an ever-shrinking middle class. Census data collected in 2010 and released in December 2011 revealed that one out of every two Americans—nearly one hundred million citizens—were considered poor or low-income. Shrinking wages and the rising cost of everyday expenses, brought on by inflation, are grinding middle-income Americans into dust.[273] Welcome to life in Obama World.

The Keynes model has failed time and again throughout history. The real solution is a simple one: look to our distant past, what great American leaders have done before us, prior to 1929 and the beginning of the era of Keynes. We need look nowhere else.

To use examples of modern men, Ron Paul has been, without question, the most outspoken proponent of the free-market solutions of Grover Cleveland, while Paul Krugman has been a fierce advocate of Keynes and his theory of economic intervention. Krugman is so convinced that using massive government spending as an effective economic stimulus that he criticized Obama's spending plan as being too *small*. Krugman wanted a stimulus bill twice as large as the $787 billion plan passed in the early part of 2009 and is, even today, pushing for more government spending. He has said that if aliens invaded the world, "a massive [military] buildup to counter the space alien threat" would pull us out of the slump in eighteen months. Since that is highly unlikely to happen, Krugman proposes we "fake it" in order to massively intervene in the economy so that the recession will end. This from a man who won a Nobel Prize in economics yet is praised in the mainstream media for his intellect. And the establishment has the temerity to call Ron Paul a kook.[274]

Unless America's leaders finally learn the lessons of the past, we are doomed to repeat its more recent mistakes. We are told, time and again, that we live in the modern world, in a global economy, and that the solutions to past depressions will not work today. But economic laws are no different than physical ones. What worked in 1893 for Grover Cleveland will work in 2012 and beyond.

V

How Cleveland's Foreign Policy Upheld American Traditions

Cleveland was a party man without answering to the ordinary conception of a politician. He had strong common sense, simplicity, and directness without subtlety, instinctive and immovable integrity, perfect courage, a kindly nature with great capacity for friendship, and with great capacity also for wrath, which made him a dangerous man to trifle with.
—*Elihu Root, Secretary of State under Theodore Roosevelt*[275]

What is the role of the United States in world affairs? It is a question asked throughout American history, in Grover Cleveland's time as well as our own. For most of the nineteenth century American foreign policy took a back seat to more pressing domestic concerns. But all that began to change as the century came to a close. America moved slowly into the realm of a world power, and overseas affairs became more prominent. During the twentieth century, the United States began to assert itself more forcefully, particularly after World War Two, as a world policeman, a role (or burden for some) it continues to carry.

JEFFERSONIAN FOREIGN POLICY

Thomas Jefferson set what became America's traditional foreign policy in his Inaugural Address in 1801, admonishing the nation to promote commerce and honest friendship with all nations but to steer clear of "entangling alliances." Washington had said much the same thing in his farewell address in 1796, warning of the dangers of a permanent alliance system, but the Jeffersonians wanted no alliances and clearly sought to remain as neutral and as isolationist as possible, making no promises that could involve the nation in a foreign war. But American ideals ran much deeper than that. In the Declaration of Independence, Jefferson enunciated the principle of self-determination, which guided US foreign policy for more than a century.

Cleveland echoed similar sentiments in both inaugural addresses, as well as in his annual messages and public speeches. The "spirit of fairness and love of justice," he wrote in his annual message in 1893, as well as "consistent fairness, characterize a truly American foreign policy."[276] He would never use diplomacy or the American military for anything other than national and hemispheric defense and certainly not for gaining new territories in distant lands, as the powers of Europe were then doing. He took Jefferson to heart.

But the attitudes of those in government, as well as across the country, were changing. The same forces of progressivism that sought a more activist government at home also wanted a more forward-looking foreign policy abroad. Just as he battled the forces of progressivism in domestic policy, Cleveland fought the same influence over the nation's foreign affairs. Progressives sought to change society for the better, to make people conform to a certain set of behaviors, to use government for the possible perfectibility of mankind and human civilization. Though we tend to think of it in terms of domestic policy, the progressive agenda also reached its tentacles across the continent and around the globe to begin the same process in alien lands. The notion of imperialism is simply progressivism applied abroad.[277] Many of the better-known progressives, such as Theodore Roosevelt and Woodrow Wilson, believed in foreign adventurism. But Cleveland hated it as much as he detested the vast changes being proposed at home.

MAINTAINING A STRONG NATIONAL DEFENSE

Not favoring an internationalist foreign policy did not mean that Cleveland preferred a weak military. Rather, he presided over a buildup of the US Navy, creating a nucleus that eventually made it one of the best in the world. In those days, before the advent of air power and nuclear weapons, naval forces were the weapons of choice and indicative of a modern power. In the late-nineteenth century, the American Navy grew into a force that easily defeated the Spanish in 1898 and helped Teddy Roosevelt exert

American influence around the globe, although that was never Cleveland's intention.

The naval buildup had actually begun under his predecessor, Chester Arthur, who earned the moniker "Father of the Modern Navy," but the expansion was greatly increased under Cleveland. But like Jefferson, Cleveland opposed the idea of a large, standing navy, one capable of offensive warfare. Such a force could lead to mischief. He saw the navy's value as a defender of the nation and the hemisphere in more troubled times, so he approved each naval appropriations bill that Congress passed, particularly large measures in 1886 and 1887. Under the watchful eye of Navy Secretary William Whitney, the fleet added 93,951 tons of new ships, compared to 11,986 tons during Arthur's administration. Whitney made sure the new steel vessels, which would replace the twenty-six wooden ships still in service, were constructed from American sources and not from foreign suppliers. Hence, Cleveland was just as responsible as his predecessor for the buildup of the great modern steel navy that performed so well in 1898 and into the twentieth century.[278]

NEW IMPERIALISM

While the United States maintained a more isolationist foreign policy for most of the nineteenth century, the powers of Europe were expanding around the globe, acquiring colonies in every corner. This great revival of Western expansion, called the New Imperialism, ran from around 1870 until 1914 and is somewhat surprising in that during most of the preceding century, imperialism had been widely seen as a fiscally unsound endeavor by most European statesmen. Yet the New Imperialism was an explosion of Western conquest that would far exceed the achievements of the Age of Discovery in the fifteenth century. It was the beginning of a new era: the Age of Empire.

The main justification behind the New Imperialism was racism—or to be more precise, scientific racism. These theories, put forward by leading scientists across Europe, including Charles Darwin, held that inferior races needed guidance and supervision from superior peoples. Britain led the way in this new way of thinking. Cecil Rhodes, an English imperialist in Africa who had large stakes in gold and diamond mining, and also served as Prime Minister of the Cape Colony from 1890–96, advised Britain to seize as much territory as possible. "We are the finest race in the world," he boasted, "and the more of the world we inhabit, the better it is for the human race." He even once told a reporter that he would annex the planets if he could.[279]

Following in Rhodes's footsteps, English author Rudyard Kipling wrote a poem called "The White Man's Burden" in 1899, where he advocated imperialism. He wrote in part:

> Take up the white man's burden
> Send forth the best ye breed
> Go bind your sons to exile
> To serve your captives' need;
> To wait in heavy harness
> On fluttered folk and wild
> Your new-caught, sullen peoples,
> Half devil and half child.

To Kipling, Third-World nations were uncivilized and childlike, and the superior races in the West had a moral obligation to introduce them to Christianity, modern education systems, and technological advancements that flowed out of "superior" Western nations. There was no way such backward peoples could go it alone, it was widely believed.[280]

As these debates raged in Europe, Americans began seeing themselves as a special people and an exceptional nation. One US senator stated in 1893, "We are sixty-five million of people, the most advanced and powerful on earth." Another believed the nation should expand throughout all of North and Central America. The "northern boundary must be the Arctic Circle and our southern boundary the Isthmus Canal," he said. Such thinking was derisively termed by its detractors as "jingoism," usually defined as an expression of extreme patriotism and the advocacy of an aggressive foreign policy to achieve territorial aspirations, a new "manifest destiny" but at a much higher level.[281]

Such boisterous statements by politicians were certainly not on the lips of everyone, as numerous Americans believed the prevailing jingoism to be "absolutely crazy," to quote one critic. Yet more and more were coming to believe the United States had been given a special mission in the world and could be as great as the powers of Europe, if not already so. But Europe was in the process of acquiring colonies, engaged heavily in a "scramble for Africa" and in attaining areas of Asia, while the United States risked falling behind the world's leaders. If it wanted to keep up, and truly be one of the most powerful nations on earth, then American foreign policy must change.[282]

In 1890, American naval officer Captain Alfred Thayer Mahan, a professor at the Naval War College, wrote one of antiquity's most important books, *The Influence of Sea Power upon History*, which argued that naval power is the key component that made nations strong. Britain, Mahan reminded his readers, dominated the world and its commerce because of its strong, powerful navy, which allowed it to control the sea-lanes, protect its merchant fleet, and, in time of war, blockade an enemy's ports. Despite its recent naval buildup, the United States possessed naval vessels that were lacking in technological advancement, far behind the forces of other great naval powers. He contended that America should abandon its policy of continental and hemispheric defense and build a truly modern blue-water naval force that could be used for offensive warfare around the globe. He also advocated the acquisition of territory for bases and refueling stops, all in order to become one of the great powers of the world. This significant work was a widely read international bestseller, even by European statesman. Kaiser Wilhelm II shifted German naval strategy after reading it, which helped pave the way for World War One. More importantly, the book greatly influenced future American leaders like Teddy Roosevelt, who would transform American foreign policy into a more aggressive strategy.[283]

Mahan's thinking fell in line with the outlook of many fellow jingoistic Americans, like Roosevelt, his good friend Senator Henry Cabot Lodge, and others in and out of government, who saw war as a good thing, a healthy and cleansing process for the nation. It was a strange concept for a country that was only one generation removed from the bloodiest war in the history of the Western Hemisphere. But many up-and-coming leaders, like TR, had been small children in the 1860s and had no real memory of the conflict between the North and South. The torch was being passed to a new generation of Americans who would take foreign policy in a new direction and away from self-determination for all peoples.

OPPOSITION TO NATION BUILDING

Cleveland did not buy into the jingoist and imperialist arguments, or in the suggestion that America needed an even larger global naval force. Unlike many jingoists, he remembered the great sectional conflict and never believed war was anything but bad. Soon after retaking office in

1893 to begin his second term, Cleveland faced a serious test of American foreign policy in a situation concerning the Hawaiian Islands and the role the United States played in a recent revolution there.

Hawaii remained an independent nation in the early 1890s, ruled by a native monarch. But the islands were in the process of undergoing major demographic changes, as native Hawaiians died out and were replaced with foreigners, namely Europeans and Americans, as well as laborers from China and Japan. The natives were holding on but by a thread only. A native population of 200,000 in 1800 had been reduced to 40,000 by 1890, with disease causing a major portion of the decline. The foreign population also swelled, with nearly 30,000 Japanese and Chinese, 9,000 Portuguese, and 2,000 Americans, who dominated the economy. And the Japanese population was growing fast.[284]

The economy of the islands centered heavily on sugar production, with the major plantations being under the thumb of non-Hawaiians, mostly Americans. A small cabal of wealthy white families, known as outlanders, so-named after an influx of European settlers, effectively controlled the economy and with it the government and all of Hawaiian society. By the early 1890s, the natives still held on to the monarchy, which served as the titular head of the government, but was, in actuality, merely a figurehead. Real power centered in the parliament, controlled by the outlanders.[285]

In the United States, liberal Republicans began seeking a much more aggressive foreign policy. After conquering the South by crushing the Confederacy and the West by subjugating the Plains Indians, Republicans turned their attention from wars of subjugation at home and looked farther to the west at the Asian realm in the new bout of jingoism. They began casting an envious eye on the lucrative and strategically located island chain. Conservative, noninterventionist Democrats did not follow suit. President John Tyler, an old Southern Democrat, had extended the Monroe Doctrine over the islands in the 1840s but left it at that. After the Civil War, as annexationist movements spread on the islands, President Andrew Johnson, another old Democrat, announced that a treaty had been negotiated that would allow Hawaii to "voluntarily apply for admission to the Union." But progressives in Congress, controlled by Republicans, rejected the voluntary offer. They wanted Hawaii by right, if not outright force. The inferior Hawaiians should have no say in the matter. In 1881, President James A. Garfield announced that the United States should be the "arbiter" of the Pacific, as well as "the controller of its commerce and chief nation that inhabits its shores," which included the Hawaiian Islands.[286]

By that time, the federal government had already become officially involved with Hawaii. Republican President Ulysses S. Grant and his Secretary of State, Hamilton Fish, negotiated a treaty in 1875 that would, in Fish's words, "bind these islands to the United States with hoops of steel." The economic agreement allowed the island's major crop of sugar to enter the American market duty-free. Likewise, US products could enter the Hawaiian market free of charge. The treaty proved prosperous for both nations, though Hawaii had become, more or less, an "economic colony" of the United States with 99 percent of its products sent to the American market, mainly sugar. This was Fish's whole intent. In 1887, during Cleveland's first term, the two governments renewed the trade agreement, but the Senate amended the original treaty to give the United States exclusive rights to a naval base at the mouth of the Pearl River, which would become Pearl Harbor. Cleveland, along with Secretary of State Thomas Bayard, was instrumental in negotiating this provision.[287]

Cleveland believed in the vitality of Hawaii for economic and military purposes only, and he agreed with Republicans on the need for trade and commerce, but he did not hold their nationalistic views on annexation, which would have destroyed Hawaiian sovereignty, an earnest progressive goal. He favored annexation, but only if native Hawaiians, through true self-determination, desired it. If not, his policy was only to uphold the Monroe Doctrine and protect the islands against outside influences. In 1887, he blocked the British from offering a loan of $2 million to Hawaii. Though it might have seemed innocent on the outside, Cleveland understood what the British were up to. In exchange for the loan, the English government asked for a share of Hawaiian revenue as collateral. This would have put the British Lion squarely in the middle of Hawaiian affairs, in a clear violation of the Monroe Doctrine. That he would not allow.[288]

The federal government had every reason to want, in the least, to maintain the status quo in Hawaii. If the islands could not be annexed, they should remain an economic colony. When Benjamin Harrison became president in 1889, following Cleveland, he ordered the landing of seventy marines from the USS *Adams* to prevent a coup against the weak monarch King Kalakaua. Harrison also mandated a permanent US naval presence in the area. But in 1891 the situation changed dramatically and threatened to overturn the status quo. A new native monarch came to the throne, a headstrong, highly nationalistic woman named Liliuokalani, sister to King

Kalakaua, who had died of an illness. She desired to run Hawaii herself with a program of "Hawaii for Hawaiians." She wanted to diminish the influence of the outlanders if not outright end it, and she proposed a new constitution that stripped all non-Hawaiians of the right to vote. Her proposal threatened the existing power structure, then in the hands of the major planters.[289]

The outlanders had to do something about the new, impulsive queen. On the night of January 14, 1893, the US minister to Hawaii, John Stevens, met secretly with a group plotting the queen's overthrow, a faction known as the "Annexation Club." Though Harrison and his jingoistic Secretary of State, James G. Blaine, denied any knowledge of the coup, it is likely that both knew of the plan and did nothing to discourage it. When the queen announced the new constitution, the scheme was launched, apparently by orders from Stevens himself, who happened to be a benefactor, business partner, and close friend of Blaine's. A US warship, the USS *Boston*, supplied American troops to assist in the revolt by keeping order, an important task. The plotters removed the queen without bloodshed and established a provisional government under the protection of US forces. Native Hawaiians were stripped of the right to vote, giving full control to the outlanders.[290]

Stevens immediately recognized the provisional government. Unsurprisingly, the new provisional authority asked for annexation to the United States, and the American flag began flying over Hawaiian government buildings. "The Hawaiian pear is now fully ripe, and this is the golden hour for the United States to pluck it," Minister Stevens announced. President Harrison wholeheartedly agreed, calling the Hawaiian monarchy "weak" and "inadequate." Secretary of State Blaine drew up a treaty to annex the Hawaiian Islands, which the president submitted to the Senate.[291]

The treaty remained in the Senate when President Cleveland came back into office on March 4, just two months after the coup, and with the economy declining rapidly. He did not like the manner in which the queen had been overthrown or that the United States's minister and Navy had been involved, which he felt caused "serious embarrassment" for the country. To get a handle on events, Cleveland named James H. Blount, a twenty-year veteran of Congress from Georgia as a commissioner to Hawaii for the purpose of discovering exactly what had happened. Blount spent four months investigating and found a military protectorate in the hands of US troops, which were even conducting regular police duties for the provisional government, as if American forces were under their control. He also discovered that a majority of Hawaiians did not favor annexation. In July he filed a report on his findings.[292]

The Blount investigation showed "beyond all question that the constitutional Government of Hawaii had been subverted with the active aid of our representative to that government and through the intimidation caused by the presence of an armed naval force of the United States, which was landed for that purpose at the instance of our minister," Cleveland told Congress in his annual message in December. "Upon the facts developed it seemed to me the only honorable course for our government to pursue was to undo the wrong that had been done by those representing us and to restore as far as practicable the status existing at the time of our forcible intervention." In order to restore the former government of the islands, the president repudiated the annexation treaty, withdrawing it from Senate consideration, and refused to annex Hawaii in any way.[293]

The Cleveland administration, however, was not able to restore Queen Liliuokalani to her throne. She vowed, upon return, to behead the rebels and seize their property. Cleveland worried about their fate and sought assurances from both sides that there would be no violence, even asking the queen to issue a general amnesty, but he was unable to get satisfactory answers. The new Democratic Congress bounced around solutions for months but remained largely indecisive, as was the president. Finally, Congress decided that the best option would be to simply recognize the provisional government that had been established after the coup, and its new president, Sanford Dole. Cleveland really had no other option but to go along. This demonstrated the complications of becoming involved in the internal affairs of other nations.[294]

Despite the setback of failing to restore the status quo, Cleveland had fought back against the growing jingoist tide and won. His paramount objective was to keep out of the affair and allow Hawaiians to determine their own future. "The thing I care most about is the declaration that the *people* of the islands instead of the *provisional government* should determine the policy," he wrote Senator William Vilas [Emphasis in the original]. The people of Hawaii were the "source of power and control" over the islands. His policy received praise from members of both parties. Charles Francis Adams Jr., of the famed Adams family, wrote him that fall. "I remember no stand taken by a government so morally sound and dignified as that now taken by … your administration," he said, a stance that would make American foreign policy stronger. "It is not easy to see how the United

States can protest against the policy of force in [British] dealings with semi-civilized natives and races, if we ourselves are quite unable to resist the temptation to have an occasional hack at them on our own account."[295]

Harrison's attempt to annex Hawaii and Cleveland's defeat of it "constitute one of the most unjustly neglected episodes in American diplomatic history," writes Allan Nevins. But Hawaii would not long remain independent. When Republican William McKinley came to the White House in 1897, annexation proceeded with vigor. Upon assuming the presidency, he lost no time negotiating a new treaty of annexation, which was sent to the Senate that summer. But the Japanese protested, fearing annexation might jeopardize treaty rights for Japanese inhabitants in Hawaii. Japan was also suspicious of American motives, annexing territory in the Asian sphere of influence rightfully reserved for Asians, so they contended. Their government was busy with its own expansion— defeating China in 1895, eventually annexing Korea in 1910, possessing Taiwan, and eyeing Manchuria. Hawaii was also on their radar.[296]

But Japan would come up short. The annexation treaty lagged in the Senate, with a stiff opposition from anti-imperialists. But in August 1898, after the Spanish-American War, Hawaii was finally annexed when it became clear to a majority that the islands were of vital importance to the United States. Americans also used fear to persuade native Hawaiians of the need for annexation. They were told the Japanese were posed to seize the islands and completely destroy Hawaiian culture, something they did after occupying any new land. To overcome anti-imperialist opposition, particularly in the Senate, Congress used a joint resolution, the same process used to annex Texas in 1845, and not a treaty, which would have taken a two-thirds majority. "Hawaii is ours," wrote Cleveland to his former Secretary of State Richard Olney upon hearing the news. "As I look back upon the first steps in this miserable business, I am ashamed of the whole affair." Though he was unable to keep the islands permanently sovereign, many native Hawaiians still honor Cleveland for his efforts to protect their native government.[297]

The aggressive, imperialist impulses of the Harrison administration, along with his overzealous Secretary of State, made most of Latin America nervous about its future. In 1893 Latin Americans breathed a collective sigh of relief and welcomed Cleveland back to the White House. Latin American leaders saw him as one who would protect the peace and security of all nations in the Western hemisphere.[298]

Closer to home, President Cleveland faced another revolution in the realm of Latin America, this one on the Spanish-controlled island of Cuba. Spain had maintained control of Cuba since Christopher Columbus, but by the late-nineteenth century much of the Cuban population was unhappy with Spanish rule, as revolutionary disturbances had broken out in the 1870s. The United States had been occupied with internal problems during the 1870s but by the 1890s was interested in foreign affairs and specifically in the construction of a canal across the Isthmus of Panama or Nicaragua. Cuba was close to the proposed canal, so this gave the United States more reason to be concerned with internal stability there. In the 1890s, another revolution broke out on the island.

Scholars generally cite two causes for the Cuban Revolution in the 1890s. An obvious reason would be the incompetent and sometimes brutal rule of the Spaniards. But a second and more important factor concerned an economic crisis in Cuba caused in part by a shift in US tariff policy, namely the adoption of the 1894 Wilson-Gorman tariff. Eighty percent of the economy of Cuba was based on sugar, and under the 1890 McKinley tariff, Cuban sugar entered the US market duty free. But the 1894 tariff placed high duties on Cuban sugar, which helped bring economic collapse to the island.[299]

Against this backdrop, the Cubans rose up against Spanish rule in February 1895, an uprising that turned into a civil war in which there were atrocities on both sides, as neither side conducted themselves in the manner a civilized nation was expected to. Under the rule of Spanish governor-general Valeriano Weyler, Cubans in rural areas were garrisoned in camps guarded by Spanish troops. This was one of the first uses of a concentration camp system in history. Anyone outside the camps was considered a rebel and could be shot on sight. For their part, the Cubans conducted a "scorched-earth" policy by burning sugar plantations and government buildings. Since US business controlled Cuban sugar, the Cuban revolutionaries wanted the business interest to intervene.[300]

And the business influence was considerable. With investments totaling $50 million, Americans had great wealth tied up on the island. Trade between Cuba and the United States amounted to nearly $100 million in 1894, quite a lucrative deal that no one wanted to see lost. But President Cleveland had no desire to intervene in Cuba on the behalf of the insurgents. The United States "is in truth the most pacific of powers and desires nothing so much as to live in amity with all the world. Its own ample and diversified domains satisfy all possible longings for territory, preclude all dreams of conquest, and prevent any casting of covetous eyes upon neighboring regions, however attractive."[301]

But the jingoistic attitude toward Cuba was at a fever pitch, which Cleveland referred to as an "epidemic of insanity." Congressional leaders traveled to Woodley, Cleveland's private residence outside Washington, in order to persuade him to change his opinion, a near impossibility once he made his mind up, and regarding Cuba he had. With the president unwilling to budge, Republicans in Congress threatened to declare war on Cuba without him, for conditions there were "intolerable," they said. Cleveland replied, "There shall be no war with Spain over Cuba as long as I am president." If Congress declared war, he would not, as commander-in-chief, mobilize the army. Why fight, he asked, when the US government could buy the island for $150 million if desired? A war would probably cost more lives and treasure than anyone realized, as well as burden the taxpayers with another long list of pensioners, all of it completely unnecessary, he felt. Instead, during the summers of 1895 and 1896 Cleveland signed two neutrality proclamations in regard to Cuba, prohibiting Americans from becoming involved with the internal disturbances on the island. The United States also made two attempts to mediate the dispute in 1896 and 1897, to no avail. Cleveland also asked the Spanish to institute political reforms but was rebuffed.[302]

Jingoists did not like Cleveland's non-aggressive approach, Theodore Roosevelt in particular, a self-described "Cuba Libre man" who wanted the president to "interfere" and send the "fleet promptly to Havana." To Teddy, war was a virtue and should be used as an instrument of national policy. As assistant secretary of the navy in 1897, Roosevelt addressed the Naval War College with this pronouncement: "All the great masterful races have been fighting races, and the minute that a race loses the hard fighting virtues, then, no matter what else it may retain, no matter how skilled in commerce and finance, in science or art, it has lost its proud right to stand as the equal of the best."[303] He had no patience for anyone who sought a softer approach.

But Cleveland believed that war with Spain, in addition to costs, would destabilize Cuba. How would the island fare if, all of a sudden, it was turned over to insurgent rebels not accustomed to governing themselves? If chaos reigned, then it might invite European intervention, a not uncommon occurrence, particularly in matters of debt default. Cleveland was every bit the nineteenth-century man on matters of race, and he did not believe the Cubans capable of self-government. Imperialists like TR believed much the same thing, but they had an alternate plan. Though Cubans, after US intervention and removal of Spain, might be in charge, at least on paper, Americans would administer the country in actuality. To Cleveland, this was just as unacceptable.

On March 4, 1897, William McKinley, who won the presidency the previous November over William Jennings Bryan, was sworn in as Cleveland's successor and would have Cuba very much on his mind. The evening before the inauguration, Cleveland hosted a dinner for him at the White House, where he told the president-elect that any conflict with Spain over Cuba, in his opinion, could be a "catastrophe." McKinley felt much the same way, or at least that's what he told Cleveland, but he was much more sympathetic to the Cuban rebels.[304]

When the tide of war came in 1898, McKinley did not have the strength to stop it even if he had wanted to, which he did not. The "splendid little war" was over in no time, allowing the United States to establish a protectorate over Cuba and then grab Guam, Puerto Rico, and, most importantly, the Philippines, which further fueled Japanese suspicion. Though not viewed as a progressive like his successor Theodore Roosevelt, McKinley did inaugurate the era of American imperialism, the application of progressivism abroad. Under McKinley, America, for the first time, bit into the "forbidden fruit of imperialism," in the words of Pat Buchanan, "leading to America's involvement in all the great wars of the twentieth century."[305]

UPHOLDING THE MONROE DOCTRINE

Many jingoists took Cleveland's noninterventionist policies for passivism, or in Theodore Roosevelt's opinion, outright cowardice. Cleveland did believe in a more aggressive foreign policy, but only if the case called for it and never for imperialistic reasons. He believed strongly in the principle of self-determination of peoples as well as in the Monroe Doctrine as an instrument to safeguard the country, having demonstrated his attachment to it with his opposition to the British loan offer to Hawaii. He even sent warships to China and Korea to protect American missionaries. He did not believe the doctrine should be used for aggressive purposes, such as acquiring more territory, but only to protect American rights. If one could sum up Cleveland's foreign policy in a short, simple phrase, it would be "maintain the status quo" if at all possible. He did not side with rebels in Hawaii, though he sympathized with them, or in Cuba, for he believed that to intervene would be worse than the current situation. He understood, better than the imperialists, that intervening militarily in the internal affairs of another nation could be a chaotic and bloody proposition, as the United States found out in the Philippines in 1898, where a five-year insurgency claimed 4,000 American lives, and later in Iraq after the 2003 invasion.

There were methods other than intervention that could be employed when trouble arose in foreign nations. In a messy internal situation in Brazil, where the government was under siege in what had become a civil war between "monarchists" and "republicans," Cleveland again came to the rescue of the government in power, sending a naval fleet of five ships to the coast to break a rebel blockade. The aggressive show of force, along with a private flotilla of armed merchant and passenger ships under Charles Flint, helped keep the republican government of Brazil intact. The grateful Brazilians, seeing Cleveland as one who would look out for their welfare, constructed a monument to honor James Monroe and his famous doctrine.[306]

But before his term was up, he faced a much more serious potential threat to the hemisphere when, upholding the Monroe Doctrine, he tangled with the British in a boundary dispute involving Venezuela. What might have been regarded as a minor disagreement involved the location of the western boundary of British Guiana, which bordered Venezuela, in an area between the Orinoco and Essiquibo rivers, encompassing a significant and lucrative chunk of Venezuelan territory. Britain had taken over the Guiana territory from the Dutch in 1814, and the exact boundary line had never really been established. The problem festered for years. Both sides thought the matter more than a minor one and suspended diplomatic relations in 1887. Venezuela, knowing President Cleveland's regard for Latin America, asked for Washington's assistance on several occasions, appeals for help that were "incessantly ringing in our ears," Cleveland wrote.[307]

Americans, as well as members of Congress, were becoming increasingly alarmed by European incursions in the Western Hemisphere, particularly by the British. Cleveland determined not to allow any further encroachment by European powers into the Americas. He believed taking even an inch of Venezuelan territory would be a violation of the Monroe Doctrine. To solve the dispute, the president sought international arbitration as the preferred method for bringing the issue to a successful conclusion. Secretary of State Richard Olney sent a non-threatening note to the British government inviting them to arbitration. But London simply ignored the inquiry.

The arrogance of the British angered Cleveland, who then ordered Olney to send a strongly worded message to get their attention. The president specified that he wanted to use the Monroe Doctrine, though Olney was a bit skeptical at first. In what became known as the Olney Corollary to the Monroe Doctrine, Olney boasted, "The United States is practically sovereign on this continent, and its fiat is law upon the subjects to which it confines its interposition," while "its infinite resources combined with its isolated position render it master of the situation and practically invulnerable as against any or all other powers."[308] Not exactly a delicate diplomatic message, but it had Cleveland's full support.

The British Prime Minister, Lord Salisbury, waited four months before responding to Olney's jab with a shot of his own, denying that the United States had any power and authority to command Britain in the Western Hemisphere. Cleveland responded with a strong message of his own on December 17, 1895. Britain had taken possession of territory of a neighboring republic "against its will and in derogation of its rights," he told Congress, making it likely that Britain will "attempt to extend its system of government to that portion of this continent which it has thus taken." This was precisely why Monroe issued his doctrine in the first place, he reminded the members. The British government might deny that the Monroe Doctrine had any authority in the matter, but to Cleveland that counted little. He vowed to use it to prevent what he perceived as an injustice toward Venezuela. The tough words led many across the nation to conclude that war was on the horizon. But that was never Cleveland's intention. Forcing Britain to arbitration was.[309]

In the end of a very long and complicated affair, the British backed down, recognizing, in principle at least, the Monroe Doctrine. A commission was then set up to determine the boundary issue. To their credit, Cleveland and Olney did not smear British noses in it but allowed them to withdraw gracefully. For their part, the British did have more pressing concerns at home and probably did not want to risk war with the United States over a small plot of jungle in the wilds of the Amazon.[310]

Historians have accused Cleveland, in the Venezuela intervention, of "wagging the dog," so as to distract the American people from the ongoing economic woes, as Bill Clinton was often accused of doing to distract from his dalliances. These opinions about Cleveland do not reflect fresh thinking and were regurgitated from what opposition politicians were saying at the time. Regardless of their origin, the theory is patently absurd. The incident with Britain did not become tense until the latter part of

1895, the last half of his presidency when the economy was on the rebound. Why would Cleveland have waited until then to "wag the dog?" The economy was in much worse shape in 1893 and 1894, and the president had a huge opportunity in Hawaii, or in Cuba, to distract attention but did not. Furthermore, an international incident with the British Empire, which many thought would lead to war, would only panic markets further, not cause a rally.

Cleveland did not believe in such tactics; he stuck to his principles instead. He did what he believed was right. Diplomatic historian Thomas A. Bailey, who does not hold Cleveland in high regard, nevertheless praised one result of the Venezuelan crisis. The "United States, having stared down the British Lion, emerged with enhanced standing among the powers of the world."[311]

Though he forced Lord Salisbury to back down, even as the Prime Minister tried to lecture him as a parent would a child, Cleveland demonstrated his toughness, and for that the British came to respect him. When Cleveland died in 1908, the *Morning Post* of London wrote that he "was one of the great men of his time. He had Bismarck's strength and Bismarck's breadth of views and more than Bismarck's honesty. As president he did not lift a finger for the Democratic Party but merely served the United States. He was the strongest man who has lived in the White House since the death of Washington."[312]

THE MONROE DOCTRINE IN MODERN TIMES

Many scholars today might ridicule the Monroe Doctrine, as well as its subsequent corollaries, as outdated. But it's the spirit of the proclamation that's still important. The whole reason behind it was to keep strong, potentially threatening powers out of our domain, or as Monroe put it, those nations "dangerous to our peace and safety." Yet our modern presidents don't seem to take the spirit of the Monroe Doctrine seriously. The Communist Chinese are in the process of building a world-class military machine to rival that of the United States. They are also expanding their intelligence-gathering capability, and gaining footholds in the Western Hemisphere. The Chinese government made great strides during Bill Clinton's presidency, when he flung open the door and allowed a foreign and hostile nation, which considers the United States an enemy, to set up shop, not to mention gain valuable technology in exchange for campaign cash.

After a failed attempt by France to dig an interoceanic canal in Central America, the United States, under Teddy Roosevelt, took over the project and completed the wondrous Panama Canal. For our efforts, Panama, which owed its very existence as a nation to the United States, granted a long-term lease to administer it indefinitely in the Panama Canal Zone. In 1977, President Jimmy Carter negotiated a treaty to give the canal back to Panama, an agreement that was finally ratified by the Senate in April 1978, despite the fact that two-thirds of the American people wisely disapproved of the deal.[313]

When Clinton came into office in 1993, he eventually got into bed with the Chinese and allowed them to take virtual control of the canal. The China Ocean Shipping Company (COSCO), in reality a front for the People's Liberation Army (PLA), gained control of major ports at each end of the canal, putting itself in perfect position to close the canal to US shipping, which makes up the bulk of canal traffic, if hostilities broke out between America and China or its allies. US economic interests would be dealt a crippling blow in such an eventuality. Clinton explained that COSCO was only there to load and unload ships. But sensible people knew better. In a letter to Defense Secretary William Cohen, Senate Majority Leader Trent Lott of Mississippi wrote, "It appears that we have given away the farm without a shot being fired." Conservatives in 1978 had previously warned of the threat to national security, to no avail.[314]

The PLA controls thousands of companies, employs hundreds of thousands of workers, and makes billions of dollars a year. COSCO serves as the merchant marine arm of the PLA, delivering arms to Chinese allies. In 1996 it was caught trying to smuggle 2,000 automatic weapons into the United States for LA gang members. US Customs seized the stash in Oakland, California. COSCO has also been used to ship nuclear components to Iran. With help from the Clinton White House, COSCO gained valuable access to space at a vacant Long Beach, California, naval base. Controlling parts of the port gave the PLA better listening capabilities for spying and intelligence gathering. COSCO also operates in the Caribbean as well as Panama.[315]

The Chinese are also greatly strengthening their ties with Cuba. There are concerns that China has plans to begin drilling for oil in the Gulf of Mexico near Cuba. Cuban rigs operating in the area now were, in fact, built in China. Many naïve politicians in Washington will presumably give the same old Clinton answer that there is nothing to be alarmed about. That might be true if that was all there was to it. In 1999, China set up a listening station in Cuba to expand its signals intelligence capability, which is to say they are spying on us. The two nations also pledged in 2010 to enhance their military ties when Chinese military officials, including the PLA's top general, visited Havana. These developments, coupled with China's extraordinary military buildup, should be cause for worry in Washington.[316]

The aggressive Chinese posture has continued under Obama. Though George W. Bush did very little to confront China, Republicans have attempted to keep them in check but have met with constant Democratic interference, as liberals consistently block bills to aid our friends, the Taiwanese. As scholars Brett M. Decker and William C. Triplett II have written, "it's predominantly Democrats who are in bed with Beijing."[317] We should have known we were in trouble the day the president of the United States, Barack Obama, bowed to the dictator of China, a humiliating gesture never before seen by the American people.

Even more troubling than Chinese expansion in the Western Hemisphere is a report that Hezbollah, the terrorist group based in Lebanon, might be establishing training camps in Cuba, as well as other parts of Central and South America, to organize and train terrorist cells to operate against the United States. The Shiite militant organization, which is nothing more than a proxy of Iran, has apparently been quite active in South America in recent years, while Iran has established its largest embassy in Caracas. The Iranian-Venezuelan relationship has grown to the extent that now the two nations are building a missile base two hundred fifty miles northwest of Caracas, an area that would put nuclear-tipped ICBMs within easy reach of the United States. But the Obama Administration has done nothing about this very serious threat to American security. Putting camps and weapons in Cuba, and possibly even missiles in South America, would be a provocative action of the highest order and should be confronted. Yet given the current state of American foreign policy and American leadership, it is likely that no action will ever be taken.[318]

When Grover Cleveland stood down the British over Venezuela, a Republican Senator, William E. Chandler of New Hampshire, spoke on the floor in praise of the president's aggressive action. "Thank God we have an American president in the White House," he said.[319] When John F. Kennedy ejected the Soviets from Cuba, the same could have been said of him, even though his weak foreign policy had led to the misguided Russian scheme. When China began creeping its way slowly into Panama and Havana under our very noses, we should have expelled them. But in the

1990s we did not have a great president in the White House; we had Bill Clinton, who seemed to be more worried about chasing skirts, collecting campaign cash—even some from China—and gaining a second term, as well as molding a lasting legacy to be proud of, than his actual obligations as president.[320] And thanks to untrustworthy politicians like Clinton and Obama, the Monroe Doctrine is dead in our time.

THE MODERN WARFARE STATE

Though the current interventionist policy, an "international meals-on-wheels," of sorts, seems to be set in stone, the debate rages on. In every presidential debate, the issue of foreign policy is paramount, as well it should be. It is an integral part of the United States and has been for more than a century.

After the Spanish-American War in 1898, another progressive president dragged us into another foreign war. Woodrow Wilson determined that the United States had a vast stake in the outcome of World War One. Though he pledged neutrality early in his administration, Wilson secretly wanted the nation in the war on the side of the Allies. He warned Americans to be neutral in "thought as well as deed," but the president himself was far from it, actively aiding the allied powers to the protest of Germany. Finally, after his successful "He Kept Us Out of War" reelection campaign in 1916, Wilson pulled the nation into the conflict within months. And the consequences were disastrous. As Jim Powell has written, the US intervention in the European conflict on the side of the Allies tipped the balance of power and eventually paved the way for Hitler, the Soviet Union, World War Two, and the Cold War.[321]

And the march goes on. After World War Two, the United States did not retreat into isolationism but took upon itself the role of global cop. Today the US military has troops in one hundred thirty nations, with nine hundred bases, encompassing more than 70 percent of the globe. For reasons beyond explanation, there are still 53,000 troops in Germany, more than 9,000 in both Italy and the United Kingdom, 28,000 in South Korea, and 33,000 in Japan, among the largest contingents, aside from Afghanistan. With the onset of the War on Terror, the Defense Department made plans for more expansion, with a string of bases in Eastern Europe, and an increase in NATO membership. While the numbers remain very small, there are now US military personnel in eleven countries of the old

Soviet Union. For many Americans, this policy is simply too much and a vast departure from the ideals of the founders.[322]

America's treaty commitments are also extensive. There are presently twenty-eight members of NATO, which means the United States is pledged to go to war on behalf of the other twenty-seven member nations, as an attack on one is considered an attack on all. There are also plans on the table for future expansion of the alliance, namely the nations of Georgia and Ukraine, two key components of the old Soviet Empire. Such a move would only antagonize Russia further, driving them closer to China, a budding relationship that is growing by the day. We are also pledged to fight China if it invades Taiwan, as well as Japan and South Korea if they are attacked. Israel, our strongest ally in the Middle East (quite possibly our only *real* ally), is another nation we must defend in the event of war in that volatile region.

The neocons, the "new jingoists," seem to believe, like the imperialists of old, that war is a good thing, and that the United States must use war as a means of national policy to destroy tyranny and forcefully impose democracy around the world in nations that may not desire it. As George W. Bush said in his second inaugural address, "The survival of liberty in our land increasingly depends on the success of liberty in other lands. The best hope for peace in our world is the expansion of freedom in all the world." He then laid out a new policy "to seek and support the growth of democratic movements and institutions in every nation and culture, with the ultimate goal of ending tyranny in our world." But that was not the reason for the creation of our Constitution. It is an absurd and utopian notion to contend that democracy in America depends on democracy in Afghanistan. The survival of liberty in our land depends upon upholding the Constitution and reigning in government, the only entity that is currently taking it away.

The United States can logically return to a more sensible, responsible, and reasonable foreign policy. We can find a happy medium between internationalism and isolationism, as it was in Cleveland's administration. President Cleveland, writes foreign policy scholar George Herring, "was not afraid to make tough foreign policy decisions. He displayed on occasion an admirable tendency to do the right thing for the right reason, injecting an element of morality into an area of endeavor and political climate where it was normally absent."[323] He believed as John Quincy Adams did that America "goes not abroad in search of monsters to destroy. She is the well-wisher to the freedom and independence of all. She is the champion and vindicator only of her own."[324] Cleveland believed in self-determination for all peoples, beautifully enunciated by Thomas Jefferson in the Declaration of Independence, a cherished right that modern politicians in Washington, sadly, seem to have forgotten.

VI

PARTY DESTROYER OR
DEFENDER OF PRINCIPLE?

I have a great respect and regard for Grover Cleveland and believe that he made a
good president. I regard him as a sound, conservative statesman whose chief fault,
in the eyes of his followers, was that he was better than his party.
—*Congressman John S. Wise of Virginia[325]*

During the debate over the debt ceiling in the summer of 2011, members of Congress who held tightly to Jeffersonian principles of small government, mainly those identifying with the Tea Party movement, like Congresswoman Michele Bachmann, stood strong against any attempt to expand the ability of Washington to borrow more money. For that principled stand they faced a barrage of criticism. After the debt deal was done, S&P downgraded the federal government's credit rating because the paltry spending cuts were not large enough to satisfy growing concern that expenditures could be controlled or the huge national debt would be paid down. Everyone from the White House to the media to liberal members of Congress blamed the Tea Party for the downgrade. The very group who wanted to cut spending to the levels called for by the leading credit agencies received blame for the reduction in the rating, as the absurd cry of "Tea Party Downgrade" swept DC. To their everlasting tribute, Tea Partiers in Congress didn't budge. What a refreshing scene, inundated as we are with flip-floppers from both parties, though the establishment was not amused.

DEFENDER OF PARTY PRINCIPLES

Grover Cleveland always stood on principle, no matter the consequences or the criticism. For that reason he was widely admired and much sought after for public office. In 1882, the New York Democratic Party found itself in a similar situation as the Republican Party did after the election of Barack Obama. A state party leader, Edgar K. Apgar, wrote to Cleveland, then the mayor of Buffalo, to see if he would consider serving as governor. The letter could just have easily been directed at the Republican Party during the Bush years, the RNC in 2009, or even today.

The Democratic Party, he wrote, "has so often, in recent years, abandoned its principles and made dishonest alliances for the sake of temporary success, which even in most cases it has failed to secure," and has "largely lost the confidence of the people." The party "has fallen, in so many instances, into bad hands," causing many to distrust "our promises of reform." The party had only itself to blame, in Apgar's eyes.

> If we had stood faithfully by Jeffersonian principles; if we had exercised all the power of legitimate party discipline to destroy corruption and demagoguism in our own ranks; if we had been content to deserve success and to wait for it, we would, in my judgment, have been for many years firmly entrenched in power in the State and nation. The weakness of our present position, in which we seem to depend more upon Republican dissensions and decay than upon any strength of our own, is, I think, much more due to our failures in the directions I have indicated than it is to any personal or factional quarrels which have existed among us.[326]

The solution was simple: to find a man of principle to head the state Democratic ticket in 1882 and maybe the national ticket in 1884. They found that man in Grover Cleveland of Buffalo, New York.

Cleveland always held the people in the highest regard, much higher than the party itself. After winning the governorship, Cleveland told a reporter from the *Buffalo Daily Courier*, "Let me rise or fall, I am going to work for the interests of the people of the state, regardless of party or anything else." When he ran for president in 1884, he chose as his campaign slogan "A Public Office is a Public Trust," a motto that perfectly captured his personal principles, of which he wrote a friend, "Above all, let us constantly be reminded that the good of the people and the protection of their interests is the supreme duty of all public officers." Today, as our politicians dodge issues, water-down past records and statements, and outright lie about their intentions, Cleveland remained true to what he believed. "I am … a Democrat attached to the principles of the party; and if elected, I desire to remain true to that organization," he wrote to a fellow reformer. He believed in the existence of the party system, but to be used as a vehicle to espouse "well-defined and understood party principles," rather than for "the hope of personal reward and advantage" for its members. The Democratic Party should rest on doing what's best for "the welfare of the country and the prosperity of our people." Throughout his great public career he desired above all "that the *party* shall demonstrate its usefulness and fitness to hold the government."[327]

When he won the nomination for president in 1884, he wrote an official letter of acceptance to the party's national committee. "We proudly call ours a government by the people," he told Democratic leaders. "It is not such when a class is tolerated which arrogates to itself the management of public affairs, seeking to control the people, instead of representing them. Parties are the necessary outgrowths of our institutions; but a government is not by the people when one party fastens its control upon the country and perpetuates its power by cajoling and betraying the people instead of serving them. A government is not by the people when a result which should represent the intelligent will of free and thinking men is or can be determined by the shameless corruption of their suffrages." He intended to bring about a "full realization of a government by the people."[328]

After he won his first White House race, he well knew the difficult task ahead. "I look upon the four years next to come as a dreadful self-inflicted penance for the good of my country," he wrote his best friend, Wilson S. Bissell, in Buffalo. "I can see no pleasure in it and no satisfaction, only a hope that I may be of service to my people."[329] He was ready to do his duty for those who elected him, tackling the major issues that would confront him, some old, some new—the never-ending battle between protectionists and free traders; emerging conflicts between labor and management; continuing arguments over monetary policy—between advocates of the gold standard and those who favored an inflationary currency; and fights between civil service reformers and hard-line machine politicians. Cleveland was prepared, according to Alyn Brodsky, "to sacrifice his influence—if need be, his presidency—in pursuit of what he believed was best for the nation."[330]

Defeated for a second presidential term in 1888, Cleveland retired and had no thought of returning to public life. The only living Democratic president was a hot commodity, and party members nationwide sought his help. But Cleveland kept his principles even when out of office. He did not think it proper for ex-presidents to be out campaigning, a situation that was "against the ideas and traditions of our people." He received an invitation to speak on behalf of the party in Ohio, a politically important state, in the midterm elections in 1890. The big issue that year, and throughout the rest of the decade, was the nation's currency—whether to maintain the gold standard or allow the free coinage of silver. Ohio had gone the way of silver and inserted a free silver plank into its platform. It was a growing movement within the party that greatly concerned Cleveland. He steadfastly advocated the gold standard throughout his life, so campaigning for a "Silver Democrat" would compromise his principles. He would never espouse free silver simply to help someone get elected. That was out of the question. Silverites, he wrote a political friend in Ohio, would most likely "resent the importation of a speaker who has put himself on record as unequivocally as I have in opposition … to free, unlimited, and independent silver coinage." And though many Democrats would accuse him of being "selfish," he would never compromise his principles to win an election.[331]

WATCHDOG OF THE TREASURY

Throughout his public life, Cleveland viciously guarded the public treasury, even in times of economic hardship for the nation, using what one cabinet officer termed "his sledgehammer veto" to keep Congress in line.[332] In his day, just like our own, liberals in Congress, state legislatures, and city councils could not quell the urge to tax and spend, but Grover Cleveland could quash their overzealous desire. He didn't just scrutinize and single out special appropriations like earmarks, pensions for veterans, or seed to farmers; he examined every spending bill that crossed his desk and killed every one he believed an unauthorized assault on the treasury, regardless of what group desired it.

"Economy in public expenditure," he repeatedly reminded Congress, "is a duty that can not innocently be neglected by those entrusted with the control of money drawn from the people for public uses." To accomplish economy in public spending, he employed a chief executive's most powerful weapon: the veto. Cleveland possessed a very strong Jacksonian concept of the veto power, even stronger than Old Hickory himself. The nation's first six presidents vetoed only legislation they believed to be in violation of the Constitution, but President Jackson, the nation's seventh chief executive, rejected any bill he ideologically disagreed with, whether constitutional or not, ushering in an era of the "unlimited veto." Presidents Washington through John Quincy Adams cancelled 10 bills; Jackson vetoed 12. But Cleveland took Jackson's policy to a whole new level, killing 414 in his first presidential term alone.[333] Whereas Jackson used the veto to strengthen the presidency, as well as his own position over Congress, Cleveland used it as a whip to discipline the people's representatives and protect taxpayers from legislative extravagance.

He was just as tough in his local and state offices. As mayor of Buffalo and governor of New York he cancelled many spending bills that legislators tried to slip by him in order to benefit and reward favored constituents. Mayor Cleveland had no tolerance or patience when it came to wasteful and unnecessary spending, particularly appropriations that violated the state constitution. On one occasion, he vetoed two resolutions that illegally provided funds for dubious purposes. The first directed $500 to the Fireman's Benevolent Association, which to some would be a fitting gesture, but Cleveland pointed out the specific clause in the state's constitution that prohibited cities and counties from spending money on such causes. The second provided another $500 to the decorating committee of the Grand Army of the Republic to be spent celebrating Decoration Day. Though he deemed the intent "a most worthy one," the bill violated the same provision of the state constitution, as well as the city's charter. Any money given to causes such as these, he wrote in his veto message, "should be a free gift of the citizens and taxpayers, and should not be extorted from them by taxation. This is so, because the purpose for which this money is asked does not involve their protection or interest as members of the community." An appropriation to such an endeavor would, in his mind, be "oppressive and unjust." The mayor then led by example in making a personal donation of $50 to the committee. The *Buffalo Daily Courier* praised his vetoes, calling his arguments "unanswerable."[334]

Cleveland also cancelled a supplemental appropriation to award $800 to each of three German newspapers in Buffalo to print the city council's proceedings. The council, and not the mayor, had the authority to designate an official paper for the city government and the politicians wanted to make sure that three German papers were included. These papers were very important within the large German community, particularly during campaign season. That being said, Mayor Cleveland, in his only annual message, reminded the council that "work of this description, like all others, should be done where it can be done the cheapest." Such an endeavor "is not accomplished when it is bestowed as a professional reward for party service or an item of political patronage."[335]

Ignoring the mayor's words, the council appropriated money to circulate their proceedings in the city's official paper but also passed a supplemental appropriation to allocate funds to the German papers. Cleveland quickly vetoed the supplemental bill. He surmised that the German papers would publish a synopsis of the proceedings on their own, in order to be of benefit to their readers. The "effect of the resolution is to give these newspapers $800 each for doing no more than they will in a sense be obliged to do without it." That did not stop the council, however. The members were determined to reward these German publications with tax dollars, passing a new appropriation to publish tax sale notices in all three German papers for $150 per paper. Cleveland again rejected the resolution. The council finally gave up.[336]

The "Veto Mayor," as he was dubbed, tackled many minor projects that were rife with corruption. He killed a warrant to pay the city comptroller an extra $27 for nine nights of overtime work because the employee was already on the payroll drawing an annual salary. He also stopped payments to city workers who wanted to use city horses and wagons for private livery services, killed the newly created job of morgue keeper, and ended the funding of unnecessary sidewalks. He then reformed the contract procedure to ensure competitive bidding for city projects, helping end many scams.[337]

His passion for saving taxpayer funds did not change when he became governor the following year. Soon after entering his duties in Albany, Cleveland quickly emerged as the "Veto Governor," swiftly killing eight bills within his first month in office, mainly issues relating to local governments. He denied Montgomery County the right to borrow money because the repayment plan involved unfair double taxation, stopped several proposals by various cities to make illegal revisions to their charters, including Buffalo and Elmira, and vetoed a proposal that would have allowed Chautauqua County to appropriate funds for a monument to its fallen soldiers, a similar action he had taken as mayor. He did not dislike such enterprises but felt such projects should be funded only by private donations and not taxpayer dollars. When a Catholic group sought state funds to establish an orphanage in New York City, he vetoed the measure on constitutional grounds.[338]

Even hometown friends, who might have believed their association with him would gain special favors, quickly found they were sadly mistaken. He vetoed a bill to reorganize the fire department in Buffalo, a scheme he believed was rife with corruption. His action led the *Albany Evening Journal* to call the veto "strong and wise." He also killed a measure that would have allowed his boyhood home of Fayetteville to borrow money to buy a fire engine. And to keep the government out of the banking business, Cleveland vetoed a measure that would authorize the state comptroller to lessen the liabilities of the First National Bank of Buffalo after it failed, a blow to the banking industry.[339]

No one received free rides on the back of taxpayers under Governor Cleveland. Public money would be used for the basic functions of government and nothing more. Not even the state's military veterans would gain from the public trough. The legislature approved a bill to provide relief to the surviving members of the First Regiment of New York Volunteers, a unit that served in the Mexican War in the 1840s. The act would provide pensions of $12 a month for the next two years, at a total cost to taxpayers of $14,976. In shades of his presidency, Governor Cleveland vetoed the pension measure as unnecessary, since the state had already appropriated $60,000 for just such a purpose during previous years and "further relief ought not be insisted on." It was, he told the legislature, a "question of principle … that justice to the taxpayer should replace the generosity of the State." Even though his party controlled the legislature, Cleveland vetoed forty-four bills during his first session and a total of two hundred during his two years as governor.[340]

When he first entered the White House in 1885, the public debt was $1.5 billion, with expenditures of only $260 million. Revenue, however, totaled $323 million, a surplus of $63 million. When he lost his bid for re-election in 1888, his frugal policies had swelled the surplus to $111 million, while the national debt had been cut by 20 percent, to $1.2 billion. In 2012, a president cutting 20 percent in debt in one term would have to shave more than $3 trillion off our gargantuan total, a staggering feat. With such high amounts of revenue and surpluses, Cleveland wanted to give it back to the taxpayers but failed twice to enact a tariff and tax cut. The high taxes had generated the surplus, which was simply over-taxation he felt, and should be given back to the people. The surplus money is "hoarded in the Treasury when it should be in their hands," he told Congress, "or we should be drawn into wasteful public extravagance, with all the corrupting national demoralization which follows in its train." He knew if the surplus remained in the treasury, Congress would spend it for sure.[341]

Today the public faces the same problem and has become especially frustrated with congressional "earmarking," the tacking of thousands of special requisitions for states and districts onto the final version of bills that often have nothing to do with its overall purpose. This practice is generally used because the spending requests are so ridiculous—everything from money for tattoo removals and cow burp research to "pancakes for yuppies" and a magic museum—that they would never survive the normal appropriations process. In December 2010 President Obama signed a 2,400-page omnibus spending bill that included a record 6,000 earmarks, even though he promised to end the practice. George W. Bush also signed numerous earmark-laden appropriations acts, as have all modern presidents. Senate Majority Leader Harry Reid ridiculously claimed that he had a "constitutional duty" to appropriate money in that fashion. But it is pure corruption, and the practice was just as common in Cleveland's day.[342]

In 1896, the final year of his second term in the White House, the Republicans, who took control of Congress during the 1894 midterms, tried again to spend more money, even though the economy was still not in good shape in terms of unemployment. But to help the situation, they sent Cleveland a bill for river and harbor construction, the major infrastructure spending at that time, what amounted to a Keynesian-style stimulus full of earmarks. Even though he had only a short time left in office, Cleveland was not buying it. "There are 417 items of appropriation contained in this bill," the president noted, "and every part of the country is represented in the distribution of its favors." Unsurprisingly, he vetoed the bill. "In view of the obligation imposed upon me by the Constitution, it seems to me quite clear that I only discharge a duty to our people when I interpose my disapproval of the legislation proposed," he wrote Congress in his veto message. "Many of the objects for which it appropriates public money are not related to the public welfare, and many of them are palpably for the benefit of limited localities or in aid of individual interests." To sign such a spending bill would be to violate fundamental principles. "Economy and the exaction of clear justification for the appropriation of public moneys by the servants of the people are not only virtues but solemn obligations."[343] From his first days as a sheriff and small-town mayor until his last day as president, Grover Cleveland never lost one ounce of his enthusiasm for the American taxpayer.

His zealous regard for public money was almost obsessive. A popular story told at the time revealed his constant concern for public money and congressional attempts to steal it. Resting at his retreat, Oak View, during a weekend, his frightened wife, Frances, shook Grover awake in the dead of night, crying out, "Wake up! There are burglars in the house!" A groggy president replied, "No, no, my dear. In the Senate maybe, but not in the House." Whether the story is true or not makes little difference. His affection for taxpayers was well known and his duty to protect them from fraud and theft would never wane during his political career.[344]

UPHOLDING THE CONSTITUTION

It can be expressed with little debate that modern-day presidents and politicians, regardless of party, have no regard for the Constitution. To some it has become what Alexander Hamilton always hoped it would be, "a frail and worthless fabric." Countless bureaucrats and politicians in Washington downright loathe it, seeing it as an impediment to progress, not a restraint on political power. When asked where Congress derived authority to pass national health-care legislation, Congressman Phil Hare, a liberal Democrat from Illinois, shocked many during a heated town hall meeting when he said, "I don't worry about the Constitution ... to be honest."[345] At least he was truthful.

All constitutional questions have been turned over to the Supreme Court in our time, though the founders never had that intention in mind. This has been done for political reasons, as much as anything else. Allowing the federal courts to take up hot-button political issues such as abortion keeps the democratically elected branches of government free to throw praise, or blame, on the unelected courts without having to really take a position on any issue that might cause them trouble at the ballot box. It's easy to dismiss an important and sensitive issue with a simple line: "The courts have already ruled on that one."

In earlier times, though, presidents believed they had as much right as Congress or the Supreme Court to rule on the constitutionality of laws. President Thomas Jefferson was skeptical about the right of the Supreme Court to exercise judicial review. "The question whether the judges are invested with exclusive authority to decide on the constitutionality of a law has been heretofore a subject of consideration with me in the exercise of official duties. Certainly there is not a word in the Constitution which has given that power to them more than to the Executive or Legislative branches." He believed the federal courts, operating under this extra-constitutional power, were establishing a judicial tyranny over the rest of the government. The Constitution, he wrote Abigail Adams, "meant that its coordinate branches should be checks on each other. But the opinion which gives to the judges the right to decide what laws are constitutional and what not, not only for themselves in their own sphere of action but for the Legislature and Executive also in their spheres, would make the Judiciary a despotic branch." Jefferson and his majority party in Congress were so hostile to the federal judiciary that they used impeachment against out-of-control judges and enacted the Judiciary Act of 1802 that abolished sixteen judgeships, nearly half the entire court system.[346]

When early presidents vetoed legislation, their messages contained constitutional arguments. In 1817, President James Madison, the Father of the Constitution, vetoed a public works bill, telling members of Congress that "such a power is not expressly given by the Constitution," nor could it "be deduced from any part of it without an inadmissible latitude of construction and reliance on insufficient precedents." His message continued: "The legislative powers vested in Congress are specified and enumerated in the eighth section of the first article of the Constitution, and it does not appear that the power proposed to be exercised by the bill is among the enumerated powers, or that it falls by any just interpretation with the power to make laws necessary and proper for carrying into execution those or other powers vested by the Constitution in the Government of the United States."[347]

Another good Jeffersonian, and a great foe of centralization, was President Franklin Pierce. "The dangers of a concentration of all power in the general government of a confederacy so vast as ours are too obvious to be disregarded," he stated in his Inaugural Address on March 4, 1853. "You have a right, therefore, to expect your agents in every department to regard strictly the limits imposed upon them by the Constitution of the United States." This was not simply high-minded rhetoric. In 1854 Pierce vetoed a bill that would have provided government funds for the mentally insane, an early attempt at paternalism on the federal level. "I can not find any authority in the Constitution for ... public charity," he told Congress. "To do so would, in my judgment, be contrary to the letter and spirit of the Constitution and subversive of the whole theory upon which the Union of these states is founded."[348] Those glorious days seem to be gone forever.

One can scarcely imagine any recent president making such an argument. Grover Cleveland was one of the last ones.

Abraham Lincoln was the first president since 1800 to abandon Jeffersonian principles and take up the centralizing role. He stretched the Constitution past its bounds, trampled the rights of the Southern states, and made a mockery of the cherished American principle of self-determination. He waged war without congressional consent, illegally suspended the writ of habeas corpus, imprisoned thousands of American citizens without charges or trial, seized and censored telegraph offices, shut down hundreds of newspapers while arresting and imprisoning editors, attacked civilians, interfered with the electoral process, and destroyed the voluntary Union of our Founders to replace it with a centralized state.[349]

Unlike Lincoln, Cleveland idolized the Jeffersonians. He held the Constitution sacred and conveyed that to the nation in his first Inaugural Address on March 4, 1885. Cleveland mentioned the Constitution eight times, elaborating at length on his strict Jeffersonian views. This would be something truly unique in modern times. In fact, of the sixteen presidential inaugural addresses since World War Two, including that of Barack Obama in 2009, the Constitution has been mentioned just five times combined. And most of these were simply casual references, not discussions of the document and the sacred rights it protects. To find a president who mentioned the Constitution nearly as much as Cleveland, one must go back to Calvin Coolidge, who mentioned it seven times in his inaugural speech in 1925.

The Constitution, said Cleveland in his first inaugural, "borne the hopes and the aspirations of a great people through prosperity and peace and through the shock of foreign conflicts and the perils of domestic strife and vicissitudes." It should be used "to promote the lasting welfare of the country and to secure the full measure of its priceless benefits to us and to those who will succeed to the blessings of our national life." In his capacity as president, Cleveland would "endeavor to be guided by a just and unstrained construction of the Constitution, a careful observance of the distinction between the powers granted to the federal government and those reserved to the States or to the people, and by a cautious appreciation of those functions which by the Constitution and laws have been especially assigned to the executive branch of the government."[350]

The Constitution and the government belonged to the people, he told his fellow citizens, and "the suffrage which executes the will of freemen is yours; the laws and the entire scheme of our civil rule, from the town meeting to the state capitals and the national capital, is yours." But with this comes great responsibility. "Your every voter ... exercises a public trust. Nor is this all. Every citizen owes to the country a vigilant watch and close scrutiny of its public servants and a fair and reasonable estimate of their fidelity and usefulness. This is the price of our liberty and the inspiration of our faith in the Republic."

As governor of New York, Cleveland maintained his strong attachment to the US Constitution as well as that of his state. One of the most controversial acts to emerge from the legislature during Cleveland's governorship was a proposal known as the "Five-Cent Fare Bill." Jay Gould, a wealthy robber baron hated throughout New York, if not the country, owned an elevated train in the city. By charter, the rail line could charge ten cents for a ride, but lawmakers wanted the fare lowered to five cents. The legislature believed Gould made far too much in profit from the deal, money he subsequently hid from the taxman, or so they contended. The *New York Times* attacked the railway as one of the "greatest monopolies" and "one of the worst swindles" in New York State. Furthermore, the great majority of the people, particularly the poor, would benefit because of the reduced rates. With the support of the major newspapers of the city and overwhelmingly passed by both houses, including the backing of Assembly Minority Leader Theodore Roosevelt, the bill was sent to Cleveland.[351]

On its face, the bill seemed like a good idea. Who would not support a law aimed at helping the poor as well as getting back at the hated Gould? Cleveland agreed with the bill's sentiments but in the end, after pondering it most of the night, vetoed the proposal. It was, he believed, an unconstitutional violation of the contract between Gould and the city, an agreement that allowed a charge of ten cents for a ticket. If Gould made lots of money from the deal, so be it. The contract could not be broken just because the government decided it no longer liked it. Though New York City scholars Edwin Burrows and Mike Wallace contend that fifty leading industrialists, such as J. P. Morgan and William H. Vanderbilt, heavily lobbied the governor to veto the "offending legislation," Cleveland acted out of a regard for the rule of law. "It seems to me that to arbitrarily reduce these fares," he wrote in his veto message, "at this time and under existing circumstances involves a breach of faith on the part of the state, and a betrayal of confidence that the state has invited."[352]

It was one of the toughest political decisions of his life, and he believed that it could very well wreck his blossoming public career. Journalist Andrew Dickson White commended him for the veto "in the face of the earnest advice of partisans who assured him that by doing so he would surely array against him the working-classes of that city and virtually annihilate his political future. To this his answer was that whatever his sympathies for the working class might be, he could not, as an honest man, allow such a bill to pass, and come what might, he would not." After issuing the veto, Cleveland retired for the evening. That night he told a friend that he expected to awaken the next morning as the most unpopular man in the state of New York. But he did what he believed was right, with no regard for the political consequences.[353]

When he peered at the papers the next morning, he realized that his initial analysis had been somewhat mistaken. For the most part, he was being praised for his political courage, which made him feel "a good deal better." The *Albany Evening Journal*, while believing the people were being injured by Gould's rail service, still called the veto "technically sound." The *New York Times* had supported the bill before its passage, editorializing that "the interests of the people cannot safely be subordinated to those of Jay Gould or any other capitalist rich and unscrupulous enough to purchase legislation." After the veto, the *Times* noted that the governor's action should not "cause much surprise." He acted to protect the "honor and good faith" of the state.[354]

The *New York Herald* praised his political courage in issuing the veto, stating that Cleveland "has done it boldly, with no attempt at disguise. We respect him for that. We expected as much from him." But the paper criticized the governor for casting "his lot on the side of the great corporations and corporate manipulators, and staked his chances for future political preferment on their favor." It is "quite touching to witness a hopeful presidential candidate choose his side in the coming struggle between them and the people for the control of the powers of government." This was among the first public mentions of Cleveland for higher office but an incorrect analysis. He was not on the side of the corporations, but that of the Constitution. He never would have acted based on politics.[355]

In 2009 President Obama destroyed the right of freedom of contract with the $85 billion auto bailout, showing his utter disregard for the Constitution and free-market principles. Car companies were in horrible shape even before the financial crisis. The best option on the table was for a declaration of bankruptcy. But the president would simply not allow that to happen because it would have legally wiped out the bloated and unrealistic contracts the union-backed autoworkers held, which paid them wages far beyond what other private sector workers received and put the companies in a competitive disadvantage. In lieu of a bankruptcy, the government offered a bailout deal, but one that heavily favored the unions, who were pushed to the head of the line, ahead of bonded creditors, whose contracts were not honored. So it was essentially a UAW bailout, a Democratic favored special interest and the very ones that destroyed the car companies in the first place, not a deal designed to get Detroit moving again. The Founding Fathers placed the right of freedom of contract in the Constitution for a reason. Without that essential right, investors will not devote large sums of capital to companies that may not be guaranteed. The free market will cease to function, but perhaps that is President Obama's goal after all.[356]

SECOND TERM POLITICAL CATASTROPHE

With the onset of the Panic of 1893, the nation's economy was a disaster, followed quickly by the fate of the Democratic Party. The contrasts between Cleveland's first term, where he enjoyed complete party unity, and his second, when the party was on the verge of collapse, could not be starker. It all began over silver. To help alleviate the country's economic ills, the Democratic Congress, which had repealed the Sherman Silver Purchase Act in August 1893, passed a modest silver bill, the Bland Act in March 1894, that would have coined the silver bullion already in the treasury and put it into circulation. Silverite members were not asking for more silver purchases, only to use that which already existed and was sitting in government vaults. They thought it a reasonable initiative. But it was still more inflation. This line of thinking was consistent with current economic planning, namely fighting inflationary depressions with more inflation. Yet this bill seemed to be more for political purposes than economic ones.

A congressional delegation from the South and West, the areas earnestly seeking inflationary silver, paid a visit to Cleveland at the White House to urge him to sign the bill, mainly for party unity. They believed that the party would take a beating at the polls during the fall midterm campaign if he did not sign the bill and show Silver Democrats that he was on their side. Those members soon discovered that they probably would have gotten a much better treatment from Cleveland had they simply slapped First Lady Francis, for the president exploded at their suggestion. Cleveland gave them such a tongue-lashing that Senator William Stewart of Nevada wrote a friend of the meeting, "I never had a man talk like that to me in my life."[357] When Cleveland vetoed the bill, many Democrats came unglued and the party nearly imploded, but he would never act on crass political expediency.

As he entered the final year of his presidency, Grover Cleveland must have been the loneliest man in the world. Scarcely has a nation's chief executive felt as alone as he did, both politically and physically. The economic depression and the policies he enacted to fix it were extremely unpopular in his own party and across the country. Members of Congress refused to visit him, even fellow Democrats, but he cared not at all. It was "very seldom that a Democratic Senator was seen at the White House," wrote Senator Shelby Cullom, an Illinois Republican who admired Cleveland. "The president became completely estranged from the members of his party in both House and Senate, but it seemed to bother him little. He went ahead doing his duty as he saw it, utterly disregarding the wishes of the members of his party in Congress."[358]

Postmaster General William L. Wilson wrote in his diary on February 1, 1896: "It must seem strange to other governments that we have in this country an administration practically without a party to support it." The president "has few to defend or comfort him." Even Cleveland recognized his own deep unpopularity with Congress. "Think of it! Not a man in the Senate with whom I can be on terms of absolute confidence," he wrote to Ambassador Thomas Bayard in London. "Not one of them comes to me on public business unless sent for, and then full of reservations and doubts." But Wilson admired his boss and friend. "What a strong, steady, conscientious worker the president is, doing each day's duty courageously and earnestly, and yet maligned and slandered perhaps as no president, perhaps as no public man ever was in all our history."[359]

In addition to his strict monetary policy, his non-jingoistic foreign policy also annoyed people and politicians on both sides of the aisle. Henry Adams, who, unlike his friends and family, supported Cleveland for president, was especially angry and wanted action in Cuba. Adams saw oppression around the globe, in Cuba and in Turkey, where an uprising among Armenians had recently been crushed. "Could not the very gentlemanly and refined philanthropist who rules us in the White House," Adams sarcastically wrote to a friend, "and who, as far as I know, has no function in office except to give our moral support to every infernal corruption on the devil's footstool of which he and his Spanish and Turkish friends are making the earth...."[360] But for Cleveland, the presidency was not about philanthropy or supporting uprisings around the world; it was about protecting Americans at home.

In the end, Cleveland's tough stand on principle cost the party dearly at the polls. In the midterm elections in 1894, the Democrats, who had finally gained control of both houses in 1892 for the first time since before the Civil War, were trounced. Republicans kept control of the House until 1910, the Senate until 1912, and held the White House for the next sixteen years. Jeffersonian government was finished in America.

THE FUTURE OF CLEVELAND'S PARTY

After turning down requests to seek a third term in 1896, Cleveland retired from public life. Progressive Democrat William Jennings Bryan gained the presidential nomination and lost to William McKinley, but, more importantly, began the change that transformed the Party of Jefferson and Jackson and ultimately led to the Party of Obama.

There is a photo of Cleveland from March 4, 1897, on the inaugural dais with his successor the day his second term ended. He is looking down as Chief Justice Melville Fuller administers the oath of office to McKinley, the incoming Republican chief executive. That photo truly represents the end of an era, the era of limited government, the era of our founding principles. From that moment on, the United States, with very few exceptions, would live under progressive government. The question would no longer be how to keep the government smaller but how to grow it larger. Washington would be, forever more, administered on the basis of a more energetic, more powerful centralized system, where the feds dictated policy and the states and local governments, as well as the people, would be under mandate to obey.

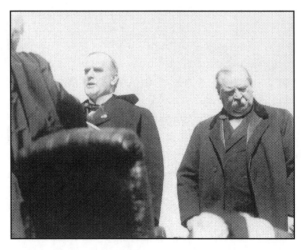

With Bryan's ascension to the top leadership role, the Democratic Party began its move to the left, severely bitten by the progressive bug. In three of the next four presidential contests, the party nominated Bryan to head the ticket. Cleveland and Bryan did not see eye-to-eye politically, as each controlled separate wings of the party, a disagreement that eventually split the National Democracy wide open and kept them from power for sixteen years. Cleveland was the leader of the Bourbons, conservatives who believed in classical liberalism, laissez faire capitalism, economy and accountability in government, sound money, individual responsibility, and a strict construction of the Constitution.

Though originally a Populist, Bryan headed what would become the Progressive wing, those who advocated more taxation, more spending, inflationary currency, and more government intervention in the lives of the people. The rupture was so decisive that Cleveland and Bryan remained at war with each other from 1895 until Cleveland's death in 1908. And with Bryan's ascension to party leadership in 1896, the Democratic Party has never returned to its philosophical roots, the principles of Mr. Jefferson, and has, instead, pushed so far to the left under modern Democrats that it is today on the verge of advocating pure socialism. At least one Cleveland cabinet member saw Bryan's movement as socialism, and even Cleveland himself was deeply suspicious of him, noting that he "has not even the remotest notion of the principles of Democracy."[361]

Spending his retirement years back in his native state of New Jersey, Cleveland was aloof from party business but remained concerned for the future of his beloved "Democracy." He wrote letters to friends for the remainder of his life, seeking a defeat of "Bryanism," ideals he considered a "disastrous heresy," and a return to true principles. If those Jeffersonian principles died out, then the Republic could very well die out with it. In 1899, he wrote his friend and former cabinet member Richard Olney. "And the poor old Democratic party! What a spectacle it presents as a tender to Bryanism and nonsense!" The party had a chance to right itself and win back the presidency in 1900, he believed, if Bryan and his followers were purged. It is advice the modern Republican Party might pay heed. "The Democratic party, if it was only in tolerable condition, could win an easy victory next year; but I am afraid it will never be in winning condition until we have had a regular knock-down fight among ourselves, and succeeded in putting the organization in Democratic hands and reviving Democratic principles in our platform." If not, the nation would get the same candidates that were on the ballot four years before. "Bryanism and McKinleyism! What a choice for a patriotic American!"[362]

Old-line Democrats around the country wrote him to ask for his support and aid in restoring conservatism to the party. He always declined to actively participate, for Bryan controlled the party, or "new Democracy," as he termed it. Cleveland knew he was not welcome at any party functions because "I have not been forgiven by Mr. Bryan for lack of support in 1896." And he had no intention of supporting him in 1900 either. Why should he speak out on a "return to the old faith" and to "reorganize under the old banners" when all it would do is increase "the volume of abuse which for a long time has been hurled at my 'defenseless head.'"[363]

Conservatives wanted him to run for president in 1900 and 1904 to rid the party of Bryanism. The calls were so strong that he had to publicly repudiate them. Many realized that he had been right in his strict conservative policies and that the party and the country were both on the wrong track. The push was, in fact, so strong in 1904 that it concerned President Theodore Roosevelt, who was seeking a term in his own right, assuming, as he did, the presidency in 1901 after McKinley's tragic assassination. "It is evident he has the presidential bee in his bonnet," TR wrote Henry Cabot Lodge about the possibility of a Cleveland candidacy, "and it is equally evident that a large number of people are desirous of running him again. Bryan would bolt him, but in spite of this I think he would be a very formidable candidate." There seemed to be "a great wave of Cleveland sentiment." In two other letters to Lodge, Roosevelt expressed his opinion that a Cleveland candidacy would be "formidable."[364]

It would be formidable because Cleveland wanted to give the nation a clear choice between the progressive "Rooseveltism" and true conservatism, not the "me-tooism" of Bryan. Cleveland saw the situation with the Democratic Party in 1900 exactly as Ronald Reagan saw the Republicans in 1975. After Watergate and the inept Gerald Ford, the GOP was in dire straits—no popular support, and bank accounts nearly empty. Many wanted a third party because the Republicans were moving so far to the left to get closer to the Democrats. Reagan, like Cleveland, wouldn't have it. "Our people look for a cause to believe in. Is it a third party we need, or is it a new and revitalized second party, raising a banner of no pale pastels, but bold colors which make it unmistakably clear where we stand on all of the issues troubling the people?" he told a CPAC (Conservative Political Action Conference) crowd. "A political party cannot be all things to all people. It must represent certain fundamental beliefs which must not be compromised to political expediency, or simply to swell its numbers."[365]

Cleveland would have wholeheartedly agreed with Reagan. "My feeling is that the safety of the country is in the rehabilitation of the old Democratic party," he wrote a supporter. "It would be a difficult task to do this," if Bryan prevailed, leading to "absurdities for which the Democratic party would be held responsible." The "old guard" had to "defeat Bryanism and the sham Democratic organization gathered about him."[366] It had to be done or both the party and country might be doomed.

Mark Twain, a steadfast and loyal Cleveland supporter, understood just how much the party, and the country, needed the former president. He wrote to his daughter in 1908, when Cleveland was asked yet again to consider a run, and as the Democratic Party began what looked to be another losing presidential campaign with Bryan. Cleveland was "a most noble public servant—and in that capacity he has been utterly without blemish," the great author wrote. "Of all our public men of today he stands first in my reverence & admiration, and the next one stands two hundred twenty-fifth. He is the only statesman we have, now. Cleveland *drunk* is a more valuable asset to this country than the whole batch of the rest of our public men *sober*. He is high-minded; all his impulses are great and pure and fine. I wish we had another of this sort." [Emphasis in the original][367]

But no other sort emerged, and at age seventy-one Cleveland was simply not up to the task. He died a few weeks after Twain's letter. Bryan captured the presidential nomination in 1908 for the third time, losing the race yet again, this time to Roosevelt's handpicked successor William Howard Taft. But progressivism would carry the Democratic Party into the future. The ideological disaster was so apparent to many old Cleveland conservatives that in 1909 one wrote that the "Democratic party, as we knew it, is dead." He was right.[368]

From McKinley's election in 1896, a series of progressive presidents, some Democrats, some Republicans, built and added on to the edifice that became our current welfare/warfare state over the course of the next century. Both parties experienced an ideological realignment during the late-nineteenth and early twentieth century. The Republicans had already been infected with progressivism from its very beginning and added to it with McKinley's imperialist foreign policy and Roosevelt's radical domestic agenda.

With McKinley's ascension, Congress raised tariff rates with the Dingley Act to one of the highest levels in history, averaging 52 percent across the board. The new tariff wiped out the modest tax cut during the Cleveland years. McKinley also caved to imperialist pressure and stretched progressive tentacles across the oceans, grabbing foreign territory for the United States, with the acquisition of Guam, Puerto Rico, and the Philippines, lands that would never be considered for statehood. McKinley also sent troops into China to aid with the Boxer Rebellion in order to get the United States in on the carving up of that populous nation and potentially lucrative market. Aside from the high tariff, with McKinley it was not domestic policy so much as it was foreign affairs that tilted to the left.

Theodore Roosevelt kicked progressivism into high gear at home. He gave us the Food and Drug Administration, greatly strengthened regulatory agencies like the Interstate Commerce Commission, and rigorously enforced the Sherman Antitrust Act with his "trust-busting" agenda. When William Howard Taft succeeded Teddy and tried to reign in the rampant liberalism, TR turned on his old friend and split the party wide open in 1912 with his Progressive Party campaign, also known as the Bull Moose Party. The breach was partially healed in 1920, when Warren Harding and Calvin Coolidge stopped the progressive tide in the GOP and the party began a march to the right. Though progressivism reared its ugly head from time to time, conservatism eventually won out in the Republican Party. It was an ideology that, though in the opposition party, Cleveland would have recognized and supported.

Interestingly, Woodrow Wilson, himself a professional historian, foretold of Cleveland's "move" to the GOP. Soon after winning the White House in 1912, because of the Republican-Progressive split, he told a group of visiting senators that he was the first Democrat to enter the presidency since James Buchanan in 1857. "This country has never had a Democratic administration since the Civil War," he told them. "You may think Cleveland's administration was Democratic. It was not. Cleveland was a conservative Republican."[369]

The Democrats experienced the same ideological shift, first with William Jennings Bryan and his silver crusade, a debasing of the nation's currency to aid the poor, as well as his wealth redistributionist ideas. But Bryan did oppose central banking and foreign adventurism, resigning as Woodrow Wilson's Secretary of State because of what he perceived as belligerent actions that would lead to American entrance into World War One.

Bryan might have sown the seeds, but it was Wilson who picked the corrupt fruit, bringing progressivism full force into the Democratic Party, increasing it both at home and abroad. Wilson gave the nation the Federal Reserve System, an income tax, and an unnecessary foreign war—an idealistic conflict to save the world for democracy—that America could have stayed out of, and if it had, the entirety of world history would have been quite different.

FDR followed and gave us the New Deal, creating for the first time a social service state, with confiscatory tax rates and central economic planning. Roosevelt decided to fight the depression by following his predecessor, Herbert Hoover, with a massive infusion of government. The results were oppressive taxes, crushing debt, overbearing government regulations and bureaucracy, and a great depression that lasted more than a decade.

LBJ stood on FDR's shoulders and expanded the social service state into a permanent welfare state, wasting trillions of dollars in the largest wealth transfer in human history and all for naught. Those programs, like Medicare, are tens of trillions of dollars in the red, and if not fixed will drag the nation into certain bankruptcy. He also involved the nation in a disastrous foreign war that continues to hang over the nation like a dark cloud. The ghosts of Vietnam have never been exorcised.

For all his many faults, Jimmy Carter didn't do much in the way of advancing progressivism because his presidency was full of incompetence, and Bill Clinton, after a massive tax hike, heightened spending, and a failure to take over the nation's healthcare system early in his administration, decided he was more interested in being reelected and remaining popular than to advance many leftwing causes. He cozied up to Republicans and triangulated on the issues in order to save his political future.

But Barack Obama, though he may seem incompetent, is not worried about his own popularity. He, and especially those around him, are socialist ideologues through and through, and are aiming to implement as much of that ideology as they can, so much so that one wonders if he cares about a second term. Obama spent a trillion dollars in a failed stimulus plan to fix the economy, took over the nation's healthcare system, strapped Wall Street with massive draconian rules and regulations, wreaked havoc on America's capitalist economic system, and divided the nation as it had not been in decades. He could very well go down in history as the nation's worst and most destructive president, and all from a party that began as a principled opposition organization to big government.

VII

Restoring the Republic

Cleveland ... seemed utterly incapable of making any bid for mob support; there had appeared not the slightest germ of demagoguism in him; he had refused to be a mere partisan tool and had steadily stood for the best ideals of government.
—*Ambassador Andrew Dickson White*[370]

As progressivism has slowly fastened itself around our government like a boa constrictor around its prey, the constitutional republic created by our founders is slowly dying—and with it the proud and prosperous nation we have come to love—if the vice of liberalism is not soon removed. Progressives, and their century-long experiment in government paternalism, have been nothing short of a complete disaster, and with the 2008 election, the future looked even grimmer. But with the hour the darkest, soon after Barack Obama took the oath of office on January 20, 2009, real hope began to arise. The Tea Party movement emerged as a counterweight to Obama's radically progressive agenda and quickly spread across the country, not mandated from the top down but spontaneously from the bottom up.

Like the elections in 1890, an outpouring of patriotic citizens led to a midterm landslide against a big government agenda. In 2010, conservatives regained control of the House with a sixty-five-seat rout and the filibuster-proof Senate was reduced to just a three-seat Democratic majority. But to complete the process and begin restoring the republic, conservatives must retake the Senate and win back the White House and must do so with strong Jeffersonian candidates, in the mold of Grover Cleveland, just as conservatives did in the early 1890s. Should we follow the more recent past and choose a "me too" Republican president, then no restoration is possible, as we have so often seen. Only a true Cleveland Conservative, a genuine Jeffersonian with admiration for the taxpayers, reverence for the Constitution, and respect for the states can restore the republic. It is Grover Cleveland's presidency that we can learn from and emulate. He is the quintessential president for conservatives to admire.

When Cleveland came to the White House during the corrupt Gilded Age, the office of the presidency had lost a great deal of its prestige. Lincoln had been a strong president, in truth much too strong, but Congress snatched that newfound power from his unfortunate and weakened successor, Andrew Johnson, and held it tight. According to Massachusetts Senator George F. Hoar, Congress was "unwilling to part with the prerogatives … which had been wrenched from the feeble hand of Johnson."[371] And after the wrenching, Congress held most of the political influence and believed itself best suited to run the nation, thereby placing the chief executive in a subservient role.

The historian Henry Adams was highly critical of the relationship between Congress and the White House, as well as the performance of the government itself. The "whole fabric of the government," he wrote, has "been violently wrenched from its original balance," for "Congress has assumed authority which it was never intended to hold." The government, he continued, "does not govern; Congress is inefficient, and shows itself more and more incompetent, as at presently constituted, to wield the enormous powers that are forced upon it, while the Executive, in its full enjoyment of theoretical independence, is practically deprived of its necessary strength by the jealousy of the Legislature."[372]

And the jealousy was strong. A president attempting to influence Congress, wrote Senator Hoar, would have been received "as a personal affront." When a member of Congress visited the White House, "it was to give, not to receive advice," he wrote. "Each of these stars kept his own orbit and shone in his sphere, within which he tolerated no intrusion from the president or from anybody else."[373]

It was Cleveland who finally broke the congressional hold on power and restored the balance of authority, returning the presidency to a more dignified position as a coequal branch. Upon his assumption of office, the Senate attempted to dictate to President Cleveland those officials he could and could not remove from office. They did this by invoking the Tenure of Office Act, the same tactic they used to impeach Andrew Johnson. But Grover Cleveland was no Andrew Johnson, and he not only won the battle over the Senate but succeeded in getting the nefarious law repealed. He even stopped the practice of presidents traveling to Capitol Hill to sign bills and instead required Congress to send newly passed laws to him in the White House so he could study them before making a decision about its future—certainly not the actions of a timid and weak chief executive.

Cleveland used the *legal* powers of the presidency to control the egos on Capitol Hill. These fights certainly restored the presidency to its distinguished position in the federal government but, more importantly, he did not strengthen the office by encroaching on the constitutional duties of Congress, like Lincoln did and future presidents would after him. In short, he did not allow the office to become the "imperial presidency" it has today. But with the onset of the new progressive philosophy of government came a change in the role of the president in public life. Chief executives after Cleveland began to take a more active part in the administration of national affairs, both domestic and foreign, as well as a more vigorous exercise of power over the states, another gift from Honest Abe. In his autobiography, Teddy Roosevelt wrote that "in all national matters, of importance to the whole people, the nation is to be supreme over state, county, and town alike."[374] As we see every day, in our own time, every issue, just as James Madison warned, has seemingly become a national one requiring a federal role.

No two philosophies were more diametrically opposed since the days of Jefferson and Hamilton than that of Grover Cleveland and Theodore Roosevelt. Cleveland idolized Jefferson and believed, as did most early Americans, that the chief executive should not take an overly active role in the government, and for that he has been unjustly criticized. His immediate presidential successors, namely William McKinley, TR, and Woodrow Wilson, developed the modern presidency as we know it today. Roosevelt Progressives revered Hamilton and Lincoln, as well as many European tyrants, such as Oliver Cromwell. Once in office, they fundamentally altered the nature of the presidency, transforming it from a constitutional image suited to Jefferson to a more powerful one envisioned by Hamilton, where it has remained ever since, save the Coolidge years.

Cleveland held a strict constructionist view of the Constitution and a narrow Jeffersonian interpretation of the constitutional powers of the presidency. He rightly recognized that the Constitution restricted power; it did not expand it. Roosevelt turned that notion on its head. He maintained that the president "was limited only by specific restrictions and prohibitions appearing in the Constitution or imposed by the Congress under its Constitutional powers." TR "declined to adopt the view that what was imperatively necessary for the nation could not be done by the president unless he could find some specific authorization to do it," the conservative view held by Jefferson and Cleveland. "My belief was that it was not only his right but his duty to do anything that the needs of the nation demanded unless such action was forbidden by the Constitution or by the laws," TR contended. "Under this interpretation of executive power I did and caused to be done many things not previously done by the president and the heads of the departments. I did not usurp power, but I did greatly broaden the use of executive power. In other words, I acted for the public welfare, I acted for the common well-being of all our people, whenever and in whatever manner was necessary, unless prevented by direct constitutional or legislative prohibition."[375]

In truth, Roosevelt did usurp power, and sadly, his erroneous, expansive view of national and presidential power has prevailed in our time, while Cleveland's conservative view has died away. And as a result of TR's power grab, the United States slowly but surely began a march toward a strong centralized state with all power held in Washington. But Teddy's notion is not a republic; it is tyranny.

Today, we need a president who will end the imperial presidency, not one who idolizes Teddy Roosevelt or Abraham Lincoln, who also ran roughshod over the Constitution. We need a president who will not get drunk on power but is willing to return the office to its original intention and restore our constitutional republic. Our republic functions when the constitutional balance between the states and the federal government is maintained. When Lincoln first destroyed the balance, the erosion of the republic began. Our republic functions when every branch of government acts as the Constitution, and the founders, prescribed. When the balance tips in any one direction, problems begin to emerge.

We need a president who does not legislate from the Oval Office and will bring the presidency back into line with its constitutional limitations. "The accumulation of all powers, legislative, executive, and judiciary, in the same hands," wrote James Madison in Federalist No. 47, "may justly be pronounced the very definition of tyranny." But modern chief executives don't see it that way, and President Obama has been no exception, taking constitutional usurpation to a whole new level. He has said time and again that he possesses the power to act on his own should he see fit. Speaking in Colorado in December 2011, he said, in reference to his economic policy, that "where Congress is not willing to act, we're going to go ahead and do it ourselves." On another occasion, he again said that if Congress would not act (which really means not do his bidding), which "hurts our economy and puts our people at risk, then I have an obligation as president to do what I can without them." At one of his Jobs Council meetings, which had just issued a report, President Obama told them to "scour" it and "identify all those areas in which we can act administratively without additional congressional authorization and just get it done." He even made what many conservatives contend are illegal recess appointments while the Senate was still in pro-forma session in the hopes of avoiding constitutionally required confirmations. Unsurprisingly, Democratic members of Congress enthusiastically urged him to follow through on each and every one of his dictatorial actions.[376]

On the volatile issue of immigration reform, of which he had no support, President Obama said in 2011, "I wish I had a magic wand and could make this all happen on my own," he told the Congressional Hispanic Caucus. "There are times where … I'd like to work my way around Congress." On the same issue he also said "the idea of doing things on my own is very tempting."[377] So for President Obama, the idea of being a dictator, enacting laws, and spending money without the approval of the people's representatives is very enticing. Not exactly what our founders envisioned.

But Obama is certainly not the first to espouse such thoughts. Chief executives before him have unilaterally ruled from the White House, starting with Lincoln, whose defenders have acknowledged the fact but say he was, at least, a "benevolent dictator." It was Teddy Roosevelt who said, "I don't think that any harm comes from the concentration of power in one man's hands." One use of unilateral rule is by executive orders, though they are not mentioned in the Constitution. Originally intended as instructions for the executive departments, today presidents routinely sign executive orders that have the force of law, particularly for "national emergencies." FDR, who set a record with more than 3,700 executive orders, criminalized the ownership of gold in 1933, interned Japanese Americans in 1942, and tried to raise the income tax rate on the wealthy to 100 percent in 1944, all with the stroke of his pen. President Kennedy created the Peace Corps with an executive order, while President Clinton illegally seized more than five million acres by executive fiat for federal wilderness areas. But the Constitution vests all legislative power in Congress, and future presidents should defer to the democratically elected lawmaking body for such actions.[378]

The federal judiciary has also attempted to rule unilaterally. We need a president who does not allow the federal courts to legislate from the bench and who will appoint constitutional justices who will actually revere and uphold the originality of the document. In shades of our modern era, liberal Republicans feared that a Cleveland presidency would fill the federal judiciary with strict constructionists judges who would erode their progressivist government. In a public rally in Massachusetts on October 29, 1884, during Cleveland's first campaign for president, Theodore Roosevelt warned his fellow Republicans, in language used in our time, that the "next president runs a chance of having to appoint four judges of the Supreme Court," and Cleveland would appoint "strict constructionists" to the bench. Such conservative justices, he said, would change the country "from a mighty and prosperous nation into a confederation of petty and wrangling republics." The Republican Party favored "loose constructionists," he said, of the "school of Marshall and Story, the Federalists, and not ... the school of Taney, the Democrat." The type of justices favored by the GOP would decide that "the national banks are constitutional, that the law by which they are created and extended is constitutional, that the law providing for the suppression of pleuro-pneumonia and of kindred diseases by the National Government should be held constitutional."[379] With Republicans, judges would allow big government to continue unopposed; with Cleveland's strict constructionist views it would come to a screeching halt. And it did under the constitutionalist Fuller Court.

We need a president with courage who will stand on principle, no matter the political consequences. Our presidential candidates should tell the people plainly what they believe and then work diligently to enact his or her agenda once in office. There can be nothing more unnerving to a freedom-loving American than to hear politicians and pundits discuss shifting positions in order to gain electoral advantage. A presidential contender must move to the right in primaries, we hear of Republican candidates, and then shift to the center for the general election, a concept mastered by Richard Nixon. But such talk is like nails on a chalkboard to me and should be to every true conservative. We should demand for our presidents not politicians who shift with the wind but statesmen who stand like a rock on principle.

We need a true conservative president who will not triangulate with critical issues in the hopes of depriving the opposition of them. In the most recent egregious example, George W. Bush signed a Medicare prescription drug benefit law in 2003, a bill supported by many so-called conservatives in Congress. Republican strategists characteristically praised the president's action because it would snatch the issue away from liberals in the presidential election in 2004. So we strapped our children and grandchildren with an estimated $19 trillion in additional debt so we can win an election? That's not statesmanship; that's stupidity. Grover Cleveland tongue lashed members of Congress for even suggesting such action. We need a president today who will do likewise.

We need a president who can and will say no to the outrageous spending schemes in Washington, like the disgraceful earmarks for a teapot museum and video game preservation, and who will aggressively use the veto pen, as Cleveland did, like a "sledgehammer" to keep government growth in check. Recent presidents, even "me too" Republicans, have been hesitant to use it because they, like Congress, seek a larger, more powerful government and look for ways to reward favored constituents, so there is no reason for them to reject big spending bills.

As of this writing Obama has vetoed only two bills in three years, while George W. Bush had just twelve in eight years, Clinton thirty-seven in eight years, George H. W. Bush forty-four in four years, and Reagan seventy-eight in eight years, an average of fewer than six vetoes per year over the previous three decades.

The last president with double-digit vetoes was Eisenhower with 181 during his two terms. Yet the best of the modern age would have to be Gerald Ford, who is never discussed as a strong president, but who vetoed 66 bills in a little less than two-and-a-half years at the helm, many of which were extravagant Democratic spending bills, making Ford the most like Cleveland, at least in that regard, during the last forty years. President Cleveland, though, averaged 73 vetoes per year as president and 100 per year as governor to stop outrageous spending. The unnecessary and unconstitutional spending Reagan and both Bushes allowed would never have been tolerated on Cleveland's watch.[380]

It is imperative that the next president begins the arduous process of dismantling the welfare state. This experiment in government paternalism has been a colossal failure. Trillions have been transferred from one class of people—those who work—to another class—those who don't, or won't. Democrats, like the closet socialists they are, think the program is fair because wealth should be shared. Good sense says it's one of the most unfair actions the federal government has ever undertaken, to "take from the mouth of labor the bread it has earned," to quote Jefferson. But we must not stop with the poor. The wealthy also gain enormous benefits from the government, most recently the gargantuan bailouts in 2008 and the Obama stimulus in 2009 that funneled billions to corporations, not to mention other goodies, like government loans, that are awarded because of the best lobbyists money can buy. No class should benefit from the government. In fact, we shouldn't even categorize the people by class. Our society is based on individuals and every individual should receive the same advantage from Washington, and nothing more or less. We need a president who will say, as Cleveland did, that spending is a "question of principle ... that justice to the taxpayer should replace the generosity of the state."[381]

A new president should also dramatically weaken the taxman. Unnecessary taxation, used to fund programs beyond the scope of federal authority, is robbery and plunder, pure and simple. President Cleveland called it "extortion." But it's even worse today. The federal government seems to think they have first rights to the wealth of the American people. Today Washington taxes income, capital gains, savings, interest, takes "contributions" for Social Security and Medicare, and levies a whole host of excise taxes, on everything from tires to tanning beds. Many on the left would love to include a socialistic Value Added Tax (VAT) to their massive tax repertoire, much like the one in Europe today, where no one really knows how much the tax actually is because it is added to the final price of products. But even without any additional levies, the government's take is enormous. And, if that's not enough, when you die, the government gets another large bite of what you have left, that is if you have enough to qualify as "rich" by then. Combine that with tens of thousands of pages of federal regulations, its little wonder businesses leave the country in droves and a major reason why the United States, the true father of economic freedom and capitalism, was ranked only the tenth freest economy in the world in 2011, falling five spots since 2008. A 2011 study by the World Bank concluded that the United States was ranked just thirteenth in the category measuring the ease of starting a business. Some of the other nations ahead of us? Armenia, Belarus, Georgia, Saudi Arabia, and Rwanda. Yes, that Rwanda.[382] Shameful.

The entire tax code should be thrown out and a new one along Jeffersonian lines should be crafted. For one hundred fifty years the federal government ran on indirect taxes, mostly tariffs and excise taxes, generating ample amounts of revenue to more than fund the legitimate operations in Washington. Chronic deficit spending was unheard of. In fact, from 1866 to 1893, the treasury ran a surplus every year, a fiscal condition we can scarcely imagine today, burdened as we have been with decades of deficits because it takes a gargantuan amount of taxes to fund the nanny state, a system never dreamed of by our founders.

In our glorious past, borrowing and running deficits in troubled times, namely during financial depressions and war, was generally to be expected, as it is now, but as soon as the calamity ended, the federal government instituted plans to begin paying down the debt. As a result, when the next crisis struck, the nation did not have an overwhelming debt load already sitting on the books. Earlier Americans used boom times to pay their bills and accumulate budget surpluses in order to be ready for the next bust they knew would come. By contrast, today we spend and spend and spend, whether boom or bust. And we find ourselves in as bad a state of affairs as we have ever been, with a world economic system on the verge of collapse.

In 1897, when Cleveland left the presidency, federal spending encompassed less than two-tenths of one percent of the economy; now it's more than a third of GDP and growing. Before the advent of progressivism, it was strongly held that the people, and not the government, owned the nation's wealth. We must return to those values. Future presidents must say no to continued deficit spending, get our fiscal house in order, and return America's vast riches to its rightful owners, the people, for when the next crisis comes, and it could be just around the corner, our current debt load may be enough to sink us.

And when an economic crisis does strike, we must stop becoming involved in the downturns in an effort to fix them, but allow the free market to work and correct the imbalance. We need a president who will not cave in to fear mongering by the Federal Reserve chairman or the Treasury Secretary when they insist on a massive infusion of government to fight any and every recession or potential depression. We need a president who will stop the inflationary schemes of the Fed and vow that the system be audited and its ever-expanding power reined in.

Our foreign policy also badly needs reform. Though America has certainly been a tremendous force for good throughout the world, today our reach around the globe has simply gotten out of hand. In 1939, Stephen Ambrose has noted in his book *Rise to Globalism*, "the United States had an army of 185,000 men with an annual budget of less than $500 million. America had no entangling alliances and no American troops were stationed in any foreign country." Today all that has dramatically changed, with a much larger military force, a massive defense budget, and alliances with more than fifty nations.[383] We have transitioned ourselves from republic to empire, from independent sovereign nation to member of the global community.

Presidents have contributed the most to this transformation, routinely waging war without congressional approval, another precedent that began with Lincoln, who raised an army and invaded the South without bothering to consult Congress, an action tantamount to treason.[384] The advent of the "imperial presidency" has only worsened the abuse in our current "perpetual war for perpetual peace" doctrine.

Dick Cheney, a man I greatly admire, wrote in his memoirs that he did not think President George H. W. Bush needed congressional approval to launch Operation Desert Storm in 1991. Since the United Nations had passed a resolution against Iraq, and since the US Senate had ratified the UN Charter, then the commander in chief needed no further authority, Cheney argued.[385] Such reasoning saddened me, seeing a solid conservative arguing for imperial power. But nothing supersedes the US Constitution. Nothing. And our leaders, as well as our soldiers, take oaths to uphold the Constitution, not the UN Charter.

If we were to derive any of our authority from the United Nations, would that not, in essence, give that organization, which is notoriously anti-American and anti-Semitic, command over our troops and our military operations in the future, as the international organization becomes more powerful? Would they be able to tell us when and how we fight? Or to negotiate a cease-fire on our behalf and force us to follow it? These are legitimate questions for any concerned citizen.

The framers of the Constitution wisely gave all war-making powers to the representatives of the people. Congress, and Congress alone, has the power to declare war or authorize the use of force and that power cannot be usurped or transferred to another entity, including the president. Congress is also given the authority to set the rules and regulations for the armed forces. To his credit, George H. W. Bush asked for congressional authority before launching Desert Storm, as did George W. Bush for conflicts in both Afghanistan and Iraq.

Democrats Bill Clinton and Barack Obama, however, did not seek authorization before launching wars, even though their party screams the loudest when Republicans *legally* go to war. Clinton expanded a restricted operation in Somalia, which began in December 1992 by George H. W. Bush, that essentially turned the US military into an international "meals on wheels" organization to help feed a starving nation. At least the Bush mission had been limited to protecting food supplies, but Clinton enlarged it to an active military operation to seek out and take down the thuggish gang leaders who were essentially holding the nation hostage. Without the proper equipment, like tanks and C-130s, which the weak president would not provide, eighteen Army Rangers lost their lives in the Battle of Mogadishu in October 1993. Clinton then tucked tail and ran out, leading Osama bin Laden to conclude the United States was a "paper tiger."

Clinton also illegally waged war with his seventy-eight-day bombing campaign against Serbia in 1999. Congress, led by conservative Republicans, would not give him the authority to launch the war, meant to oust Serbian dictator Slobodan Milosevic. When Clinton did not get congressional approval or a UN mandate, he used the NATO alliance in an illegal fashion. NATO was originally crafted as a defensive coalition, but the 1999 Serbian campaign saw the use of the organization in an offensive mode for the first time in its history. Clinton's actions are all the more disturbing when you factor in the fact that he cut the military nearly in half.[386]

For his part, Obama, who also instituted large defense cuts, joined a NATO campaign against Libya, telling Congress that he did not need any authorization to do so. He also sent one hundred special operations forces to Uganda, in Africa, to help combat the Lord's Resistance Army, which almost no Americans had ever heard of. The president claimed, in a letter to Speaker of the House John Boehner, that the mission would further "US national security interests and foreign policy and will be a significant contribution toward counter-LRA efforts in central Africa."[387] Obama opposed getting involved in a "civil war" in Iraq, as well as military options to confront and possibly strike Iran, as being against US national security interests, but a civil war in Central Africa is apparently another story.

Many national security conservatives support such missions and routinely argue that a president has this constitutional authority as commander-in-chief, but they are flat out wrong. We need a president who will not get into these "feel-good" missions but will use the US military for the right reasons—for the defense of the nation and its people, who will scale back our foreign commitments and entanglements and end humanitarian and nation-building ventures. War should be the absolute last resort, to be used only when there is a vital threat to our national security and when all other avenues have been exhausted and failed.

To advocate such a position doesn't mean that one is a "raise the draw bridge" isolationist. It doesn't mean we allow a thuggish regime like Iran to possess a nuclear weapon, send warships to our coastline, or build missile bases in South America. Nor does it mean that we shouldn't launch a preemptive strike to stop an attack before it begins. It simply means we are presently stretched too thin and have taken on too much, especially when our fiscal situation is so bad that we borrow billions from nations in order to defend them. We must stop this insanity and tailor our foreign policy to meet modern threats. We can responsibly scale back our obligations abroad, as well as withdraw from some of our most pressing entangling alliances, and still maintain a strong national defense. To borrow a phrase from Newt Gingrich, we can be hawks but "cheap hawks."

Some of our alliances could, and should, be realistically retained, like our support of Israel, but the question is, do we really need to keep all of them? Should we continue to pledge the blood and treasure of our children to defend half the globe? In the absence of a Cold War, is NATO still needed? Does it need to be expanded, particularly into Eastern Europe, as we are now doing? We simply cannot in good faith attempt to expel China and Iran from the Western Hemisphere while we maintain alliances and a ground presence in Japan and South Korea, a close friendship with Taiwan, and warships and ground troops in the Middle East. That would be base hypocrisy. But these are important questions that we, as a society, need to ask of ourselves and formulate answers that best suit our needs as a nation.

We must ask ourselves another question. Do we fight for freedom around the globe and build democracies, or do we stay out of the internal affairs of other nations as we historically have done? For the most part, on the right it's the so-called neocons who believe in, and most often advocate, the position that we should fight for liberty in foreign lands and push democratic governments onto foreign nations. But would they sacrifice Los Angeles for Taipei, or Chicago for Kiev? Would they, with an honest mind, sacrifice American troops for India, Taiwan, South Korea, Poland, or Ukraine? And most importantly, could they give up their children for the cause of worldwide democracy? If the answer to the last question is no, then they have no business telling others they should sacrifice theirs.

How backward have we become in our foreign policy? In Cleveland's day, the federal government kept a close eye on every nation that attempted to make any inroads into the Western Hemisphere and confronted them if necessary. But at the same time, the United States had no interest in the internal happenings of Europe or Asia. Today, however, we have a presence all around the globe while China and Iran, nations who are not our friends no matter how much we pretend, are busy working to expand military and intelligence capabilities on our very doorstep, and we have done nothing to stop them.

We must have a president who, when war does come, will use all the resources at his disposal to bring the conflict to a swift and sudden end, rather than worry about what the world will think of us if harsh force is applied. We must no longer allow silly and unwise Pentagon lawyers to determine how our men and women fight, nor rely on the restrictions of international rules of conduct written by European bureaucrats. We should fight as we did in the days of World War Two.

Consider President Truman's statement on August 6, 1945, about the continuing war with Japan. "We are now prepared to obliterate more rapidly and completely every productive enterprise the Japanese have above ground in any city. We shall destroy their docks, their factories, and their communications. Let there be no mistake; we shall completely destroy Japan's power to make war," he said. If the Japanese "do not now accept our terms, they may expect a rain of ruin from the air, the likes of which has never been seen on this earth. Behind this air attack will follow sea and land forces in such numbers and power as they have not yet seen and with the fighting skill of which they are already well aware."[388] Truman, like FDR before him, did not mince words when it came to war. They meant business and did what was necessary to win, without regard to the opinions of those in the media or anywhere else. They concerned themselves first and foremost with the overwhelming destruction of an enemy, which generally precludes further aggression, as we saw with both Germany and Japan.

Our current mess in Afghanistan is a perfect example of the foolishness of nation-building ventures. Instead of simply destroying al Qaeda and the Taliban regime, we decided to build a new democratic Afghanistan, though George W. Bush campaigned against the nation-building tendencies of his predecessor. After a decade of fighting, losing nearly 2,000 troops, and spending half a trillion dollars, we have what has turned out to be a corrupt regime that has continued its dope peddling and squashing of Christianity. Not the wisest investment.

Ronald Reagan is the perfect modern model for US foreign affairs, a close resemblance to Cleveland. He was neither a nation-builder nor a believer in humanitarian operations. He did not send the US military into foreign lands to topple governments, build democracies, or construct schools and roads. He never placed one boot on the ground in Eastern Europe but stood with those oppressed peoples for whom he remains today a great hero. He believed in peace through strength, that we should build up our forces to the point that a war with the United States was unthinkable. He also understood the uses of economic strength as a major foreign policy weapon, a tactic that is of little use today with our economy in steep decline. Combine those positions with a president whose very presence struck fear into our enemies, rather than laughter and derision, and you have a strong national defense policy. Then and only then will we truly know peace.

Finally, our future presidents must also change the aura of the office from that of a king to its original role as a servant of the people. They should insist on complete honesty in government, faithfully uphold the Constitution, and be a president that is closer to the people, by reducing the White House staff, ending the extravagant parties and gatherings, ceasing from unnecessary travel and vacations, and working diligently on behalf of the public. These are the marks of a great American president.

Grover Cleveland is the embodiment of the ideal president: honest, hardworking, frugal, dedicated to the needs of the people, and committed to upholding constitutional ideals. He was the epitome of pure Jeffersonian thought. Conservatives today often invoke the names of staunch Republicans Barry Goldwater and Ronald Reagan as the chief personifications of our movement, and both are important modern heroes to be sure, but we must also turn back to the very root of our philosophy, to Thomas Jefferson and his Democratic-Republican Party, the ideological forerunner to Reagan's Republicans. Cleveland brought those ideals back to the Democratic Party, which had started a drift to the left. He was totally beholden to Jefferson's political philosophy, the true ideals of the American Revolution. But true Jeffersonianism ended with Cleveland. And today, other than the Tea Party, we have no major political party that truly advances these important principles.

Like others, I have dubbed Cleveland the last Jeffersonian, but he might also be called the first Tea Partier. If he were alive today, he would certainly join the grassroots crusade of action against an overbearing federal government, just as he stood against the growing tide of progressivism in his day. For all his strengths, he was ultimately unable to hold back the deluge of progressivism, a political philosophy that eventually overtook the Democratic Party in 1896 and became a permanent fixture in Democratic politics, as well as in national governance, for decades to come. As a result of progressivism, the federal government would reign supreme over the "new nation."

But today we have a distinct advantage. When Cleveland stood squarely for the old ways, he did so against a mighty whirlwind. Today we have the wind at our back, as more and more Americans are coming to the realization that things are terribly wrong with our country and are mobilizing to set things right. In our effort, we must not fail to return America to its constitutional republic by expressing pure Jeffersonian virtue, just as Cleveland did, for it is the only expression of true conservatism. If we do not fight for better government, our children and their children will pay the price of a future under socialism. We owe them, as well as the millions yet unborn, that much.

To do that we must have a new American Revolution, not a violent affair as we had against the British, but one conducted at the ballot box, as Jefferson had in 1800 and Cleveland during the 1880s and 1890s. As Jefferson wrote of his triumph, the "revolution of 1800 … was a real revolution in the principles of our government as that of 1776 was in its form; not effected indeed by the sword, as that, but by the rational and peaceable instrument of reform, the suffrage of the people."[389] And the American people today, through the Tea Party, are gearing up for another revolt against the powers of progressivism. Let us hope we find the right leader.

When Grover Cleveland's great public career ended on March 4, 1897, one of his cabinet officers, Postmaster General William L. Wilson, confided to his diary, asking, "When will another Cleveland occupy the White House?"[390] We have been waiting for more than one hundred years, but let us pray for our sakes and that of posterity that the wait will soon be over.

ENDNOTES

1 Patrick J. Buchanan, *Day of Reckoning: How Hubris, Ideology, and Greed Are Tearing America Apart* (New York: Thomas Dunne Books, 2007), 86.

2 Chuck Norris, *Black Belt Patriotism: How to Reawaken America* (Washington: Fidelis, 2008).

3 This quote is most often attributed to Henry Ford.

4 Ronald Reagan, Farewell Address, January 11, 1989, http://www.reagan.utexas.edu/archives/speeches/1989/011189i.htm.

5 Larry Schweikart, *What Would the Founders Say? A Patriot's Answers to America's Most Pressing Problems* (New York: Sentinel Books, 2011), 9.

6 Thomas Jefferson, *Notes on the State of Virginia*, in Merrill D. Peterson, comp., *Jefferson: Writings* (New York: Library of America, 1984), 274.

7 Grover Cleveland to Herbert Bissell, September 30, 1885, Allan Nevins, ed., *Letters of Grover Cleveland* (Boston: Houghton Mifflin Company, 1933), 80–1.

8 David N. Mayer, The Mayer Blog, "Rating the US Presidents," http://users.law.capital.edu/dmayer/index.asp; Thomas DiLorenzo, "The Last Good Democrat," Lewrockwell.com, July 8, 2004; Paul Whitfield, "Grover Cleveland, The Last Libertarian President," *Investor's Business Daily*, August 31, 2011, http://news.investors.com/Article/583350/201108311413/Grover-Cleveland-The-Last-

Libertarian-President.htm; Larry Schweikart and Michael Allen, *A Patriot's History of the United States: From Columbus's Great Discovery to the War on Terror* (New York: Sentinel, 2004), 455.

9 The books I am referring to are numerous, but a few major examples would be Thomas DiLorenzo's *Hamilton's Curse: How Jefferson's Archenemy Betrayed the American Revolution and What It Means for America Today* (New York: Crown Forum, 2008); and *The Real Lincoln: A New Look at Abraham Lincoln, His Agenda, and an Unnecessary War* (Roseville, CA: Forum Prima, 2002); Jim Powell's *Bully Boy: The Truth about Theodore Roosevelt's Legacy* (New York: Crown Forum, 2006); *Wilson's War: How Woodrow Wilson's Great Blunder Led To Hitler, Lenin, Stalin & World War II* (New York: Crown Forum, 2005); *FDR's Folly: How Roosevelt and His New Deal Prolonged the Great Depression* (New York: Crown Forum, 2003); Burton Folsom's *New Deal or Raw Deal: How FDR's Economic Legacy Has Damaged America* (New York: Threshold Editions, 2008) and *FDR Goes to War: How Expanded Executive Power, Spiraling National Debt, and Restricting Civil Liberties Shaped Wartime America* (New York: Threshold Editions, 2011).

10 Allan Nevins, *Grover Cleveland: A Study in Courage* (New York: Dodd, Mead & Company, 1932);, 4. Nevins's book, the best of the Cleveland biographies, won the 1933 Pulitzer Prize.

11 Cleveland, Veto of Texas Seed Bill, February 16, 1887, James D. Richardson, *A Compilation of the Messages and Papers of the Presidents*, 13 vols. (New York: Bureau of National Literature, 1897), XI, 5142-5143.

12 Jean Edward Smith, *FDR* (New York: Random House, 2008), 23.

13 Richard Hofstadter, *The American Political Tradition* (New York: Vintage, 1948), 232.

14 *Life*, November 1, 1948; *The New York Times*, July 29, 1962.

15 *Chicago Tribune* magazine, January 10, 1982; Robert K. Murray and Tim H. Blessing, "The Presidential Performance Study: A Progress Report" *Journal of American History* (December, 1983), 540, 541, 543, 545; *Wall Street Journal*, September 12, 2005. The *Wall Street Journal*/Federalist Society study has been published in book format,

Presidential Leadership: Rating the Best and the Worst in the White House, edited by James Taranto and Leonard Leo (New York: Free Press, 2004).

16 Siena College Research Institute, Siena College, Press Release, August 19, 2002; C-SPAN, Historians Presidential Leadership Survey, February 16, 2009, www.cspan.org.

17 Siena College Research Institute, Siena College, Press Release, July 1, 2010.

18 Alvin Stephen Felzenberg, *The Leaders We Deserved (And A Few We Didn't): Rethinking the Presidential Rating Game* (New York, 2008), 12, 378.

19 Ibid., 79, 114, 173, 257, 333.

20 Ivan Eland, *Re-carving Rushmore: Ranking the Presidents on Peace, Prosperity, and Liberty* (Oakland, CA: The Independent Institute, 2009). In Eland's list, John Tyler ranked number one.

21 Schweikart and Allen, *Patriot's History*, 446.

22 R. Emmett Tyrrell, Jr., "Conservatism's Next Coming" *Human Events*, September 24, 2009.

23 Lewis L. Gould, *Grand Old Party: A History of the Republicans* (New York: Random House, 2003), 106.

24 Steven R. Weisman, *The Great Tax Wars: Lincoln to Wilson—The Fierce Battles over Money and Power that Transformed the Nation* (New York: Simon & Schuster, 2002), 115.

25 Sherman Antitrust Act, "Our Documents, http://www.ourdocuments. gov/doc.php?doc=51; Shelby M. Cullom, *Fifty Years of Public Service: The Personal Recollections of Shelby M. Cullom* (Chicago: A. C. McClurg & Co, 1911), 254.

26 DiLorenzo, "The Last Good Democrat"; Schweikart and Allen, *Patriot's History*, 449; Susan Carter, et al., eds., *Historical Statistics of the United States* (New York: Cambridge University Press, 2006), V, 92.

27 Gould, *GOP*, 109.

28 Susan B. Carter, et al., eds., *Historical Statistics of the United States*, 5 vols. (Cambridge: Cambridge University Press, 2006), V, 80–1.

29 Gould, *GOP*, 108; Elizabeth Harrington, "Education Spending up 64 Percent under No Child Left Behind but Test Scores Improve Little," CNSNews, September 26, 2011, http://cnsnews.com/news/article/education-spending-64-under-no-child-left-behind-test-scores-improve-little.

30 "Obama and ACORN," *Wall Street Journal*, October 14, 2008, http://online.wsj.com/article/SB122394051071230749.html; Matthew Vadum, "How Obama and Acorn are Sabotaging America," *Human Events*, June 9, 2011, http://www.humanevents.com/article.php?id=44040; Homer E. Socolafsky and Allan B. Spetter, *The Presidency of Benjamin Harrison* (Lawrence, Kansas: University Press of Kansas, 1987), 65–8.

31 Cleveland to Vilas, September 15, 1889, Nevins, *Letters*, 210–11.

32 Cleveland to Vilas, September 15, 1889, Cleveland to Representative John G. Carlisle, April 7, 1890, Nevins, *Letters*, 210–11 and 221–2.

33 Gould, *GOP*, 110; Cleveland to L. Clarke Davis, November 5, 1890, Nevins, *Letters*, 233. The House in the Fifty-First Congress consisted of 179 Republicans and 152 Democrats; the Fifty-Second would seat 238 Democrats, 86 Republicans, and 8 Populists.

34 Grover Cleveland, Speech, "The Principles of True Democracy," George F. Parker, ed., *The Writings and Speeches of Grover Cleveland* (New York, 1892), 263–71.

35 Mark Twain to Grover Cleveland, in *Mark Twain's Autobiography*, edited by Albert Bigelow Paine, 2 vols. (New York: Harper & Brothers Publishers, 1924), II, 164.

36 Nevins, *Cleveland*, 10; H. Paul Jeffers, *An Honest President: The Life and Presidencies of Grover Cleveland* (New York: Harper Collins, 2000), 2. The surname was originally spelled Cleaveland, for which the "a" was dropped during the next three generations. George F. Parker, *Recollections of Grover Cleveland* (New York: The Century Co., 19011), 14.

37 Denis Tilden Lynch, *Grover Cleveland: A Man Four-Square* (New York: H. Liveright, Inc, 1932) 2; Parker, *Recollections*, 16.

38 John Frost and Harry French, *The Presidents of the United States from Washington to Cleveland* (Boston: Lee and Shepard Publishers, 1889), 539; Parker, *Recollections*, 14.

39 Frost and French, 539-540; Robert M. McElroy, *Grover Cleveland: The Man and the Statesman*. 2 vols. (New York: Harper and Brothers Publishers, 1923), I, 3; Graff, *Cleveland*, 4.

40 Henry Graff, *Grover Cleveland* (New York: Times Books, 2002), 5; Parker, *Recollections*, 16.

41 McElroy, I, 4–6; Chauncey M. Depew, *My Memories of Eighty Years* (New York: Charles Scribner's Sons, 1924), 128. Depew was a prominent attorney and served in the New York State Assembly, as New York Secretary of State, as President of the New York Central Hudson River Railroad, and in the United States Senate. When asked by Depew how he obtained his writing and speaking style, Cleveland told him from his father, who had provided the majority of his education.

42 Parker, *Recollections*, 19.

43 McElroy, I, 13–15; Graff, *Grover Cleveland*, 4.

44 Richard Hofstadter, *Age of Reform* (New York: Vintage, 1960), 232–3.

45 William Allen White, "Cleveland," *McClure's Magazine*, XVIII, February 1902, No. 4, 322.

46 Parker, *Recollections*, 22–3.

47 Lynch, 31.

48 Charles H. Armitage, *Grover Cleveland As Buffalo Knew Him* (Buffalo: Buffalo Evening News, 1926), 1, 8; Horace Samuel Merrill, *Bourbon Leader: Grover Cleveland and the Democratic Party* (Boston, 1957), 4; Parker, *Recollections*, 28; Lynch, 35, 42. Armitage was the political writer for the *Buffalo Evening News* during Cleveland's years in the city.

49 Lynch, 36.

50 Armitage, 16; Parker, *Recollections*, 31; Lynch, 36, 39.

51 Lynch, 37. According to Charles H. Armitage, Cleveland's Uncle Lewis was prominent enough in the Whig and Republican parties to entertain Daniel Webster, Henry Clay, Winfield Scott, Millard Fillmore, William H. Seward, and Horace Greeley in his Buffalo home, though this, more than likely, would have been in the years before Cleveland arrived, particularly since Webster and Clay were already dead when he moved to Buffalo. Aside from an acquaintance with Fillmore, if Cleveland ever met any other prominent men, he never mentioned it. See Armitage, 4.

52 Ibid., 38; Richard Watson Gilder, *Grover Cleveland: A Record of Friendship* (New York: The Century Co., 1910), 224.

53 Parker, *Recollections*, 33–4.

54 Alyn Brodsky, *Grover Cleveland: A Study in Character* (New York: St. Martin's Press, 2000), 26; Jeffers, 27-28; Armitage 18, 42.

55 Merrill, 11.

56 Ibid.; Jeffers, 30.

57 Schweikart and Allen, 448.

58 Brodsky, 28; Parker, *Recollections*, 32.

59 Merrill, 11–12.

60 Armitage, 42.

61 Ibid., 57.

62 Brodsky, 30–1; Armitage, 52.

63 Brodsky, 31–2.

64 Ibid; Jeffers, 34.

65 Jeffers, 34; Armitage, 58–9.

66 Merrill, 12; Armitage, 55.

67 Lynch, 39–40; White, "Cleveland," 323.

68 Armitage, 34; Jeffers, 13.

69 Parker, *Recollections*, 39–40; Armitage, 48; Frost and French, 541.

70 Merrill, 5; William Allen White, "Cleveland," 323; Parker, *Recollections*, 39–40.

71 Merrill, 5-6; Armitage, 43-44; White, "Cleveland," 323; Lewis L. Gould, *Modern American Presidency* (Lawrence, Kansas: University Press of Kansas, 2009), 1.

72 Depew, 124–5.

73 Armitage, 28–9.

74 Ibid., 31.

75 Parker, *Recollections*, 40.

76 Hofstadter, *Age of Reform*, 233; Henry Jones Ford, *The Cleveland Era: A Chronicle of the New Order in Politics* (New Haven: Yale University Press, 1921), 42.

77 Henry Watterson, *"Marse Henry": An Autobiography.* 2 vols. (New York, 1919), II, 118.

78 John Steele Gordon, *An Empire of Wealth: The Epic History of American Economic Power* (New York: Harper Perennial, 2004), 205.

79 William McKinley, "The Tariff of 1890," House Speech, May 7, 1890, *Speeches and Addresses of William McKinley*, compiled by Joseph P. Smith (New York: D. Appleton and Company, 1893), 428.

80 Henry Kissinger, *Diplomacy* (New York: Simon and Schuster, 1994), 37; George C. Herring, *From Colony to Superpower: US Foreign Relations since 1776* (Oxford: Oxford University Press, 2008), 285.

81 Paul Kennedy, *The Rise and Fall of the Great Powers: Economic Change and Military Conflict from 1500 to 2000* (New York, 1987), 200–2, 211; Alfred E. Eckes, *Opening America's Market: US Foreign Trade Policy Since 1776* (Chapel Hill: University of North Carolina Press, 1995), 53; Patrick J. Buchanan, *The Great Betrayal: How American*

Sovereignty and Social Justice Are Being Sacrificed to the Gods of the Global Economy (New York: Little, Brown and Company, 1998), 222-224; Carter, *Historical Statistics*, III, 550; Andrew Carnegie, "The Silver Problem," *North American Review*, September 1893, 354.

82 Carter, *Historical Statistics*, I, 28.

83 H. Wayne Morgan, *From Hayes to McKinley: National Party Politics, 1877–1896* (Syracuse, New York: Syracuse University Press, 1969), vi.

84 H. Wayne Morgan, *Hayes to McKinley*, vii.

85 Newton D. Baker, "Introduction," in Festus P. Summers, ed., *The Cabinet Diary of William L. Wilson, 1896–1897* (Chapel Hill: University of North Carolina Press, 1957), xxv. Baker served as William Wilson's private secretary before serving as Woodrow Wilson's Secretary of War.

86 For a more complete understanding of this topic, see Joel Silbey, *A Respectable Minority: The Democratic Party in the Civil War Era, 1860–1868* (New York: W. W. Norton, 1977).

87 David Barry, *Forty Years in Washington* (Boston: Little, Brown, and Company, 1924), 193.

88 R. Hal Williams, *Realigning America: McKinley, Bryan, and the Remarkable Election of 1896* (Lawrence, Kansas, 2010), xii, 2; Carter, *Historical Statistics*, V, 165.

89 Henry Adams, *The Education of Henry Adams: An Autobiography* (Boston: Houghton Mifflin Company, 1918), 294, 255.

90 Henry Graff, *Grover Cleveland* (New York: Times Books, 2002).

91 Governor Richard Yates, Final Message to the Illinois General Assembly, January 2, 1865, *Chicago Tribune*, January 5, 1865, as quoted in Jeffrey Rogers Hummel, *Emancipating Slaves, Enslaving Free Men: A History of the American Civil War* (Chicago: Open Court Publishing Company, 1996), 332; Taylor quote in James M. McPherson, *Abraham Lincoln and the Second American Revolution* (New York: Oxford University Press, 1991), vii.

92 George Ticknor, as quoted in Morton Keller, *Affairs of State: Public Life in Late Nineteenth Century America* (Cambridge, Massachusetts: Belknap Press, 1977), 2.

93 McPherson, *Lincoln and the Second American Revolution*, viii.

94 Heather Cox Richardson, *The Greatest Nation of the Earth: Republican Economic Policies During the Civil War* (Cambridge, Massachusetts: Harvard University Press, 1997), vii, 1.

95 H. L. Mencken, "A Good Man in a Bad Trade," *American Mercury*, Vol. XXVIII, No. 109, January 1933, 127.

96 Samuel S. Cox, *Union-Disunion-Reunion: Three Decades of Federal Legislation, 1855 to 1885.* (Providence, RI: J. A. and R. A. Reid, Publishers, 1885), 683-684. Cox is referring to Cato the Younger (95 BC to 46 BC), who fought the corruption of the Roman Republic under Caesar and whose characteristics are eerily similar to Grover Cleveland—moral integrity, incorruptibility, dedication to duty, distaste for luxury, and a sacred belief in the past. See Tom Holland, *Rubicon: The Triumph and Tragedy of the Roman Republic* (London: Abacus, 2003), 194–5.

97 O. O. Stealy, *Twenty Years in the Press Gallery: A Concise History of Important Legislation* (New York: Publishers Printing Company, 1906), 28–9

98 John C. Calhoun to George McDuffie, December 4, 1843, in Clyde Wilson, ed., *The Essential Calhoun: Selections from Writings, Speeches, and Letters* (New Brunswick, NJ: Transaction Publishers, 1992), 345.

99 Merrill, 54; David Saville Muzzey, *James G. Blaine: A Political Idol of Other Days* (New York, 1934), 311.

100 Merrill, 24.

101 Gould, *GOP*, 100.

102 Cleveland to Charles W. Goodyear, July 23, 1884, Nevins, *Letters*, 37.

103 A new book focused entirely on this story was published in 2011 and authored by Charles Lachman, entitled *A Secret Life: The Lies and Scandals of President Grover Cleveland* (New York: Skyhorse Publishing). In the book, Lachman, the executive producer of the television tabloid *Inside Edition*, takes Halpin's side and makes the shocking claim that Cleveland raped her. His evidence is an affidavit produced by Halpin. Yet her testimony was taken, not at the time of the incident, but just weeks before the 1884 presidential election, and then sent out to *Republican* newspapers in an "October Surprise." Lachman's argument is so completely ridiculous that it is not worthy of any prominence other than this endnote.

104 Cleveland to Daniel N. Lockwood, July 31, 1884, Ibid., 38–9.

105 William C. Hudson, *Random Recollections of an Old Political Reporter* (New York, 1911), 185-190.

106 Bruce Chadwick, *Lincoln for President: An Unlikely Candidate, An Audacious Strategy, and the Victory No One Saw Coming* (Naperville, Il: Source Books, 2009), 82–4; Richard Hofstadter, *The American Political Tradition: And the Men Who Made It* (New York, Vintage Books, 1948), 223.

107 Details of the meeting can be found in Thomas C. Platt, *The Autobiography of Thomas Collier Platt* (New York: B. W. Dodge & Company, 1910), 126-132. Platt was in attendance at the meeting to speak for Conkling. Also see Kenneth C. Ackerman, *Dark Horse: The Surprise Election and Political Murder of President James A. Garfield* (New York: Da Capo Press, 2004), 174–5.

108 Lincoln Steffens, *The Shame of the Cities* (New York: McClure, Phillips & Co., 1904), 6–7; Hofstadter, *American Political Tradition*, 223.

109 William C. Hudson, *Random Recollections of an Old Political Reporter* (New York: Cupples and Leon Company, 1911), 240; Hofstadter, *American Political Tradition*, 234.

110 Cleveland to George W. Curtis, October 24, 1884 and Cleveland to Daniel Lamont, August 11, 1884, Nevins, *Letters*, 47, 40.

111 Brodsky, 207–8.

112 Ronald Kessler, *In the President's Secret Service: Behind the Scenes with Agents in the Line of Fire and the Presidents They Protect* (New York: Crown Publishers, 2009), 75.

113 Stealy, 29; Burton J. Hendrick, *The Life and Letters of Walter H. Page* (New York: Doubleday, Page & Company, 1922), 41; Nevins, *Cleveland*, 127 and 214.

114 Thomas Pendel, *Thirty-Six Years in the White House: A Memoir of the White House Doorkeeper from Lincoln to Roosevelt* (Washington: The Neal Publishing Company, 1902), 148; Irwin Hood Hoover, *Forty-Two Years in the White House* (Boston: Houghton Mifflin Company, 1934), 13.

115 Hudson, 148–9; Barry, 167.

116 Graff, 75.

117 Mrs. James G. Blaine to M., March 13, 1882, *Letters of Mrs. James G. Blaine*, edited by Harriet S. Blaine Beale, 2 vols. (New York: Duffield and Company, 1908), II, 4–5.

118 W. H. Crook, *Memories of the White House: The Home Life of Our Presidents From Lincoln to Roosevelt* (Boston: Little, Brown and Company, 1911), 172–4, 176, 179, 188.

119 Ike Hoover, 12.

120 Kessler, 71.

121 Greta Van Sustren show, "Trump: Obama 'Takes More Vacations than Any Human Being I've Ever Seen,'" Fox News, August 16, 2011,

http://nation.foxnews.com/donald-trump/2011/08/16/trump-obama-takes-more-vacations-any-human-being-ive-ever-seen; Fox News, "Obama off to Hawaii for seventeen-day vacation," December 3, 2011, located at: http://nation.foxnews.com/president-obama/2011/12/03/obama-hawaii-17-day-vacation.

122 Andrea Tantaros, "Material girl Michelle Obama is a modern-day Marie Antoinette on a glitzy Spanish vacation," *New York Daily News*, August 4, 2010, http://www.nydailynews.com/opinions/2010/08/04/2010-08-04_material_girl_michelle_

obama_is_a_modernday_marie_antoinette_on_a_glitzy_spanish. html#ixzz0vka65lxZ; "Obama gets into the swing of things on his Martha's Vineyard vacation ... after increasing his personal debt ceiling with rare sighting of the First Credit Card," *Daily Mail*, August 20, 2011,

http://www.dailymail.co.uk/news/article-2027541/Obama-golfs-Marthas-Vineyard-increasing-personal-debt-ceiling.html; "Expensive massages, top shelf vodka and five-star hotels: First Lady accused of spending $10m in public money on her vacations," *Daily Mail*, August 24, 2011,
http://www.dailymail.co.uk/news/article-2029615/Michelle-Obama-accused-spending-10m-public-money-vacations.html; Paul Bedard, "Michelle Obama's Africa Trip Cost More Than $424,142," Washington Whispers, *US News & World Report*, October 4, 2011,
http://www.usnews.com/news/blogs/washington-whispers/2011/10/04/michelle-obamas-africa-vacation-cost-more-than-432142.

123 Daniel Halper, "Obama: 'We Never Need an Excuse For a Good Party,'" *Weekly Standard*, December 8, 2011,

http://www.weeklystandard.com/blogs/obama-we-never-need-excuse-good-party_611765.html; Karen Travers, "Obamas Spotlight American Music at White House," ABC News, July 22, 2009, http://abcnews.go.com/Politics/story?id=8140337&page=1#.TuWFVJi1m-8; Michael Gartland and Cynthia R. Fagen, "White House threw secret 'Alice in Wonderland bash during recession," NYPost.com, January 8, 2012, http://www.nypost.com/p/news/national/in_blunderland_hKpNQkHfvpEWe4F51kI4dP; Lynn Sweet, "Obama Super Bowl Party 2011 Party Menu: White House sports bar," *Chicago Sun Times*, February 6, 2011,
http://blogs.suntimes.com/sweet/2011/02/obama_super_bowl_party_2011_pa.html.

124 Steven Thomma, "Obama's No. 1—most foreign travel by first-year president," *McClatchy Newspapers*, October 28, 2011,

http://www.mcclatchydc.com/2009/10/07/v-print/76725/obamas-no-1-most-foreign-travel.html; Penny Starr, "FLASHBACK--George W. Bush Gives Up Golf: 'Playing Golf During a War Sends Wrong

Message,'" CNSNews.com, August 22, 2011, http://cnsnews.com/news/article/flashback-george-w-bush-gives-golf-playing-golf-during-war-sends-wrong-message; J. P. Freire, "Obama's jetset fitness trainer helps shed pounds, adds to global warming," *Washington Examiner*, February 28, 2011,

http://washingtonexaminer.com/blogs/beltway-confidential/2011/02/obamas-jetset-fitness-trainer-helps-shed-pounds-adds-ozone; Nile Gardiner, "The Obama presidency increasingly resembles a modern-day Ancien Régime: extravagant and out of touch with the American people," *The Telegraph*, August 7, 2010, http://blogs.telegraph.co.uk/news/nilegardiner/100050002/the-obama-presidency-increasingly-resembles-a-modern-day-ancien-regime-extravagant-and-out-of-touch-with-ordinary-people/.

125 Roy Morris Jr., *Fraud of the Century: Rutherford B. Hayes, Samuel Tilden, and the Stolen Election of 1876* (New York: Simon and Schuster, 2003), 100; Edwin G. Burrows and Mike Wallace, *Gotham: A History of New York City to 1898* (New York: Oxford University Press, 1999), 1009.

126 Morris, *Fraud*, 100; Burrows and Wallace, 1009.

127 Nevins, *Cleveland*, 79.

128 Cleveland, Speech Accepting Nomination for Mayor before City Convention in Buffalo, October 25, 1881, Parker, *Writings and Speeches*, 1–2.

129 Nevins, *Cleveland*, 82–3; *Buffalo Daily Courier*, October 26, 1881 and November 5, 1881.

130 Cleveland, Mayoral Message, January 2, 1882, Parker, *Writings and Speeches*, 28–30.

131 Armitage, 103, 105.

132 Ibid., 104–5, 109; *Buffalo Daily Courier*, June 27, 1882.

133 Nevins, *Cleveland*, 135–6.

134 Cleveland, Proclamation against the Violation of Laws Governing Elections, *Public Papers of Grover Cleveland, Governor, 1883*–1884, 2 vols. (Albany: Argus Company, Printers, 1883), I, 149–50.

135 Cleveland, Mayoral Message, January 2, 1882, Parker, *Writings and Speeches*, 28–30.

136 Cleveland, Letter Accepting Nomination for President, August 18, 1884, Parker, *Writings and Speeches*, 9–13; Cleveland to John Temple Graves, July 30, 1887, Nevins, *Letters*, 147.

137 Cleveland, Executive Order, July 14, 1886, in Grover Cleveland Presidential Papers, The American Presidency Project, University of California at Santa Barbara, www.presidency.ucsb.edu.

138 Cleveland to A. Bush, August 1, 1885, Nevins, *Letters*, 69-70.

139 *New York World*, August 13, 1885, as quoted in Nevins, *Cleveland*, 215.

140 Nevins, *Cleveland*, 4.

141 Parker, *Recollections*, 112.

142 Graff, 74-75; Jeffers, 137; Richard V. Oulahan, "Presidents & Publicity," 15–16, unpublished book manuscript, Richard V. Oulahan Papers, Herbert Hoover Presidential Library, West Branch, Iowa. Oulahan served as an assistant reporter during Cleveland's second term.

143 Hudson, 138; *New York Herald*, January 4, 1883.

144 For more on this story, see Matthew Algeo, *The President is a Sick Man: Whereas the Supposedly Virtuous Grover Cleveland Survives a Secret Surgery at Sea and Vilifies the Courageous Newspaperman Who Dared Expose the Truth* (Chicago: Chicago Review Press, 2011), although I do not agree with his interpretation.

145 Andrew Malcolm, "A Little Secret about Obama's Transparency," *Los Angeles Times*, March 21, 2010, http://articles.latimes.com/2010/mar/21/nation/la-na-ticket21-2010mar21; Ed O'Keefe, "Obama Finally Accepts his Transparency Award...Behind Closed Doors," Washington Post, March 3, 2011, http://www.washingtonpost.com/

blogs/federal-eye/post/obama-finally-accepts-his-transparency-award-behind-closed-doors/2011/03/31/AFRplO9B_blog.html.

146 Martin L. Gross, *National Suicide: How Washington is Destroying the American Dream From A to Z* (New York: Berkley Books, 2009), 313–16.

147 Ibid.

148 "Grover Cleveland Library Envisioned," *North Buffalo Journal and Review*, March 15, 2007, http://nbjr.speakupwny.com/grover-cleveland-presidential-library-envisioned-newsdaycom/2007/03/15/.

149 Cleveland to Vilas, September 15, 1889, Nevins, *Letters*, 210–11.

150 Cleveland to William E. Russell, June 9, 1891, Nevins, *Letters*, 256; Cleveland to L. Clarke Davis, March 9, 1891, Ibid., 249–50.

151 Terence P. Jeffrey, "Obama: 'I Don't Think Ethics' Was My Favorite Subject," CNSnews.com, September 29, 2011, http://www.cnsnews.com/news/article/obama-i-dont-think-ethics-was-my-favorite-subject; Michelle Malkin, *Culture of Corruption: Obama and His Team of Tax Cheats, Crooks, and Cronies* (Washington DC: Regnery, 2009), 6, 35, 147–9.

152 McClatchy Blog, Planet Washington, "Open Negotiations? Obama Said What?" January 5, 2010.

153 "Top Obamateurisms," *Townhall* magazine, February 2012, 25.

154 Kevin Bogardus, "Pelosi's Wealth Grows by 62 Percent," *The Hill*, June 15, 2011.

155 Robert Lincoln O'Brien, "Cleveland as Seen by His Stenographer, July, 1892–November, 1895," *Proceedings of the Massachusetts Historical Society* (Oct 1950–May 1953), 142.

156 Nicholas Ballasy, "Pelosi: 'My Work in Politics' Is 'An Extension of My Role as a Mom,'" CNSnews.com, July 28, 2011, http://www.cnsnews.com/news/article/pelosi-my-work-politics-extension-my-role-mom.

157 *New York Times*, June 24, 2005, http://www.nytimes.com/2005/06/24/opinion/24fri1.html.

158 Terry Eastland, "Chief Justice Roberts," *Weekly Standard*, September 26, 2005, http://www.weeklystandard.com/Content/Public/Articles/000/000/006/092cavxd.asp?pg=2.

159 Audrey Hudson, "Don't Let Obama Kill 'Tony the Tiger,'" *Human Events*, October 18, 2011, http://www.humanevents.com/article.php?id=46934.

160 *Boston Herald*, June 8, 1880.

161 Rutherford B. Hayes, Diary Entry, January 24, 1886, in Charles Richard Williams, ed., *The Diary and Letters of Rutherford B. Hayes, Nineteenth President of the United States* (Columbus, Ohio: Ohio State Archeological and Historical Society, 1922), IV, 261–2.

162 Donald L. McMurray, *Coxey's Army: A Study of the Industrial Army Movement of 1894* (Boston: Brown, Little & Company, 1929), 22, 25–6.

163 Cleveland to Hon. William L. Wilson, and others, Committee, etc., Letter of Acceptance, September 26, 1892, *Official Proceedings of the National Democratic Convention*, edited by Edward B. Dickinson (Chicago: Cameron, Amberg & Co., 1892), 234–40.

164 Cleveland, Veto of Texas Seed Bill, February 16, 1887, James D. Richardson, *A Compilation of the Messages and Papers of the Presidents*, 13 vols. (New York: Bureau of National Literature, 1897), XI, 5142–3.

165 *Houston Daily Post*, February 18, 1887; *Dallas Morning News*, February 17, 1887.

166 Marvin Olasky, *The American Leadership Tradition: Moral Vision from Washington to Clinton* (New York: The Free Press, 1999), 160.

167 William H. Glasson, *Federal Military Pensions in the United States* (New York: Oxford University Press, 1918), 277; Morton Keller, *Affairs of State: Public Life in Late Nineteenth Century America* (Cambridge: Belknap Press of Harvard University, 1977), 311.

168 Cleveland, Veto of a Pension Bill for William Bishop, June 23, 1886, Richardson, *Messages and Papers*, XI, 5028.

169 Cleveland, Veto of a Pension Bill for Cudbert Stone, February 4, 1887, Ibid., 5131–2; Cleveland, Veto of a Pension Bill for John W. Farris, June 21, 1886, Ibid., 5020–1; Cleveland, Veto of a Pension Bill for William H. Hester, May 19, 1888, Ibid., 5252; Cleveland, Veto of a Pension Bill for Rebecca Eldridge, May 28, 1886, Ibid., 5009–10.

170 Donald L. McMurry, "The Political Significance of the Pension Question," *Mississippi Valley Historical Review* (June 1922), 21, 23; Glasson, 331; *New York Times*, February 8, 1887.

171 Cleveland, Veto of the Dependent Pension Bill, February 11, 1887, Richardson, *Messages and Papers*, XI, 5134-5142; Nevins, *Cleveland*, 330-331.

172 Vincent P. De Santis, "Grover Cleveland," in Morton Borden, ed., *America's Eleven Greatest Presidents* (Chicago: Rand McNally, 1971), 162–4.

173 Charles Gasparino, *Bought and Paid For: The Unholy Alliance Between Barack Obama and Wall Street* (New York: Sentinel, 2010), ix–xi, 50.

174 Zachary A. Goldfarb, "Wall Street's resurgent prosperity frustrates its claims, and Obama's," *Washington Post*, November 6, 2011.

175 Theodore Roosevelt, *Autobiography*, edited by Louis Auchincloss (New York: Library of America edition, 2004), 333-334.

176 Cleveland, Second Message to the New York Legislature, *Public Papers*, II, 3–59.

177 Ibid.

178 Carter Goodrich, *Government Promotion of Canals and Railroads, 1800-1900* (Westport, Connecticut: Greenwood Press, 1974), 271; Cleveland, Second Inaugural Address, March 4, 1893, Richardson, *Messages and Papers*, XII, 5821–25.

179 Burton W. Folsom, Jr., *The Myth of the Robber Barons: A New Look at the Rise of Big Business in America* (Herndon, VA: Young America's Foundation, 1996), 18; Goodrich, 271.

180 DiLorenzo, *Capitalism*, 120.

181 Eland, *Re-carving Rushmore*, 170.

182 Parker, *Recollections*, 296–8.

183 Barack Obama, Address to Joint Session of Congress, February 24, 2009, http://www.whitehouse.gov/the-press-office/remarks-president-barack-obama-address-joint-session-congress.

184 For more on the failure of the transcontinental lines, see Burton W. Folsom, *The Myth of the Robber Barons*, 17–39; and Thomas J. DiLorenzo, *How Capitalism Saved America*, 116–21.

185 Cleveland to Charles L. Seeger, May 30, 1890, Nevins, *Letters*, 224–5.

186 Cleveland to the Tammany Society, June 29, 1887, in Everett P. Wheeler, *Sixty Years of American Life: Taylor To Roosevelt, 1850 to 1910* (New York: E. P. Dutton & Company, 1917), 132–3.

187 H. Wayne Morgan, *Hayes to McKinley*, 271; Richard E. Welch Jr., *The Presidencies of Grover Cleveland* (Lawrence: University Press of Kansas, 1988), 85.

188 Eckes, 49. According to data in *Historical Statistics of the United States*, government revenue in 1885 amounted to $323 million, of which $181 million came via customs duties. See volume V, 83.

189 Gould, *GOP*, 105; Charles Calhoun, *Minority Victory: Gilded Age Politics and the Front Porch Campaign of 1888* (Lawrence, Kansas: University Press of Kansas, 2008), 126, 128.

190 Willie D. Halsell, "The Appointment of L. Q. C. Lamar to the Supreme Court," *Mississippi Valley Historical Review* (Dec. 1941), 403–4.

191 Congressional Budget Office, "Trends in the Distribution of Household Income Between 1979 and 2007," October 2011, http://www.cbo.gov/doc.cfm?index=12485; Scott Rasmussen, "5 Things Voters are Looking for in 2012," *Townhall* magazine, December 2011, 39.

192 National Taxpayers Union, "Who Pays Income Taxes?" http://www.ntu.org/tax-basics/who-pays-income-taxes.html; Phil Izzo, "What Percent Are You?" *Wall Street Journal*, October 19, 2011, http://blogs.wsj.com/economics/2011/10/19/what-percent-are-you.

193 Keller, 308.

194 Cleveland, Fourth Annual Message (First Term), Richardson, *Messages and Papers*, XI, 5358-5385.

195 Brodsky, 241.

196 Ibid.

197 Cleveland, Fourth Annual Message (First Term), Richardson, *Messages and Papers*, XI, 5358-5385.

198 *New York Times*, April 13, 1891.

199 John Goode, *Recollections of a Lifetime* (New York: The Neale Publishing Company, 1906), 173–4.

200 New Orleans *Daily Picayune*, July 21, 1892.

201 Jack Beatty, *Age of Betrayal: The Triumph of Money in America, 1865-1900* (New York: Vintage Books, 2008), 195.

202 Ibid.

203 James Madison to Edmund Pendleton, January 21, 1792, *Papers of James Madison: Congressional Series*, edited by Robert A. Rutland et al, (Charlottesville: University Press of Virginia, 1983), XIV, 195–6. Emphasis in the original.

204 James Madison, Speech in Congress, February 6, 1792, Ibid., XIV, 221.

205 John C. Calhoun, Senate Speech, February 3, 1837, in Wilson, *Essential Calhoun*, 182.

206 Cleveland, Second Inaugural Address, March 4, 1893, Richardson, *Messages and Papers*, XII, 5821–25.

207 Lewis L. Gould, *Progressives and Prohibitionists: Texas Democrats in the Wilson Era* (Austin: University of Texas Press, 1973), 26.

208 Franklin D. Roosevelt, State of the Union Address, January 4, 1935, http://www.presidency.ucsb.edu/ws/index.php?pid=14890#axzz1Y9fj5Jwr; Bruce J. Schulman, *Lyndon B. Johnson and American Liberalism:*

A Brief Biography with Documents (Boston: Bedford/St. Martin's, 1995), 91-93; Lyndon B. Johnson, Annual Message to Congress, January 8, 1964, http://www.presidency.ucsb.edu/ws/index.php?pid=26787#axzz1WxucAPfl

209 Star Parker, *Uncle Sam's Plantation: How Big Government Enslaves America's Poor and What We Can Do about It* (Nashville, TN: WND Books, 2003).

210 John Melloy, "Welfare State: Handouts Make Up One-third of US Wages," CNBC.com, http://www.cnbc.com/id/41969508; Sara Murray, "Nearly Half of US Lives in Household Receiving Government Benefit," *Wall Street Journal*, October 5, 2011, http://blogs.wsj.com/economics/2011/10/05/nearly-half-of-households-receive-some-government-benefit/; David Morgan, "Number of Poor hit record 46 million in 2010," Reuters, September 13, 2011, http://in.reuters.com/article/2011/09/14/idINIndia-59318920110914?feedType=RSS&feedName=everything&virtualBrandChannel=11709; Liz Goodwin, "Twenty-two percent of American children lived in poverty last year," Yahoo! News, September 13, 2011, http://news.yahoo.com/blogs/lookout/22-percent-american-children-lived-poverty-last-142535015.html; Kristina Cooke, "USA becomes Food Stamp Nation but is it sustainable?", August 22, 2011, http://news.yahoo.com/usa-becomes-food-stamp-nation-sustainable-160645036.html.

211 Heritage Foundation, "Fact sheet #82: Welfare Reform the Next Steps," March 17, 2011, http://www.heritage.org/Research/Factsheets/2011/03/Welfare-Reform-The-Next-Steps; Heritage Foundation, Solutions for America, "The Unsustainable Growth of Welfare," August 17, 2010, http://www.heritage.org/Research/Reports/2010/08/The-Unsustainable-Growth-of-Welfare; John Merline, "Is Obama Creating a Nation of Dependents?" *Investor's Business Daily*, January 26, 2012, http://news.investors.com/Article/598993/201201260805/entitlements-soar-under-president-obama.htm; Fred Lucas, "Obama Will Spend More on Welfare in the Next Year Than Bush Spent on Entire Iraq War, Study Reveals," CNSNews.com, September 22, 2009, http://www.cnsnews.com/news/article/54400.

212 Heritage Foundation Reports; Howard Husock, *America's Trillion Dollar Mistake: The Failure of American Housing Policy* (Chicago: Ivan R. Dee, 2003), 5.

213 Heritage Foundation Reports; Kimberly Brown, "Shocking Need: American Kids Go Hungry," ABCNews.com, August 24, 2011, http://abcnews.go.com/US/hunger-home-american-children-malnourished/story?id=14367230.

214 Audrey Hudson, "Rep. Rosa DeLauro Pushes Bill That Gives Free Diapers to the Poor," October 19, 2011, http://www.humanevents.com/article.php?id=46958.

215 Star Parker, 19, 25, 29; Thomas Sowell, "War on Poverty Revisited," *Capitalism* magazine, August 17, 2004.

216 Stephen Grocer, "Banks Set for Record Pay," *Wall Street Journal*, January 14, 2010, http://online.wsj.com/article/SB100014240527487042812045750033517739831 36.html.

217 Franklin D. Roosevelt, State of the Union Address, January 4, 1935, http://www.presidency.ucsb.edu/ws/index.php?pid=14890#axzz1Y9fj5Jwr.

218 Burton Folsom, Jr. and Anita Folsom, "Did FDR End the Depression?" Wall Street Journal, April 12, 2010, http://online.wsj. com/article/SB10001424052702304024604575173632046893848. Html.

219 Cullom, 225–6.

220 Steve Kroft, "Obama on the Economy: 'I didn't over-promise,'" CBSNews.com, December 9, 2011,

http://www.cbsnews.com/8301-18563_162-57340578/obama-on-the-economy-i-didnt-over-promise/.

221 The whole story of the Panic of 1837 is much more complicated than I have laid out here but for a more complete view see Murray Rothbard, *A History of Money and Banking in the United States* (Auburn, AL: Ludwig von Mises Institute, 2002), 90–114.

222 Martin Van Buren, Special Session Message, September 4, 1837, Richardson, *Messages and Papers*, IV, 1561; Jeffrey Rogers Hummel, "Martin Van Buren: The American Gladstone," in John V. Denson,

Reassessing the Presidency: The Rise of the Executive State and the Decline of Freedom (Auburn, Alabama: Ludwig von Mises Institute, 2001), 188.

223 Thomas J. DiLorenzo, *How Capitalism Saved America: The Untold History of Our Country, From the Pilgrims to the Present* (New York: Crown Forum, 2004), 159; Eland, 73; Hummel, "Van Buren," 188.

224 Irwin Unger, *The Greenback Era: A Social and Political History of American Finance, 1865-1879* (Princeton: Princeton University Press, 1964), 15–6.

225 Kermit L. Hall, ed., *The Oxford Companion to the Supreme Court of the United States* (New York: Oxford University Press, 1992), 685, 498–9; Sidney Ratner, "Was the Supreme Court Packed by President Grant?" *Political Science Quarterly* (September 1935): 343–58.

226 Milton Friedman, "The Crime of 1873" *Journal of Political Economy* (December 1990): 1159–94.

227 Ray B. Westerfield, *Our Silver Debacle* (New York: The Ronald Press Company, 1936), 7; Unger, 81, 89–91.

228 Several economists, such as Murray Rothbard, have conclusively proven that there was no economic depression after the panic. Historians and some economists, citing deflation, have long argued that a depression lasted until 1879 but the economy, as well as the money supply, greatly expanded during that period. See Rothbard, *A History of Money and Banking in the United States*, 154–5.

229 John Sherman, *Recollections of Forty Years*, 2 vols (Chicago: The Werner Company, 1895), II, 1187; Welch, 128.

230 Rothbard, 168.

231 Henry Villard, *Memoirs of Henry Villard, Journalist and Financier, 1835–1900*, 2 vols. (Boston: Houghton, Mifflin and Company, 1904), II, 357–9.

232 Nevins, *Cleveland*, 525; Stanley Lebergott, *Manpower in Economic Growth: The American Record Since 1800* (New York: McGraw-Hill, 1964), 522; Carter, *Historical Statistics*, IV, 80–1; John Steele Gordon,

Hamilton's Blessing: The Extraordinary Life and Times of Our National Debt (New York: Walker & Company, 2010), 85.

233 Benjamin Harrison, Fourth Annual Message to Congress, December 6, 1892, Richardson, *Messages and Papers*, XII, 5741, 5744; Carl Schurz, "Cleveland's Second Administration," in Frederic Bancroft, ed., *Speeches, Correspondence and Political Papers of Carl Schurz*, 6 vols., (New York: G. P. Putnam's Sons, 1913), IV, 347.

234 Nevins, *Cleveland*, 525; *Wall Street Journal*, May 5, 1893; Harold U. Faulkner, *Politics, Reform and Expansion, 1890–1900* (New York: Harper & Row, Publishers, 1959), 141; *Wall Street Journal*, February 27, 1893.

235 Faulkner, 145.

236 Charles A. Collman, *Our Mysterious Panics, 1830–1930* (New York: Greenwood Press, 1968), 161; Lebergott, 522; Carter, *Historical Statistics*, III, 550, 24–5; O. M. W. Sprague, *History of Crises under the National Banking System* (Washington: Government Printing Office, 1910), 400–3.

237 Henry Adams, *Education*, 338; Cullom, 264; R. Hal Williams, *Years of Decision: American Politics in the 1890s* (New York: John Wiley & Sons, 1978), 77; *Bankers' Magazine* of London, September 1893, as quoted in Samuel Rezneck, *Business Depressions and Financial Panics* (New York: Greenwood Press, 1968), 324.

238 Robert Higgs, *Crisis and Leviathan: Critical Episodes in the Growth of American Government* (New York: Oxford University Press, 1987), 86.

239 Ron Paul, *End the Fed* (New York: Grand Central Publishing, 2009), 195.

240 Cleveland to Governor W. J. Northern, September 25, 1893, Nevins, *Letters*, 335–6.

241 Cleveland, Special Session Message, August 8, 1893, Richardson, *Messages and Papers*, XII, 5833-5837.

242 Sprague, 208; Rothbard, 169.

243 Rothbard, 169.

244 Olasky, 164; Nevins, *Cleveland*, 201.

245 Charles Kadlec, "Nixon's Colossal Monetary Error: The Verdict 40 Years Later," *Forbes*, August 15, 2011, http://www.forbes.com/sites/charleskadlec/2011/08/15/nixons-colossal-monetary-error-the-verdict-40-years-later/

246 Carl Schurz, "The Issues of the National Campaign of 1892," September 18, 1892, *Papers of Schurz*, IV, 100; *New York Times*, January 31, 1894.

247 Cleveland, First Annual Message to Congress, December 4, 1893, Richardson, *Messages and Papers*, XII, 5866–92.

248 John Sharp Williams to Davie Crompton, February 14, 1894, John Sharp Williams Papers, Mississippi Department of Archives and History, Jackson, MS; Welch, 132–3; William Jennings Bryan, Speech on the Income Tax, House of Representatives, January 30, 1894, *Speeches of William Jennings Bryan* (New York: Funk & Wagnalls Company, 1909), 164.

249 Hummel, *Freeing Slaves*, 223; Gordon, *Hamilton's Blessing*; 70–1; Charles Adams, *Those Dirty Rotten Taxes: The Tax Revolts that Built America* (New York: The Free Press, 1998, 141.

250 Higgs, 99; Adams, *Those Dirty Rotten Taxes*, 141; Gordon, *Hamilton's Blessing*, 80; Charles Adams, *For Good and Evil: The Impact of Taxes on the Course of Civilization* (Lanham, Maryland: Madison Books, 1999), 364.

251 Roger Q. Mills, "The Wilson Bill," *North American Review* (February, 1894), 237–8; Weisman, 122–3.

252 Thomas G. Shearman to Roger Q. Mills, June 12, 1893, Mills Papers, Dallas Historical Society, Dallas, TX.

253 Cleveland, First Annual Message to Congress, December 4, 1893, Richardson, *Messages and Papers*, XII, 5866–92.

254 Adams, *Dirty Rotten Taxes*, 131, *New York Times*, January 31, 1894.

255 Cleveland to Wilson, July 2, 1894, Nevins, *Letters*, 357; Josephus Daniels, *Editor in Politics* (Chapel Hill: University of North Carolina Press, 1941), 76; Nevins, *Cleveland*, 565; John Sharp Williams to Davie Crompton, February 14, 1894, John Sharp Williams Papers, Mississippi Department of Archives and History, Jackson, MS.

256 Cullom, 265; Schurz, "Second Administration," 361. The "deadly blight of treason" comment can be found in Cleveland to Thomas C. Catchings, August 27, 1894, Thomas C. Catchings Papers, Tulane. This letter can also be found in Nevins, *Letters*, 364–6.

257 Daniels, *Editor in Politics*, 74; Welch, 134.

258 Barry, 193, Nevins, *Cleveland*, 568.

259 Welch, 134.

260 Cleveland to Wilson, July 2, 1894, Nevins, *Letters*, 354–7.

261 Cleveland to Catchings, August 27, 1894, Catchings Papers, Tulane.

262 Keller, 308; Lawrence W. Reed, "A Supreme Court to Be Proud Of," The Freeman, March 2006, http://www.thefreemanonline.org/columns/ideas-and-consequences-a-supreme-court-to-be-proud-of/.

263 Cleveland, First Annual Message to Congress, December 4, 1893, Richardson, *Messages and Papers*, XII, 5866–92; Carter, *Historical Statistics*, V, 80–1.

264 Carter, *Historical Statistics*, III, 24–5; Lebergott, 522.

265 Sherman, II, 1187. For more on Cleveland's stance on the monetary issue during his first term, see Cleveland, First Annual Message to Congress, December 8, 1885, Richardson, *Messages and Papers*, X, 4927-4931 and Cleveland to the Honorable A. J. Warner and others, February 28, 1885, Nevins, *Letters*, 56-57.

266 Depew, 127; Horace White to Cleveland, April 16, 1894, Nevins, *Letters*, 350.

267 Herbert Hoover, *The Memoirs of Herbert Hoover: The Great Depression, 1929–41* (New York: Macmillan, 1952), 29.

268 DiLorenzo, *Capitalism*, 168.

269 Margaret Hoover, *American Individualism: How a New Generation of Conservatives Can Save the Republican Party* (New York: Crown Forum, 2011), 15.

270 Burton Folsom, Jr., New Deal or Raw Deal?: How FDR's Economic Legacy Has Damaged America (New York: Threshold Editions, 2008), 144.

271 Burton Folsom, Jr. and Anita Folsom, "Did FDR End the Depression?" *Wall Street Journal*, April 12, 2010, http://online.wsj.com/article/SB1 0001424052702304024604575173632046893848.html DiLorenzo, *Capitalism*, 184.

272 James Carville, "What Should the White House Do? Panic!" CNN. com, September 14, 2011, http://www.cnn.com/2011/09/14/opinion/ carville-white-house-advice/index.html; First House vote: http://clerk. house.gov/evs/2008/roll674.xml; Senate vote: http://www.senate.gov/ legislative/LIS/roll_call_lists/roll_call_vote_cfm.cfm?congress=110& session=2&vote=00213; Second House vote: http://clerk.house.gov/ evs/2008/roll681.xml.

273 Hope Yen, "Census shows 1 in 2 people are poor or low-income," Associated Press, December 15, 2011, http://finance.yahoo.com/news/ census-shows-1-2-people-103940568.html.

274 Noel Sheppard, "Paul Krugman Calls for Space Aliens to Attack Earth Requiring Massive Defense Buildup to Stimulate Economy," Newsbusters.org, August 14, 2011, http://newsbusters.org/blogs/ noel-sheppard/2011/08/14/paul-krugman-calls-space-aliens-attack- earth-requiring-massive-defens; "Bush says sacrificed free-market principles to save economy," Breitbart.com, December 16, 2008, http://www.breitbart.com/article.php?id=081216215816.8g97981o& show_article=1.

275 Elihu Root, "Introduction," in McElroy, I, x, xi.

276 Cleveland, First Annual Message to Congress, December 4, 1893, Richardson, *Messages and Papers*, XII, 5866–92.

277 This theory has been put forward by William E. Leuchtenburg, "Progressivism and Imperialism: The Progressive Movement and

American Foreign Policy, 1898–1916," *Mississippi Valley Historical Review* (December 1952), 483–504.

278 Mark D. Hirsch, *William C. Whitney: Modern Warwick* (New York: Archon Books, 1948), 297-302, 335–6; Graff, 77.

279 Robert I. Rotberg, *The Founder: Cecil Rhodes and the Pursuit of Power* (New York: Oxford University Press, 1988), 100; Matthew Sweet, "Cecil Rhodes: A Bad Man in Africa," *The Independent*, March 16, 2002, http://www.independent.co.uk/news/world/africa/story.jsp?story=274990.

280 Rudyard Kipling, "The White Man's Burden," 1899, http://www.poetryloverspage.com/poets/kipling/white_mans_burden.html.

281 Herring, 299; John James Ingalls, *A Collection of the Writings of John James Ingalls: Essays, Addresses, and Orations* (Kansas City, MO: Hudson-Kimberly Publishing Co., 1902), 507.

282 E. L. Godkin to Charles Eliot Norton, December 29, 1895, *The Gilded Age Letters of E. L. Godkin*, edited by William M. Armstrong (Albany, NY: State University of New York Press, 1974), 475.

283 Herring, 303; Warren Zimmerman, *First Great Triumph: How Five Americans Made Their Country a World Power* (New York: Farrar, Straus and Giroux, 2004), 87–95.

284 Nevins, *Cleveland*, 551.

285 Ibid.

286 Robert Kagan, *Dangerous Nation: America's Place in the World from Its Earliest Days to the Dawn of the Twentieth Century* (New York: Alfred A. Knopf, 2006), 324–5.

287 Ibid; Nevins, *Cleveland*, 550.

288 Nevins, *Cleveland*, 550.

289 Ibid., 325; Herring, 296.

290 Stephen Kinzer, *Overthrow: America's Century of Regime Change from Hawaii to Iraq* (New York: Times Books, 2006), 9; Tom Coffman,

The Island Edge of America: A Political History of Hawaii (Honolulu: University of Hawaii Press, 2003), 9–10.

291 Nevins, *Cleveland*, 551; Kagan, 326; Herring, 296–7.

292 Cleveland, First Annual Message to Congress (Second Term), December 4, 1893, Richardson, *Messages and Papers*, XII, 5866–92; Nevins, *Cleveland*, 554.

293 Cleveland, First Annual Message to Congress (Second Term), December 4, 1893, Richardson, *Messages and Papers*, XII, 5866–92.

294 Herring, 306.

295 Cleveland to Senator William F. Vilas, May 29, 1894, and Charles Francis Adams, Jr., to Cleveland, November 18, 1893, Nevins, *Letters*, 339, 353.

296 Coffman, 19–20.

297 Nevins, *Cleveland*, 549; Cleveland to Olney, July 8, 1898, Nevins, *Letters*, 502.

298 Nevins, Cleveland, 549–50.

299 Buchanan, *The Great Betrayal*, 216–7.

300 Kagan, 376.

301 Kagan, 376; Herring, 310; Cleveland, Fourth Annual Message (Second Term), December 7, 1896, Richardson, *Messages and Papers*, XIII, 6146–77.

302 Richard Watson Gilder to H. G., September 1896, *Letters of Richard Watson Gilder*, edited by Rosamond Gilder (Boston: Houghton Mifflin Company, 1916), 298-299; A. B. Farquhar, *The First Million the Hardest: An Autobiography* (New York: Doubleday, 1922), 270–71; Cleveland, Proclamation 377, June 12, 1895 and Proclamation 387, July 27, 1896, Richardson, *Messages and Papers*, XIII, 6023–4 and 6126–7.

303 Jim Powell, *Bully Boy: The Truth About Theodore Roosevelt's Legacy* (New York: Crown Forum, 2006), 36.

304 Parker, *Recollections*, 249.

305 Pat Buchanan, *A Republic, Not an Empire: Reclaiming America's Destiny* (Washington DC: Regnery Publishing, Inc., 1999), 141.

306 Herring, 306; Kagan, 368.

307 Nevins, *Cleveland*, 630; Grover Cleveland, *Presidential Problems* (New York: The Century Company, 1904), 247.

308 Henry James, *Richard Olney and His Public Service* (Boston: Houghton Mifflin, 1923), 109.

309 Cleveland, Special Message on Venezuela, December 17, 1895, Richardson, *Messages and Papers*, XIII, 6087–90.

310 Gerald G. Eggert, *Richard Olney: Evolution of a Statesman* (University Park, PA: Penn State University Press, 1974), 232–3.

311 Thomas A. Bailey, *Presidential Greatness: The Image and the Man from George Washington to the Present* (New York: Appleton-Century, 1966), 300.

312 *The New York Times*, June 25, 1908.

313 Steven F. Hayward, *The Real Jimmy Carter: How Our Worst Ex President Undermines American Foreign Policy, Coddles Dictators, and Created the Party of Clinton and Kerry* (Washington DC: Regnery Publishing, Inc., 2004), 118–9.

314 Edward Timberlake & William C. Triplett II, *Red Dragon Rising: Communist China's Military Threat to America* (Washington DC: Regnery Publishing, Inc., 1999), 143–4.

315 Ibid., 74–5, 128; Edward Timberlake & William C. Triplett II, *Year of the Rat: How Bill Clinton Compromised US Security for Chinese Cash* (Washington DC: Regnery Publishing, Inc., 1998), 190.

316 "China, Cuba pledge to boost military ties," *China Daily*, April 25, 2010, http://www.chinadaily.com.cn/china/2010-04/25/content_9772114.htm.

317 Brett M. Decker and William C. Triplett II, *Bowing to Beijing: How Barack Obama is Hastening America's Decline and Ushering in a Century*

of Chinese Domination (Washington DC: Regnery Publishing, Inc., 2011), 143, 145.

318 Menachem Gantz, "Report: Hezbollah Opens Base in Cuba," Ynet News, September 1, 2011, http://www.ynetnews.com/articles/0,7340,L-4116628,00.html; Lee DeCovnick, "Blog: Iran Building Missile Base in Venezuela, *American Thinker*, January 5, 2012, http://www.americanthinker.com/blog/2012/01/iran_building_missile_base_in_venezuela.html.

319 Barry, 176.

320 For more on Clinton's campaign funds from China, see Edward Timberlake & William C. Triplett II, *Year of the Rat: How Bill Clinton Compromised US Security for Chinese Cash* (Washington DC: Regnery Publishing, Inc., 1998).

321 Jim Powell, *Wilson's War: How Woodrow Wilson's Great Blunder Led to Hitler, Lenin, Stalin & World War II* (New York: Crown Forum, 2005).

322 Global Security Reports, http://www.globalsecurity.org/military/library/report/2009/hst0906.pdf.

323 Herring, 278.

324 John Quincy Adams, Address of July 4, 1821, in Walter LaFeber, ed., *John Quincy Adams and American Continental Empire: Letters, Papers and Speeches* (Chicago: Quadrangle Books, 1965), 45.

325 John S. Wise, *Recollections of Thirteen Presidents* (Freeport, New York: Books for Libraries Press, 1968), 172.

326 Edgar K. Apgar to Cleveland, August 23, 1882, in Parker, *Recollections*, 49–50.

327 Cleveland to William E. W. Ross and Robert G. King, December 18, 1885, Nevins, *Letters*, 97; Cleveland to George W. Curtis, October 24, 1884, Ibid., 47; Cleveland to Herbert P. Bass, September 30, 1885, Ibid., 80–1; Cleveland to Wilson S. Bissell, December 24, 1885, Ibid., 98; *Buffalo Daily Courier*, August 10, 1884.

328 Cleveland, Letter Accepting Nomination for President, August 18, 1884, Parker, *Writings and Speeches*, 9–13.

329 Cleveland to Wilson S. Bissell, November 13, 1884, Nevins, *Letters*, 48.

330 Brodsky, 108.

331 Cleveland to D-Cady Herrick, July 26, 1891, Cleveland to Michael D. Harter, August 3, 1891, and Cleveland to Governor William E. Russell, July 23, 1891, Nevins, *Letters*, 263–5.

332 Wilson Diary, May 12, 1896, 82.

333 Cleveland, First Annual Message to Congress (Second Term), December 4, 1893, Richardson, *Messages and Papers*, XII, 5866-5892; List of Presidential Vetoes, http://www.presidency.ucsb.edu/data/vetoes.php.

334 Cleveland, Veto of an Appropriation for Celebrating Decoration Day, May 8, 1882, in Parker, *Writings and Speeches*, 433-435; Armitage, 117; *Buffalo Daily Courier*, May 9, 1882.

335 Jeffers, 48–9; Armitage, 120–1.

336 Armitage, 121–2.

337 Ibid., 125–6; Jeffers, 48–9.

338 Cleveland, Veto Messages, *Public Papers*, I, 28–9, 35–6, 103–27.

339 Jeffers, 67-68; McElroy, I, 51; Cleveland, Veto Messages, *Public Papers*, I, 64–6, 38–9, 68–9; *Albany Evening Journal*, April 10, 1883.

340 Cleveland, Veto Message, Assembly Bill No. 360, For Relief of Surviving Members of First Regiment, N.Y. Mexican Volunteers, *Public Papers*, I, April 25, 1883, 79–80.

341 Carter, *Historical Statistics*, V, 80-81; Cleveland, Second Annual Message (First Term), Richardson, *Messages and Papers*, XI, 5082–5114.

342 Wilson Diary, May 12, 1896, 82; Senator Tom Coburn, "Wastebook 2011: A Guide to Some of the Most Wasteful and Low Priority

Government Spending of 2011," http://www.coburn.senate.gov/public//index.cfm?a=Files.Serve&File_id=b69a6ebd-7ebe-41b7-bb03-c25a5e194365; David A. Patten, "GOP Slams 6,000 Earmarks in Trillion-Dollar Omnibus Spending Bill," Newsmax.com, December 15, 2010, http://www.newsmax.com/Headline/gop-omnibus-spending-earmarks/2010/12/15/id/380064; Anjeanette Damon, "Harry Reid accentuates the positive in final campaign push," *Las Vegas Sun*, October 7, 2010, http://www.lasvegassun.com/news/2010/oct/07/and-now-look-some-positives/.

343 Cleveland, Veto of the River and Harbor Bill, May 29, 1896, Richardson, *Messages and Papers*, XIII, 6109–11.

344 Jeffers, 186.

345 Publius, "Phil Hare: 'I Don't Worry About the Constitution,'" Biggovernment.com, April 1, 2010, http://biggovernment.com/publius/2010/04/01/rep-phil-hare-d-il-i-dont-worry-about-the-constitution.

346 Thomas Jefferson to W. H. Torrance, June 11, 1815, in Andrew A. Lipscomb and Albert E. Bergh, eds., *The Writings of Thomas Jefferson*, 20 vols (Washington DC: Thomas Jefferson Memorial Association, 1904), XIV, 302–6; Jefferson to Abigail Adams, September 11, 1804, in Lester J. Cappon, ed., *The Adams-Jefferson Letters: The Complete Correspondence between Thomas Jefferson & Abigail & John Adams* (Chapel Hill: University of North Carolina Press, 1987), 278-280.

347 James Madison, Veto Message, March 3, 1817, Richardson, *Messages and Papers*, II, 569–70.

348 Franklin Pierce, First Inaugural Address, March 4, 1853, Richardson, *Messages and Papers*, VI, 2730–6; Pierce, Veto Message, May 3, 1854, Ibid., 2782.

349 For an excellent account of Lincoln's abuses of power, see Thomas J. DiLorenzo, *The Real Lincoln: A New Look at Abraham Lincoln, His Agenda, and an Unnecessary War* (Roseville, CA: Prima Publishing, 2002) and *Lincoln Unmasked: What You're Not Supposed to Know about Dishonest Abe* (New York: Crown Forum, 2006).

350 Cleveland, First Inaugural Address, March 4, 1885, Richardson, *Messages and Papers*, X, 4884-4888.

351 McElroy, I, 52; *New York Times*, March 3, 1883.

352 Burrows and Wallace, 1056; Cleveland, Veto Message, Assembly Bill No. 58, To Regulate Fares on Elevated Railroads in New York City, *Public Papers*, I, 47.

353 Andrew Dickson White, *The Autobiography of Andrew Dickson White*, 2 vols. (New York: The Century Co., 1904), I, 207; Parker, *Recollections*, 62.

354 Brodsky, 59; *Albany Evening Journal*, March 2, 1883; *New York Times*, March 3, 1883.

355 *New York Herald*, March 3, 1883.

356 Nathan B. Oman, "The Hidden Costs of Auto Bailouts," *Washington Times*, August 10, 2010, http://www.washingtontimes.com/news/2010/aug/10/the-hidden-cost-of-auto-bailouts/.

357 J. Rogers Hollingsworth, *The Whirligig of Politics: The Democracy of Cleveland and Bryan* (Chicago: University of Chicago Press, 1963), 26.

358 Cullom, 269.

359 Wilson Diary, February 1, 1896, 19–20; Cleveland to Ambassador Thomas F. Bayard, February 13, 1895, Nevins, *Letters*, 377; Wilson Diary, March 4, 1896, 39.

360 Henry Adams to William Woodville Rockhill, September 10, 1896, in Harold Dean Carter, ed., *Henry Adams and his Friends: A Collection of His Unpublished Letters* (Boston: Houghton Mifflin Company, 1947), 386.

361 Wilson Diary, May 30, 1896, 93; Parker, *Recollections*, 209.

362 Cleveland to Wilson S. Bissell, September 16, 1900, Nevins, *Letters*, 536–7; Cleveland to Richard Olney, March 19, 1899 and April 12, 1899, Ibid., 512–3; Cleveland to Charles S. Hamlin, September 13, 1900, Ibid., 536.

363 Cleveland to Judson B. Harmon, July 17, 1900, Ibid., 532–3; Cleveland to Wilson S. Bissell, September 16, 1900, Ibid., 536–7.

364 Theodore Roosevelt to Henry Cabot Lodge, May 4, 1903, May 11, 1903, and May 23, 1903, Henry Cabot Lodge, *Selections from the Correspondence of Theodore Roosevelt and Henry Cabot Lodge, 1884–1918*. 2 vols. (New York: Charles Scribner's Sons, 1925), 10, 13, 17.

365 Ronald Reagan, "Let Them Go Their Way," CPAC Speech, March 1, 1975, http://www.conservative.org/cpac/archives/cpac-1975-ronald-reagan/#ixzz1Wlq0ztow.

366 Cleveland to Judson B. Harmon, July 17, 1900, Nevins, *Letters*, 532–3.

367 Mark Twain to Jean Clemens, June 19, 1908, Mark Twain Papers, University of California, Berkeley.

368 Merrill, 207.

369 Wilson quoted in De Santis, "Grover Cleveland," in Borden, 164.

370 White, I, 207.

371 George F. Hoar, *Autobiography of Seventy Years* (New York: Charles Scribner's Sons, 1903), II, 46.

372 Henry Adams, "The Session," *North American Review*, Vol. 111, No. 228 (July 1870), 29–62.

373 Hoar, II, 46.

374 Roosevelt, *Autobiography*, 607–8.

375 Ibid., 614.

376 James Madison, Federalist No. 47, *The Federalist Papers*, edited by Clinton Rossiter (New York: Mentor, 1961), 301; Real Clear Politics Video, December 14, 2011, http://www.realclearpolitics.com/video/2011/12/14/obama_where_congress_is_not_willing_to_act_were_going_to_go_ahead_and_do_it_ourselves.html; Real Clear Politics Video, October 11, 2011, http://www.realclearpolitics.com/video/2011/10/11/obama_tells_advisers_to_find_how_to_approve_stimulus_projects_without_additional_congressional_authorization.

html; Real Clear Politics Video, January 5, 2012, http://www. realclearpolitics.com/video/2012/01/05/obama_i_have_an_ obligation_as_president_to_do_what_i_can_without_congress.html; Susan Jones, "The Heck with the Senate: Obama Skips 'Advise and Consent' in Naming 3 Members to NLRB," CNSNews.com, January 5, 2012, http://cnsnews.com/news/article/heck-senate-obama-skips-advise-and-consent-naming-3-members-nlrb.

377 Byron York, "Obama: 'I'd Like to Work My Way Around Congress," Washington Examiner, September 15, 2011, http://campaign2012. washingtonexaminer.com/blogs/beltway-confidential/obama-id-work-my-way-around-congress; Edwin Mora, "Obama: Idea of Changing Laws on My Own 'is very tempting,'" CNSNews.com, July 26, 2011, http://www.cnsnews.com/news/article/obama-idea-changing-immigration-laws-my.

378 For Roosevelt quote, see Powell, *Bully Boy*, 1; Todd Gaziano, "The Use and Abuse of Executive Orders and Other Presidential Directives," Heritage Foundation, February 21, 2001, http://origin.heritage.org/ research/reports/2001/02/the-use-and-abuse-of-executive-orders-and-other-presidential-directives; Also see Burton Folsom, *New Deal or Raw Deal* and *FDR Goes to War*. The Historian James G. Randall, in *Constitutional Problems Under Lincoln*, referred to him as a "benevolent dictator."

379 Theodore Roosevelt, "Party Rallies: Roosevelt Answerers Josiah Quincy," *Letters of Roosevelt and Lodge,* 22-23.

380 Presidential Vetoes, Washington-Obama, http://www.presidency.ucsb. edu/data/vetoes.php.

381 Cleveland, Veto Message, Assembly Bill No. 360, For Relief of Surviving Members of First Regiment, N.Y. Mexican Volunteers, *Public Papers*, I, April 25, 1883, 79–80. The Jefferson quote is from his first inaugural address.

382 Cato Institute, "Economic Freedom of the World: 2011 Annual Report," September 12, 2011, http://www.cato.org/pubs/efw/; "The World's Top Ten Freest Economies," Human Events, February 14, 2008, http:// www.humanevents.com/article.php?id=25018; International Finance

Corporation, "Doing Business," June 2011, http://www.doingbusiness. org/rankings.

383 Stephen Ambrose, *Rise to Globalism: American Foreign Policy Since 1938* (New York: Penguin Books, 1988), xi.

384 Professor Thomas J. DiLorenzo has pointed out that the US Constitution defines treason this way: "Treason against the United States shall consist only in levying War against them, or in adhering to their Enemies, giving them Aid and Comfort." It is obvious that "them" refers to the individual states so Lincoln committed treason with his invasion of the South. See Thomas J. DiLorenzo, "Another Court Historian's False Tariff History," Lewrockwell.com, January 18, 2011, http://www.lewrockwell.com/dilorenzo/dilorenzo199.html.

385 Dick Cheney, *In My Time: A Personal and Political Memoir* (New York: Threshold Editions, 2011), 207–8.

386 Rich Lowry, *Legacy: Paying the Price for the Clinton Years* (Washington: Regnery Publishing, Inc., 2003), 249. Also see *Dereliction of Duty: The Eyewitness Account of How Bill Clinton Compromised America's National Security* (Washington: Regnery Publishing, Inc., 2003).

387 Jake Tapper, "Obama Sends 100 US Troops to Uganda to Help Combat Lord's Resistance Army," ABCNews.com, October 14, 2011, http://abcnews.go.com/blogs/politics/2011/10/obama-sends-100-us-troops-to-uganda-to-combat-lords-resistance-army.

388 Harry Truman, Statement on Japan, August 6, 1945, http://www. trumanlibrary.org/whistlestop/study_collections/bomb/small/mb10. htm.

389 Jefferson to Spencer Roane, September 6, 1819, Lipscomb and Bergh, *Writings*, XV, 212.

390 Wilson Diary, March 4, 1897, 250.